T0210878

Lecture Notes in Computer Science   9070

Commenced Publication in 1973
Founding and Former Series Editors:
Gerhard Goos, Juris Hartmanis, and Jan van Leeuwen

More information about this series at http://www.springer.com/series/8637

Abdelkader Hameurlain · Josef Küng
Roland Wagner · Sherif Sakr
Lizhe Wang · Albert Zomaya (Eds.)

Transactions on Large-Scale Data- and Knowledge-Centered Systems XX

Special Issue on Advanced Techniques for Big Data Management

 Springer

Editors-in-Chief

Abdelkader Hameurlain
IRIT, Paul Sabatier University
Toulouse
France

Roland Wagner
FAW, University of Linz
Linz
Austria

Josef Küng
FAW, University of Linz
Linz
Austria

Guest Editors

Sherif Sakr
King Saud bin Abdulaziz University
   for Health Sciences
Riyadh
Saudi Arabia

Albert Zomaya
The University of Sydney
Sydney
Australia

Lizhe Wang
Chinese Academy of Sciences
Beijing
China

ISSN 0302-9743   ISSN 1611-3349   (electronic)
Lecture Notes in Computer Science
ISBN 978-3-662-46702-2   ISBN 978-3-662-46703-9   (eBook)
DOI 10.1007/978-3-662-46703-9

Library of Congress Control Number: 2015934899

Springer Heidelberg New York Dordrecht London

Printed on acid-free paper

Springer-Verlag GmbH Berlin Heidelberg is part of Springer Science+Business Media
(www.springer.com)

Preface

Data constitute a key resource in the modern world. Big data is a popular term which has been recently used to describe the exponential growth and availability of data. In particular, big data is a new phenomenon which represents the outcome of the development and the convergence of a range of technological advances in communication and computing sciences. In particular, the radical expansion and integration of computation, networking, digital devices, and data storage has provided a robust platform for the explosion in big data as well as being the means by which big data is generated, processed, shared, and analyzed. Big Data has commonly been characterized by 3V properties which refer to huge in _Volume_, consisting of terabytes or petabytes of data; high in _Velocity_, being created in or near real time; and diverse in _Variety_ of type, being structured and unstructured in nature. IDC predicts that the worldwide volume of data will reach 40 zettabytes by 2020 where 85% of all of this data will be of new data types and formats including server logs and other machine generated data, data from sensors, social media data, and many more data sources. All these varieties of data types need to be harnessed to provide a more complete picture of what is happening in various application domains.

In general, data are not useful in and of themselves. They only have utility if meaning and value can be extracted from them. Therefore, given their utility and value, there are always continuous increasing efforts devoted to producing and analyzing them. In principle, big data discovery enables data scientists and other analysts to uncover patterns and correlations through analysis of large volumes of data of diverse types. Insights gleaned from big data discovery can provide businesses with significant competitive advantages, such as more successful marketing campaigns, decreased customer churn, and reduced loss from fraud. In practice, the growing demand for large-scale data processing and data analysis applications spurred the development of novel solutions from both industry and academia.

This TLDKS Special Issue presents a representative selection of articles covering a wide range of important topics in the domain of advanced techniques for big data management. The first article "A Proxy Service for Multi-tenant Elastic Extension Tables" by Haitham Yaish et al. proposes a multi-tenant database proxy service called Elastic Extension Tables Proxy Service (EETPS) that combines each tenant relational tables and virtual relational tables and makes them act and operate virtually as one single database schema for each tenant. In particular, the service allows data to be accessed by calling functions and avoids efforts associated with writing SQL queries and backend data management code. In addition, the proposed scheme allows the service provider tenants to focus on their core business and easily create their SaaS, mobile, web, and desktop software applications.

In recent years, consumption of video streams has risen sharply. This phenomenon has played a role in shaping Internet traffic. In their article "Boosting Streaming Video Delivery with WiseReplica" Guthemberg Silvestre et al. introduce WiseReplica as an adaptive replication scheme for peer-assisted VoD systems that enforces the average bitrate for Internet videos. WiseReplica relies on machine-learned ranking in order to save storage and bandwidth from the vast majority of non-popular contents for the most watched videos.

In the past decade, the Web has been evolving to a sink of disparate information sources which are totally isolated from each other. The technology of Linked Data promises to connect such information sources in order to enable their better exploitation by humans or automated programs. The article "A Cloud-Based, Geospatial Linked Data Management System" by Kyriakos Kritikos et al. proposes a novel, cloud-based geospatial LD management system which can scale out or scale in according to the incoming load in order to serve the respective user requests with the appropriate service level. On top of this system lies an LD-as-a-service offering which abstracts away the user from any LD publishing complexities and provides all the appropriate functionality for enabling a full LD management.

The Random Prism classifier has recently been proposed as an alternative to the popular Random Forests classifier, which is based on decision trees. In principle, Random Prism is based on the Prism family of algorithms, which is more robust to noise. The article "A Scalable Expressive Ensemble Learning Using Random Prism: A MapReduce Approach" by Frederic Stahl et al. provides a detailed and exhaustive description of Random Prism and Parallel Random Prism approaches. Additionally, the article also provides a formal theoretical scalability analysis of Random Prism and Parallel Random Prism, which examines the scalability to much larger computer clusters. This examination provides a theoretical underpinning that can be used for scalability of the MapReduce framework. It also presents a thorough experimental study of Parallel Random Prism's scalability.

In practice, popular frameworks which are supporting the MapReduce programming model for Big Data applications do not flexibly adapt to these environments. Instead, these frameworks, including Hadoop, typically divide data evenly among worker nodes which induces the well-known problem of stragglers on slower nodes. The first invited article of this special issue "Performance Analysis of Adapting a MapReduce Framework to Dynamically Accommodate Heterogeneity" by Jessica Hartog et al. presents an alternative MapReduce framework, called MARLA, which divides each worker's labor into subtasks, delays the binding of data to worker processes, and thereby enables applications to run faster in performance-heterogeneous environments. In addition, the article explores and characterizes the opportunity for performance gains, and identifies when the benefits outweigh the costs of the proposed approach.

In general, a Content Distribution Network (CDN) is a distributed network of servers and file storage devices that replicates content/services (e.g., files, video, audio, etc.) on a large number of surrogate systems placed at various locations, distributed across the globe. In practice, CDNs that are using cloud resources such as storage and compute have started to emerge. Unlike traditional CDNs hosted on private data centers, cloud-based CDNs take advantage of the geographical availability and the pay-as-you-go model of cloud platforms. Therefore, the Cloud-based CDNs (CCDNs) promote the content-delivery-as-a-service cloud model. The second invited article of this special issue "An overview of Cloud-Based Content Delivery Networks: Research Dimensions and State of the Art" by Meisong Wang et al. presents a comprehensive study of Cloud CDNs. In particular, the article presents a state-of-the-art survey on current commercial and research-driven Cloud CDNs and presents an analysis of current Cloud CDN based on a comprehensive taxonomy. In addition, the article identifies some of the promising research opportunities in the Cloud CDN area.

We would like to note that the publication of this TLDKS Special Issue would not have been possible without the help of many people. First, we would like to thank all the authors who submitted their articles to this special issue. We are grateful to all the reviewers for their very valuable efforts to ensure the high quality of the selected articles for this special issue. We also acknowledge the work of Abdelkader Hameurlain, Josef Küng, and Roland Wagner, Editors-in-chief of the TLDKS journal, for their confidence and help. Finally, we are particularly grateful to Gabriela Wagner for her valuable guidance and administrative assistance during the whole process of preparing this special issue.

January 2015

Sherif Sakr
Lizhe Wang
Albert Zomaya

Organization

Editorial Board

Reza Akbarinia	Inria, France
Bernd Amann	Laboratoire d'Informatique de Paris 6 / Université Pierre et Marie Curie, France
Dagmar Auer	FAW, University of Linz, Austria
Stéphane Bressan	National University of Singapore, Singapore
Francesco Buccafurri	Università degli Studi Mediterranea di Reggio Calabria, Italy
Qiming Chen	HP Laboratories, USA
Tommaso Di Noia	Politecnico di Bari, Italy
Dirk Draheim	University of Innsbruck, Austria
Johann Eder	Alpen-Adria-Universität Klagenfurt, Austria
Stefan Fenz	Vienna University of Technology, Austria
Georg Gottlob	Oxford University, UK
Anastasios Gounaris	Aristotle University of Thessaloniki, Greece
Theo Härder	Technical University of Kaiserslautern, Germany
Andreas Herzig	IRIT, Paul Sabatier University, France
Hilda Kosorus	FAW, University of Linz, Austria
Dieter Kranzlmüller	Ludwig-Maximilians-Universität München, Germany
Philippe Lamarre	INSA Lyon, France
Lenka Lhotská	Czech Technical University in Prague, Czech Republic
Vladimir Marik	Czech Technical University in Prague, Czech Republic
Mukesh Mohania	IBM Research, India
Franck Morvan	IRIT, Paul Sabatier University, France
Kjetil Nørvåg	Norwegian University of Science and Technology, Norway
Gultekin Ozsoyoglu	Case Western Reserve University, USA
Themis Palpanas	Paris Descartes University, France
Torben Bach Pedersen	Aalborg University, Denmark
Günther Pernul	University of Regensburg, Germany
Klaus-Dieter Schewe	Johannes Kepler University of Linz, Austria
David Taniar	Monash University, Australia
A Min Tjoa	Vienna University of Technology, Austria
Chao Wang	Oak Ridge National Laboratory, USA

Contents

A Proxy Service for Multi-tenant Elastic Extension Tables

Haitham Yaish[1,2(✉)], Madhu Goyal[1,2], and George Feuerlicht[2,3,4]

[1] Centre for Quantum Computation and Intelligent Systems,
University of Technology Sydney,
P.O. Box 123, Broadway, NSW 2007, Australia
[2] Faculty of Engineering and Information Technology,
University of Technology Sydney,
P.O. Box 123, Broadway, NSW 2007, Australia
{haitham.yaish,madhu.goyal-2,
george.feuerlicht}@uts.edu.au
[3] Unicorn College, Prague, Czech Republic
[4] University of Economics, Prague, Czech Republic

Abstract. An important challenge in the design of multi-tenant databases that support Software as a Service (SaaS) applications is providing a platform that manages multiple tenants' data in single database storage. To address this challenge, we have previously proposed a multi-tenant database schema called Elastic Extension Tables (EET) that uses single shared database and shared schema for all tenants. In this paper, we extend this work with a multi-tenant database proxy service called Elastic Extension Tables Proxy Service (EETPS) that combines tenants' relational tables with virtual relational tables into single database schema for each tenant. This service enables data access by calling functions in order to avoid writing SQL queries and backend data management code. It allows the tenants to focus on their core business and easily create SaaS, mobile, web, and desktop software applications. We present the EETPS algorithms and perform several experiments to assess their feasibility and effectiveness by comparing the performance of retrieving data from traditional physical tables, virtual tables, and integrated physical and virtual tables.

Keywords: Cloud Computing · Software as a Service · Multi-tenancy · Multi-tenant database · Elastic Extension Tables

1 Introduction

Software as a service (SaaS) is a Cloud Computing service model that exploits economies of scale for SaaS service providers by offering single configurable software and computing environment for multiple tenants. It is an emerging software application service model and a significant current topic in the software industry. Also, SaaS can be defined as a model where the service provider hosts the applications and customers accesses these applications via the internet [19]. Configuration is one of the main characteristics of multi-tenant SaaS applications that allows SaaS vendors to run a single instance of the application. This requires a multi-tenant aware design with a single

© Springer-Verlag Berlin Heidelberg 2015
A. Hameurlain et al. (Eds.): TLDKS XX, LNCS 9070, pp. 1–33, 2015.
DOI: 10.1007/978-3-662-46703-9_1

codebase and metadata capability. Multi-tenant aware application enables each tenant to design different parts of the application, and automatically configure its behaviour during runtime without redeploying the application [3]. Multi-tenant databases manage two types of data: shared data and tenant's isolated data. Combining these two types of data gives tenants a complete view of the data which suits their business requirements [6, 16]. There are various approaches of multi-tenant database schema designs and techniques that address multi-tenant database challenges [21, 23], but there are also remaining challenges [2].

Designing and developing a configurable multi-tenant SaaS application is a complicated task due to the lack of support for a manageable database schema, and the complexities associated with providing configurable database fields [8, 9, 14, 18]. In [21, 23], we proposed a configurable database design technique for multi-tenant applications called Elastic Extension Tables (EET) that consists of Common Tenant Tables (CTT), Extension Tables (ET), and Virtual Extension Tables (VET). This design enables tenants to build their virtual database schema by creating the required number of tables and columns, creating virtual database relationships, and assigning suitable data types and constraints for table columns during multi-tenant application runtime. In this paper, we propose a multi-tenant database proxy service called Elastic Extension Tables Proxy Service (EETPS). This service is based on EET, and it integrates, generates, and executes tenants' queries by using a codebase solution that converts multi-tenant queries into traditional database queries and execute them in a RDBMS. It provides new features, include: (1) allowing cloud database service providers to offer three EET database models, and database tenants to choose from any of these database models; (2) allowing extensions to the traditional Relational Database Management Systems (RDBMS) during applications' runtime; (3) avoiding the need to write SQL queries, learning special programming languages, and writing backend data management codes by calling functions from EETPS. This service retrieves simple and complex queries including join operations, filtering on multiple properties, and filtering of data based on subquery results. We present sample algorithms for five EETPS functions, and we carry out five types of experiments to verify the effectiveness of EETPS. The results of these experiments indicate that EET multi-tenant schema and EETPS is suitable for storing and retrieving data for software applications in general and SaaS applications in particular.

The remainder of this paper is organized as follows. Section 2 reviews related work. Section 3 describes the Elastic Extension Tables. Section 4 describes the Elastic Extension Tables Proxy Service. Section 5 presents the Elastic Extension Tables Proxy Service algorithms. Section 6 gives our experimental results, and Sect. 7 concludes this paper and describes the future work.

2 Related Work

A number of multi-tenant database schema designs and techniques have studied and implemented to address multi-tenant database challenges. This section presents seven multi-tenant database schema techniques, including Private Tables, Extension Tables, Universal Table, Pivot Tables, Chunk Table, Chunk Folding, and XML Table [1, 2, 8,

9, 12, 15]. All of these seven multi-tenant database schema techniques are based on traditional RDBMS [5, 17]. Moreover, we describe the storage model design of SalesForce and discuss its special programming and query languages. Furthermore, we discuss some of the limitations of NoSQL (Not Only SQL).

The **Private Tables** technique allows each tenant to have his own private tables, which can be extended and changed [1, 2]. Using this multi-tenant query technique can be transformed from one tenant to another by renaming tables, and metadata without using extra columns like 'tenant_id' to distinguish and isolate the tenants' data. In contrast, many tables are required to satisfy each tenant needs. Therefore, this technique can be used if there are fewer tenants using it, to produce sufficient database load and good performance [2].

The **Extension Tables** are separated tables joined with the base tables by adding tenants' columns to construct logical source tables [1, 2]. This technique has been adapted from the Decomposed Storage Model that splits up n-column table into n 2-column tables joined using surrogate keys [1]. Multiple tenants can use the base tables as well as the extension tables [9]. This technique is considered superior to the Private Tables approach described above. Nevertheless, in this approach, the number of tables increases with increasing number of tenants, and with the variety of their different business requirements [1].

The **Universal Table** is a table that contains additional columns of the base application schema columns, which enable tenants to store their required columns. It is structured with two main columns 'tenant_id' and 'table_id', and other generic data columns, which have a flexible VARCHAR data type in which different data types with different data values can be stored in these columns [1, 15]. It is a flexible technique that enables tenants to extend their tables in different ways according to their business needs. However, the rows of the universal table can be too wide with an overhead in the number of NULL values, which the database has to handle [1].

In the **Pivot Tables** technique, the application maps the schema into generic structure in the database, in which each column of each row in a logical source table is given its own row in the Pivot Table. The rows in the Pivot Table comprise of four columns, including tenant, table, column, and row that specifies which row in the logical source table they represent. As well as a single data type column that stores the values of the logical source table rows according to their data types in the designated pivot Table [1, 9]. For example, the Pivot Tables can have two pivot tables, the first table 'pivot_int' to store INTEGER values, and the second table 'pivot_str' to store STRING values. The performance benefits are achieved by avoiding NULL values and by selectively reading from smaller numbers of columns [1].

The **Chunk Table** is another generic structure technique that is similar to Pivot Table. Except, it has a set of data columns with a mixture of data types that replacing the column 'col' in the Pivot Table with 'chunk' column in the Chunk Table. This technique partitions the logical source table into groups of columns. Each group assigned to a chunk ID and mapped into an appropriate Chunk Table. This technique has four advantages over Pivot Table. (1) Reducing metadata storage ratio, (2) reducing the overhead of reconstructing the logical source tables, (3) reducing the number of columns, and (4) providing indexes. This technique is flexible, but it adds complexity to the database queries [1].

The **Chunk Folding** is a schema mapping technique that partition logical source tables into chunks vertically [1, 9]. These chunks are folded in different physical tables and joined together, where a chunk of columns is partitioned into a group of columns and each group has a chunk id [9]. Aulbach et al. (2008) perform experiments to measure the efficiency of Chunk Table and Chunk Folding techniques, and they found that Chunk Folding technique outperform the Chunk Table technique. Additionally, they state that the performance of this technique is enhanced by mapping the most frequently used tenants' columns of the logical schema into conventional tables, and the majority of tenants do not use the remaining columns in the Chunk Tables. However, the main limitation of the Chunk Folding technique is that the common schema must be known in advance, which is not a practical solution for multi-tenant databases. This issue also exists in Extension Tables, Pivot Tables, and Chunk Table.

The **XML Table** database extension technique is a combination of relational database systems and Extensible Markup Language (XML) [2, 8, 9]. The extension of XML can be provided as native XML data type, or storing the XML document in the database as a Character Large Object (CLOB) or Binary Large Object (BLOB) [2]. XML data type facilitating the creation of database tables, columns, views, variables and parameters, and isolating the application from relational data model [8]. This technique satisfies tenants' needs because their data can be handled without changing original database relational schema, and XML data type can be supported by several relational database products [8, 9]. In contrast, this technique reduces the data access performance using XML files [2], and Heng et al. (2012) state that this technique has the highest response time, in other words, it was the slowest technique in comparison with Private Tables, Universal Tables, Pivot Tables, Chunk Table and Chunk Folding techniques.

In summary, although Heng et al. (2012) use the Elastic Extension Tables (EET) name that proposed in [21], but using this name for the Salesforce storage model is incorrect. Heng et al.'s paper [12] conducted a number of significant experiments to evaluate retrieving data from six different multi-tenant schemas used in multi-tenant SaaS applications including Private Tables, Universal Tables, Pivot Tables, Chunk Table, Chunk Folding, and XML Table. The results of these experiments show that retrieving data from Universal Table is faster than from other schemas except the Private Tables schema. Aulbach et al. (2009) conduct experiments that compare Private Tables schema and the Universal Table (Spare Columns) schema. The results of these experiments show that the Universal Table schema has the same or better performance than the Private Tables schema when retrieving or inserting data, except when inserting a large number of data, the Universal Table schema is slower than the Private Tables schema. Such experimental results lead to the conclusion that the performance of the Universal Table schema is the best out of the five multi-tenant schemas, as the Private Tables schema is only suitable for a small number of tenants. Overall, the experimental results make the Universal Table schema the optimal schema to use for a multi-tenant database when it is compared to Pivot Tables, Chunk Table, Chunk Folding, and XML Table. However, as noted earlier the Universal Table can be too large introducing overhead with the number of NULL values, which the database has to handle. Ultimately, this suggests that the current available multi-tenant database schemas still have remaining challenges and issues. Based on this conclusion, we proposed in [21] EET multi-tenant schema and in [23] we evaluated this schema by comparing it with the Universal Tables schema that is the optimal commercially available multi-tenant database schema, which is used by Salesforce. The experiments of EET evaluation show significant performance improvements obtained using EET when compared to Universal Tables, making EET schema a good candidate for the management of multi-tenant data in SaaS applications.

Salesforce, the pioneer of SaaS CRM applications has designed and developed a storage model to manage its virtual database structure by using a set of metadata, universal data table, and pivot tables. This set of metadata and tables get converted to objects that the Universal Data Dictionary (UDD) keeps track of them, their fields and relationships, and other object definition characteristics. In addition, it provides a special object-oriented procedural programming language called Apex that has the following functions. First, declare program variables, constants and execute traditional flow control statements. Second, declare data manipulation operations. Third, declare the transaction control operations. Then Salesforce compiles Apex code and stores it as metadata in the UDD [20]. In addition, it has its own Query Languages, first, Salesforce Object Query Language (SOQL), which retrieve data from one object at a time. Second, Salesforce Object Search Language (SOSL), which retrieve data from multiple objects simultaneously [10, 20]. NoSQL is a non-relational database management system approach designed to handle storing and retrieving large quantities of data, and it includes services such as MongoDB, Cassandra, CouchDB, Google App Engine Datastore, and others. This technique avoids joining operations, filtering on multiple properties, and filtering of data based on subqueries results. Therefore, the efficiency of its simple query is very high, but this is not the case for complex queries. Moreover, unless configuring NoSQL consistency models in protective modes of operation, NoSQL database typically do not ensure data consistency [4, 11]. Indrawan-Santiago [13] states that NoSQL should be seen as a complimentary solution to relational databases in providing enhanced data management capability, not as a replacement for it.

3 Elastic Extension Tables

The proposed Elastic Extension Tables (EET) database schema is a novel way of designing and creating a multi-tenant database that consists of three types of tables [21, 23]. The first type is Common Tenant Tables (CTT) which are physical tables shared between tenants using a RDBMS. These physical relational tables can be applied to any business domain database such as CRM, Accounting, Human Resource (HR), or other business domains. The second type is Virtual Extension Tables (VET), which allow tenants to extend the existing business domain database, or have their own configurable database through creating their virtual database structures from scratch by creating (1) virtual database tables, (2) virtual database relationships, and (3) other database constraints. The third type is Extension Tables (ET), which consists of eight physical tables that are used to construct VETs [21, 23]. The data architecture details of the eight ETs of EET are shown in Fig. 1 and listed as follows: (1) the 'db_table' ET allows tenants to create virtual tables and give them unique names. (2) The 'table_column' ET allows tenants to create virtual columns for a virtual table stored in the 'db_table' ET. (3) The table row ETs store records of virtual extension columns in three separate tables. These tables are separated to store small data values in the 'table_row' ET such as NUMBER, DATE-and-TIME, BOOLEAN, VARCHAR and other data types. While the large data values stored in two other tables: the first one is the 'table_row_blob' ET, which stores a Uniform Resource Identifier (URI) for virtual columns of Binary Large Object (BLOB) data type. The second one is the 'table_row_clob' ET, which stores Character Large Object (CLOB) values for virtual columns with TEXT data type. These three row ETs are capable to store data types, including traditional relational data, texts, audios, images, videos, and XML in structured, unstructured, and semi-structured format. The structured data, such as traditional relational data can be stored in CTTs and VETs using ETs. The unstructured data files such as images, audios, videos can be stored in EET, by storing the URI of a file in the 'table_row_blob' ET. Then the actual physical file can be stored in a folder of a file system, and then this file can be accessed using the URI that stored in the 'table_row_blob' ET and mapped to the physical file that stored in a folder. The semi-structured data such as XML files can be stored in two ways. Firstly, using the same method as used for storing unstructured data, then accessing the XML file using the URI that stored in the 'table_row_blob' ET and mapped to the physical XML file that stored in a folder. Secondly, XML files can be stored as text in the 'table_row_clob' ET as a CLOB file, and then accessed from the 'table_row_clob' ET. (4) The 'table_relationship' ET allows tenants to create virtual relationships for their virtual tables with any of CTTs or VETs. (5) The 'table_index' ET is used to add indexes to virtual columns. These indexes reduce the query execution time when tenants retrieve data from the VET. (6) The 'table_primary_key_column' ET allows tenants to create single or composite virtual primary key for virtual extension columns that are stored in the 'table_column' ET [21, 23]. Figure 1 shows the details of multi-tenant EET database schema.

The effectiveness of accessing data from EET was evaluated in [23], and it will be confirmed in this paper. Furthermore, the multi-tenant schema includes access control data architecture that allows each tenant to have a number of users with different types of access privileges [22].

4 Elastic Extension Tables Proxy Service

This paper proposes a multi-tenant database proxy service called EETPS that combines, generates, and executes tenants' queries by using a codebase solution that first converts multi-tenant queries into traditional database queries, and then executes the queries in a RDBMS. This service has three objectives: (1) to allow the tenants' applications to retrieve table rows from CTTs, VETs, or both CTTs and VETs. (2) to allow tenants to extend a business domain database that based on traditional RDBMS during their applications' runtime; (3) to avoid efforts associated with writing SQL queries and backend data management code by calling functions from this service, which retrieves simple and complex queries including join operations, union operations, filtering on multiple properties, and filtering of data based on subqueries results. These functions return a two dimensional array (Object $[\alpha]$ $[\beta]$), where α is the number of array rows

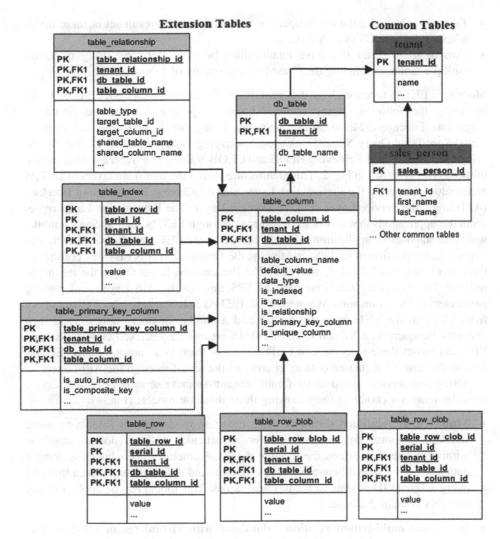

Fig. 1. Elastic Extension Tables

that represents a number of retrieved rows, and β is the number of array columns that represent a number of retrieved columns for a particular CTT or VET. These functions are designed to retrieve tenants' data from the following tables:

- One table, either a CTT or a VET.
- Two tables have One-to-One, One-to-Many, Many-to-One, Many-to-Many, or Self-referencing relationships. These relationships can be between two VETs, two CTTs, or one VET and one CTT.
- Two tables based on a common field between them, by using different types of joins including Left Join, Right Join, Inner Join, Outer Join, Left Excluding Join, Right Excluding Join, and Outer Excluding Join. The Join operations can be used between two VETs, two CTTs, or a VET and a CTT.

- Two tables by using the union operator that combines the result-set of these tables whether they are CTTs or VETs.
- Two or more tables that have relationships between them, by using filters on multiple tables, or filtering data based on the results of subqueries.

Moreover, EETPS functions have the capabilities of retrieving data from CTTs or VETs by using the following query options: Logical Operators, Arithmetic operators, Aggregate Functions, Mathematical functions, Using Single or Composite Primary Keys, Specifying Query SELECT clauses, Specifying Query WHERE Clause, Specifying Query Limit, and Retrieving BLOB and CLOB Values. The overview architecture of the service is shown in Fig. 2. This architecture shows the four main layers of EETPS architecture, including the Presentation Layer, the Application Programming Interface (API) layer, the Service Layer, and the Domain Layer. The Presentation Layer represents the applications that access EET database through EETPS such as SaaS, mobile, web, and stand-alone applications. The API Layer is the EET Data Retrieval API. The Service Layer consists of EETPS, and finally, the Domain Layer is EET that consists of three types of tables CTT, ET, and VET. The Presentation Layer allows the tenants to retrieve data by calling functions from EETPS through the API Layer, and passing parameters to these functions. When invoked, EETPS function generates a tenant query from CTTs and/or VETs by using the ET and a number of query options, and then executes the query in a RDBMS. The RDBMS returns the retrieved table rows from EET and passes these rows back to EETPS to store them in an array. Finally, EETPS returns the tenant's requested data in an array to the tenant through the API Layer.

Using this service on top of EET multi-tenant database schema gives the service provider tenants a choice of the following three database models (Fig. 4):

- **Multi-tenant relational database**. This database model allows tenants to use a standard relational database schema for a particular business domain database without the need to extend the existing database structures. This business domain database can be shared between multiple tenants and differentiate between them by using a Tenant ID column in the physical tables. This model can be applied to any business domain database.

- **Integrated multi-tenant relational database with virtual relational database.** This database model allows tenants to use a standard relational database schema or a particular business domain, extend it by adding additional virtual database tables, and combine these tables with the existing database structure by creating virtual relationships between them.

- **Multi-tenant virtual relational database**. This database model allows tenants to use their own configurable database through creating their virtual database schema from the scratch, by creating virtual database tables, virtual database relationships, and other database constraints to satisfy the requirements of their business applications.

For example, if a service provider offers a Sales database schema to be used by multiple tenants, and on top of this database schema the service provider uses EETPS, then this service provider is able to use the three database models listed above that fulfill various

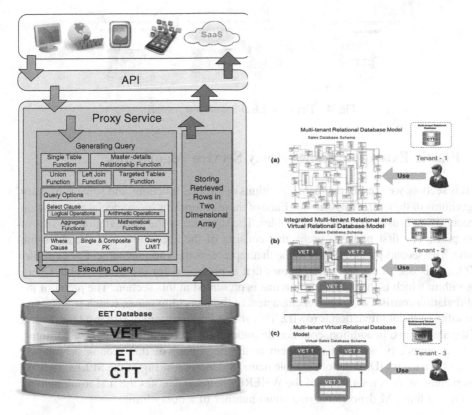

Fig. 2. EETPS overview architecture

Fig. 3. The EETPS three database models example

business requirements. In this example, we assume that the service provider has three tenants. The first user has evaluated the Sales database and found that this database suits his business requirements without any modifications. Therefore, this user will use the Sales database schema as originally provided by the service provider as illustrated in Fig. 3(a). The second user has evaluated the Sales database schema and found that he needs to add extra tables to fulfill his business needs. Thus, this user created VET 1, VET 2, and VET 3, and then, created virtual database relationships between these VETs and the existing physical tables (CTTs) in the sales database schema. The database model for this user is shown in Fig. 3(b). The third user has evaluated the same database schema and found that it did not suit his business requirements, and decided not to use the Sales database schema at all, and instead created virtual relational tables from scratch and established database relationships between them as shown in Fig. 3(c). When these three users have created and configured their database structures, they can retrieve data from their databases by calling functions from EETPS. This example illustrates the three database models that EETPS and EET schema provide. Using these database models, users can design their databases and automatically configure their behaviors during runtime. For more details about how to manage EET, we refer the reader to [24].

Fig. 4. The three EETPS database models

5 Elastic Extension Tables Proxy Service Algorithms

In this section, we present the main algorithms of EETPS functions and some subsidiary algorithms of these main algorithms. Each of these algorithms has a special abbreviation structure that is used to define its variables. The structure of the abbreviation consists of two parts. The first part is a prefix that consists of the abbreviation of the algorithm name. The second part is a suffix name that represents the variable name. For example, STQ_{rowID} is one of the definition names that is presented for the Single Table Query algorithm, which is the first algorithm that is presented in this section. The prefix of the abbreviation consists of the initial characters of the algorithm name, which is STQ, and the suffix of the abbreviation is rowID. This abbreviation pattern is also used for the rest of the algorithms. In addition, common definitions are used in the following algorithms, and for simplicity we are listing them at the beginning of this section as follows: T denotes a tenant ID. B denotes a table name. S denotes a string of the SELECT clause parameters. W denotes a string of the WHERE clause. F denotes the first result number of a query limit. M denotes the maximum number of a query limit.

5.1 Single Table Query Algorithm

This section presents the main algorithm and some subsidiary algorithms of the Single Table function that retrieves table rows from a CTT or a VET. This algorithm has three different cases to retrieve table rows from a VET. Firstly, retrieving rows from a VET by specifying a set of primary keys. Secondly, retrieving rows from a VET by specifying a set of table rows IDs that are stored in 'table_row' ET. Thirdly, retrieving all rows of a CTT or a VET without specifying any primary key or row ID.

Single Table Main Algorithm: This algorithm is used to retrieve table rows from one single table either a CTT or a VET, and it is outlined in Algorithm 1.

Definition 1 (Single Table Query Main Algorithm). STQ_{rowID} denotes a set of table rows IDs. STQ_{PK} denotes a set of primary keys. STQ_{type} denotes the table type (CTT or VET). STQ_{index} denotes a set of VET indexes. $STQ_{PKIndex}$ denotes a primary key indexes of a VET. STQ_{CTT} denotes a set of retrieved rows from a CTT. STQ_{VET} denotes a set of retrieved rows from a VET. STQ_{array} denotes a two dimensional array that stores the retrieved rows.

Algorithm 1. SingleTableQuery (STQ)

Input: T, B, STQ_{rowID}, STQ_{PK}, S, W, F, M, and STQ_{type}
Output: STQ_{array}

1. **if** STQ_{type} = 'CTT' **then**
2.   W ← Concatenate (W, STQ_{PK})
3. STQ_{CTT} ← **CovertCTTtoVETStructure**(T, B, S, W, F, M) /* Algorithm 4 */
4. **else if** STQ_{type} = 'VET' **then**
5.   **if** $STQ_{PK} \neq$ null **then**
6. STQ_{VET} ← **GetTableRowQuery**(T, B, Nil, STQ_{PK}, S, W, F, M) /*Algorithm 2 */
7.   **else if** $STQ_{rowID} \neq$ null **then**
8. STQ_{VET} ← **GetTableRowQuery**(T, B, STQ_{rowID}, Nil, S, W, F, M) /*Algorithm 2 */
9.   **else**
10. $STQ_{PKIndex}$ ← retrieve the primary key index column from table_column ET using T,
           and B query filters
11. STQ_{index}← retrieve indexes from table_index ET using T, B, and $STQ_{PKIndex}$ query
           filters
12.   **if** $STQ_{index} \in$ B **then**   /* If B has indexes */
13. STQ_{VET} ← **GetTableRowQuery**(T, B, STQ_{index}, Nil, S, W, F, M)
14.   /* Algorithm 2 */
15.   **else**
16. STQ_{VET} ← **GetTableRowQuery**(T, B, Nil, Nil, S, W, F, M)
17.   /* Algorithm 2 */
18.   **end if**
19.   **end if**
20. **end if**
21. **if** STQ_{type} = 'CTT' **then**
22. STQ_{array} ← **StoreRowsInArray**(T, B, STQ_{CTT}) /* Algorithm 3 */
23. **else if** STQ_{type} = 'VET' **then**
24. STQ_{array} ← **StoreRowsInArray**(T, B, STQ_{VET}) /* Algorithm 3 */
25. **end if**
26. **Return** STQ_{array}

Get Table Row Query Algorithm: This subsidiary query algorithm is used to retrieve tenant's table rows from a VET. The database query of this algorithm uses UNION operator keyword to combine the result-set of three SELECT statements for three tables, including the 'table_row', the 'table_row_blob', and the 'table_row_clob' ETs when the VET contains BLOB and/or CLOB. However, if the VET does not contain BLOB and CLOB then this algorithm do not use the UNION operator in the query and instead it retrieve data from only the 'table_row' ET. The details of this algorithm are outlined in Algorithm 2.

Definition 2 (Get Table Row Query Algorithm). $GTRQ_{rowID}$ denotes a set of table rows IDs. $GTRQ_{PK}$ denotes a primary key row matrix with 2 rows and n columns. The first row stores a $GTRQ_{PK0,i}$ that denotes a value of virtual primary key column ID stored in the 'table_column_id' column of any of the three ETs, including the 'table_row', the 'table_row_blob', and the 'table_row_clob'. The second row stores a $GTRQ_{PK1,i}$ that denotes the value of the $GTRQ_{PK0,i}$. $GTRQ_M$ denotes the maximum amount number of a query limit that will be retrieved from the 'table_row' ET. $GTRQ_{queryStr}$ denotes a string contains the structure of a select statement that is executed in this algorithm. $GTRQ_{rows}$ denotes the retrieved rows from RDBMS after executing the $GTRQ_{queryStr}$.

Algorithm 2. GetTableRowQuery (GTRQ)

Input: T, B, $GTRQ_{rowID}$, $GTRQ_{PK}$, S, W, F, and $GTRQ_M$
Output: $GTRQ_{rows}$
1. W ← Concatenate(W, $GTRQ_{PK}$)
/* Store the select statement string into $GTRQ_{queryStr}$ */
2. $GTRQ_{queryStr}$ ← Retrieve rows from table_row ET using T, B , $GTRQ_{rowID}$, S, and W ∪
   Retrieve rows from table_row_blob ET using T, B, $GTRQ_{rowID}$, S, and W ∪
   Retrieve rows from table_row_clob ET using T, B, $GTRQ_{rowID}$, S, and W using a limit of
   the rows result between F and $GTRQ_M$
3. $GTRQ_{queryStr}$ ← execute $GTRQ_{queryStr}$ in RDBMS
4. **Return** $GTRQ_{rows}$

Store Rows in Array Algorithm: This subsidiary algorithm is used to store the retrieved data from a CTT or a VET in a two-dimensional array. The number of array rows corresponds a number of retrieved rows, and the number of array columns corresponds a number of retrieved columns. The column names are stored in the first element of the two-dimensional array, and the columns' values are stored in the rest of the array elements. The details of this algorithm are outlined in Algorithm 3.

Definition 3 (Store Rows in Array Algorithm). $SRA_{rowsList}$ denotes a set of retrieved rows from a CTT or a VET where each of these rows is denoted by SRA_{row}. Each SRA_{row} is a set of columns and each column is denoted by SRA_{col}. $SRA_{rown}(SRA_{colm})$ denotes a value stored in the SRA_{colm} of the SRA_{rown}. $SRA_{rowsListSize}$ denotes the size of the $SRA_{rowsList}$. $SRA_{rowSize}$ denotes the size of the SRA_{row}. $SRA_{colNames}$ denotes a set of column names of a CTT or a VET. $SRA_{colNamesSize}$ denotes the size of the $SRA_{colNames}$. SRA_{array} denotes a two dimensional array to store the retrieved rows.

Algorithm 3. StoreRowsInArray (SRA)

Input: T, B, and $SRA_{rowsList}$
Output: SRA_{Array}
1. $SRA_{colNames}$ ← retrieve the column names from table_column ET using T and B query
    filters
2. Initialize SRA_{array} $[SRA_{rowsListSize}]$ $[SRA_{colNamesSize}]$
3. **for** i ← 0 **to** $SRA_{colNameSize}$ **do** /* This loop stores the row columns' names */
4. $SRA_{array}[0][i]$ ← $SRA_{colNames\,i}$
5. i ← $i + 1$
6. **end for**
7. **for** n ← 0 **to** $SRA_{rowsListSize}$ **do** /* This loop stores the rows columns' values */
8.   **for** m ← 0 **to** $SRA_{rowSize}$ **do**
9. $SRA_{array}[n+1][m]$ ← $SRA_{row\,n}(SRA_{col\,m})$
10. m ← $m + 1$
11.   **end for**
12. n ← $n + 1$
13. **end for**
14. **Return** SRA_{array}

Convert CTT Structure to VET Structure Algorithm: This subsidiary algorithm is used to convert the retrieved data from a CTT into VET structure that consists of two-dimensional array, the number of array rows represents a number of retrieved rows, and the number of array columns represents a number of retrieved columns of a CTT. The column names are stored in the first element of the two-dimensional array, and the data in these columns are stored in the rest of the array elements. The details of this algorithm are outlined in Algorithm 4.

Definition 4 (Convert CTT to VET Structure Algorithm). $CCVS_{rowList}$ denotes a set of retrieved rows from a CTT where each row is denoted as $CCVS_{row}$. Each $CCVS_{row}$ is a set of columns and each column is denoted by $CCVS_{col}$. $CCVS_{rown}(CCVS_{colm})$ denotes a value stored in the $CCVS_{colm}$ of the $CCVS_{rown}$. $CCVS_{rowListSize}$ denotes the size of $CCVS_{rowList}$, and the size of each $CCVS_{row}$ in the $CCVS_{rowList}$ is denoted by $CCVS_{rowSize}$. $CCVS_{colNames}$ denotes a set of a CTT columns'names. $CCVS_{colNamesSize}$ denotes the size of the $CCVS_{colNames}$. $CCVS_{array}$ denotes a two dimensional array that stores the retrieved row s from a CTT.

Algorithm 4. CovertCTTtoVETStructure (CCVS)

Input: T, B, S, W, F, and M
Output: $CCVS_{array}$
1. $CCVS_{colNames} \leftarrow$ retrieve the column names of a CTT from
      INFORMATION_SCHEMA.COLUMNS view using B query filter
2. $CCVS_{rowList} \leftarrow$ retrieve rows from B using T, S, W, F, and M query filters
3.   **for** $i \leftarrow 0$ **to** $CCVS_{colNamesSize}$ **do**
4. $CCVS_{array}[0][i] \leftarrow CCVS_{colNames\ i}$
5. $i \leftarrow i + 1$
6.   **end for**
7.   **for** $n \leftarrow 0$ **to** $CCVS_{rowListSize}$ **do**
8.   **for** $m \leftarrow 0$ **to** $CCVS_{rowSize}$ **do**
9. $CCVS_{array}[n+1][m] \leftarrow CCVS_{row\ n}(CCVS_{col\ m})$
10. $m \leftarrow m + 1$
11.   **end for**
12. $n \leftarrow n + 1$
13.**end for**
14.**Return** $CCVS_{array}$

5.2 One-to-Many Query Algorithm

This algorithm retrieves table rows from two CTTs, two VETs, or one VET and one CTT. These two tables may have any of the following database relationships between them: One-to-One, One-to-Many, Many-to-One, Many-to-Many, or Self-referencing. In this section, a sample algorithm of the One-to-Many relationship is presented as outlined in Algorithm 5.

Definition 5 (One-to-Many Query Algorithm). $OTMQ_{master}$ denotes the master table of the One-to-Many relationship. $OTMQ_{details}$ denotes the details table of the One-to-Many relationship. $OTMQ_{masterPK}$ denotes a row matrix with 2 rows and n columns. The first row stores $OTMQ_{masterPK0,i}$ that denotes a primary key column name of a table. The second row stores $OTMQ_{masterPK1,i}$ that denotes a table primary key value of the

$OTMQ_{masterPK0,i}$. $OTMQ_{type}$ denotes the $OTMQ_{details}$ type (CTT or VET). $OTMQ_{detailsFK}$ denotes a set stores foreign keys columns' names of the details table. $OTMQ_{swapPK}$ denotes a row matrix with 2 rows and n columns to store. The first row stores a $OTMQ_{swapPK0,i}$ that denotes the column name of a foreign key. This foreign key belongs to the details table and refers to a primary key in the master table. The second row stores $OTMQ_{swapPK1,i}$ that denotes a value of the $OTMQ_{swapPK0,i}$. $OTMQ_{rows}$ denotes a set of retrieved rows from a VET. $OTMQ_{array}$ denotes a two dimensional array to store the retrieved rows.

Algorithm 5. OneToManyQuery (OTMQ)

Input: T, $OTMQ_{master}$, $OTMQ_{details}$, $OTMQ_{masterPK}$ S, W, F, M, and $OTMQ_{type}$
Output: $OTMQ_{array}$
1. **if** $OTMQ_{type}$ = 'CTT' **then**
2.   W ← Concatenate (W, $OTMQ_{masterPK}$)
3. $OTMQ_{array}$ ← **CovertCTTtoVETStructure**(T, B, S, W, F, M)
       /* Algorithm 4 */
4. **else if** $OTMQ_{type}$ = 'VET' **then**
5. $OTMQ_{detailsFK}$ ← retrieve the foreign keys of $OTMQ_{details}$ which has a master details
       relationship with $OTMQ_{master}$ from the table_relationship ET using T, B query filters
6.   **for** i ← 0 to $OTMQ_{masterPK}$ **do**
7.   **for** j ← 0 to $OTMQ_{detailsFK}$ **do**
8.   **if** $OTMQ_{detailsFK\ j}$ ∈ $OTMQ_{masterPK\ 0,i}$ **then**
9. $OTMQ_{swapPK\ 0,i}$ ← $OTMQ_{detailsFK\ j}$
10. $OTMQ_{swapPK\ 1,i}$ ← $OTMQ_{masterPK\ 1,i}$
11.   **end if**
12. j ← j + 1

13.   **end for**
14. i ← i + 1
15. **end for**
16. $OTMQ_{rows}$ ← **GetTableRowQuery**(T, B, Nil, $OTMQ_{swapPK}$,S, W, F, M)
       /* Algorithm 2 */
17. $OTMQ_{array}$ ← **StoreRowsInArray**(T, B, $OTMQ_{rows}$)   /* Algorithm 3 */
18.**end if**
19.**Return** $OTMQ_{array}$

5.3   Union Query Algorithm

This algorithm retrieves a combined result-set of two or more tables, whether they are CTTs, VETs or a combination of CTTs and VETs, and then stores the result-set in an array. The details of this algorithm are outlined in Algorithm 6.

Definition 6 (Union Query Algorithm). UQ_{tables} denotes a set of CTTs and/or VETs tables names. $UQ_{colNames}$ denotes a matrix with 1 row and n columns. Each column in this matrix contains of a set of arbitrary table columns which are related to a table in UQ_{tables}. UQ_W denotes a set of WHERE clauses which are related to the UQ_{tables} and the columns are ordered according to the table orders of UQ_{tables}. UQ_{Wi} denotes an element of the set UQ_W. UQ_{rows} denotes a set of retrieved rows from a CTT or a VET where each row is denoted as UQ_{row}. Each UQ_{row} is a set of columns and each column is denoted by UQ_{col}. $UQ_{rown}(UQ_{colm})$ denotes a value stored in UQ_{colm} of UQ_{rown}. $UQ_{tablesSize}$ denotes the size of UQ_{tables}. $UQ_{rowSize}$ denotes the size of UQ_{row}. $UQ_{colNamesSize}$ denotes the size of $UQ_{colNames}$. UQ_{array} denotes a two dimensional array that stores the retrieved rows.

Algorithm 6. UnionQuery (UQ)

Input: T, UQ_{tables}, $UQ_{colNames}$, UQ_W, F, and M
Output: UQ_{array}
1. **for** $i \leftarrow 0$ to $UQ_{tablesSize}$ **do**
2.   **if** $UQ_{table\ i} \in$ CTTs **then**
3. $UQ_{row} \leftarrow$ retrieve rows from $UQ_{table\ i}$ by using $UQ_{colNames\ i}$, $UQ_{W\ i}$, F, and M query
        filters
4.   **else if** $UQ_{table\ i} \in$ VETs **then**
5. $UQ_{row} \leftarrow$ **GetTableRowQuery**(T, $UQ_{table\ i}$, Nil, Nil, $UQ_{colNames\ i}$, $UQ_{W\ i}$, F, M x
        $UQ_{colNamesSize}$) /* Algorithm 2 */
6.   **end if**
7.   **for** $n \leftarrow 0$ to $UQ_{rowSize}$ **do**
8.   **for** $m \leftarrow 0$ to $UQ_{rowSize}$ **do**
9. $UQ_{array}[n+1][m] \leftarrow UQ_{row\ n}(UQ_{col\ m})$
10. $m \leftarrow m + 1$
11.   **end for**
12. $n \leftarrow n + 1$
13.   **end for**
14. $i \leftarrow i + 1$
15. **end for**
16. **Return** UQ_{array}

5.4 Join Query Algorithm

This algorithm retrieves a combined table rows from two CTTs, two VETs, or a VET and a CTT based on a common field between them using different types of joins including Left Join, Right Join, Inner Join, Outer Join, Left Excluding Join, Right Excluding Join, and Outer Excluding Join. In this section, a sample algorithm of the Left Join is outlined in Algorithm 7.

Definition 7 (Left Join Query Algorithm). $LJQ_{leftTable}$ denotes a left table of the left join operation. $LJQ_{rightTable}$ denotes a right table of the left join operation. $S_{leftTable}$ denotes a string of the SELECT clause for the left table. $S_{rightTable}$ denotes a string of the SELECT clause for the right table. $W_{leftTable}$ denotes a string of the WHERE clause for the left table. $W_{rightTable}$ denotes a string of the WHERE clause for the right table. LJQ_{leftPK} denotes a set of primary keys of the left table. $LJQ_{rightPK}$ denotes a set of primary keys of the right table. $LJQ_{rightFK}$ denotes a set of foreign keys of the right table refrencing the primary keys of the left table. $LJQ_{twoVETs}$ denotes a row matrix with n rows and 2 columns. The first column stores a $LJQ_{twoVETsn,0}$ that denotes a 'table_row_id' of the $LJQ_{leftTable}$. The second column stores a $LJQ_{twoVETsn,1}$ that denotes a 'table_row_id' of the $LJQ_{rightTable}$. $LJQ_{CTTandVET}$ denotes a row matrix with n rows and 2 columns. The first column stores a $LJQ_{CTTandVETn,0}$ that denotes the primary key of the $LJQ_{leftTable}$ which is a CTT. The second column stores a $LJQ_{CTTandVETn,1}$ that denotes a 'table_row_id' of the $LJQ_{rightTable}$ which is a VET. $LJQ_{leftRows}$ denotes a set of rows of the left table.

Algorithm 7. LeftJoinQuery (LJQ)

Input: T, $LJQ_{leftTable}$, $LJQ_{rightTable}$, $S_{leftTable}$, $S_{rightTable}$, $W_{leftTable}$, $W_{rightTable}$, F, and M
Output: LJQ_{array}
/* Left join for two CTTs */
1. if $LJQ_{leftTable}$ is CTT $\wedge$ $LJQ_{rightTable}$ is CTT **then**
2. $LJQ_{rightPK}$ ← get the primary keys of the CTT $LJQ_{rightTable}$ from the
           INFORMATION_SCHEMAviews
3. LJQ_{leftPK} ← get the primary keys of the CTT $LJQ_{leftTable}$ from the
           INFORMATION_SCHEMA views
4. LJQ_{rows} ← retrieve rows from $LJQ_{leftTable}$ and $LJQ_{rightTable}$ from RDBMS using the
           left join operator and using LJQ_{leftPK}, $LJQ_{rightPK}$, $S_{leftTable}$, $S_{rightTable}$,
           $W_{leftTable}$, $W_{rightTable}$, F, and M query filters
5. LJQ_{array} ← store LJQ_{rows} in two dimensional array
/* Left join for two VETs */
6. else if $LJQ_{leftTable}$ is VET $\wedge$ $LJQ_{rightTable}$ is VET **then**
7. LJQ_{leftPK} ← get the primary keys of the $LJQ_{leftTable}$ from table_column ET
8. $LJQ_{rightFK}$ ← get the foreign keys of the $LJQ_{rightTable}$ from table_relationship ET

9. $LJQ_{twoVETs}$ ← retrieve rows from the table_index ET using a join operator, and using
           LJQ_{leftPK} and $LJQ_{rightFK}$ query filters
10. $LJQ_{leftRows}$ ← **GetTableRowQuery**(T, $LJQ_{lefttTable}$, $LJQ_{twoVETs (1, 2, … ,n),0}$, Nil,
           $S_{leftTable}$, $W_{leftTable}$, F, M)
           /* Algorithm 2*/
11. $LJQ_{rightRows}$ ← **GetTableRowQuery**(T, $LJQ_{rightTable}$, $LJQ_{twoVETs (1, 2, … ,n),1}$,
           Nil, $S_{rightTable}$, $W_{rightTable}$, F, M)
           /* Algorithm 2*/
12. LJQ_{set} ← Concatenate($LJQ_{leftRows}$, $LJQ_{rightRows}$)
13. LJQ_{array} ← store LJQ_{set} in two dimensional array
/* Left join for a CTT and a VET */
14. else if ($LJQ_{leftTable}$ is CTT $\wedge$ $LJQ_{rightTable}$ is VET) **then**
15. LJQ_{leftPK} ← get the primary keys of the $LJQ_{leftTable}$ from the
           INFORMATION_SCHEMAviews
16. $LJQ_{rightFK}$ ← get the foreign keys of the $LJQ_{rightTable}$ from table_relationship ET
17. $LJQ_{CTTandVET}$ ← retrieve rows for $LJQ_{leftTable}$ and $LJQ_{rightTable}$ from the CTT
           $LJQ_{leftTable}$ and the table_index ET using a join operator and using LJQ_{leftPK},
           $LJQ_{rightFK}$ query filters
18. $LJQ_{leftRows}$ ← retrieve rows from the CTT $LJQ_{leftTable}$ using $S_{leftTable}$, $W_{leftTable}$, F,
           and M query filters
19. $LJQ_{rightRows}$ ← **GetTableRowQuery**(T, $LJQ_{rightTable}$, $LJQ_{CTTandVET (1, 2, … ,n),1}$,
           Nil, $S_{rightTable}$, $W_{rightTable}$, F, M)
           /* Algorithm 2*/
20. LJQ_{set} ← Concatenate($LJQ_{leftRows}$, $LJQ_{rightRows}$)
21. LJQ_{array} ← store LJQ_{set} in two dimensional array
/* Left join for a VET and a CTT */
22. else if ($LJQ_{leftTable}$ is VET $\wedge$ $LJQ_{rightTable}$ is CTT) **then**
23.   [...] /* Symmetric to lines 15 to 21, but the difference is that the left table is a VET and
           the right table is a CTT */
24. **end if**
25. **Return** LJQ_{array}

$LJQ_{rightRows}$ denotes a set of rows of the right table. LJQ_{set} denotes a set which consist of two elements. The first element is the $LJQ_{rightRows}$, and the second element is the $LJQ_{leftRows}$. LJQ_{rows} denotes a set of rows for a left CTT and right CTT. LJQ_{array} denotes a two dimensional array that stores the retrieved rows.

5.5   Targeted Tables Query Algorithm

This algorithm combines the result-set of two, or more tables, whether they are CTTs, VETs or a combination of both types of tables. It uses query filters on multiple tables or filtering of data based on the results of subqueries. These complex queries can be executed by calling the function that executes this algorithm. Figure 5 shows an example of a set of tables that have relationships between them. Table A (Root Table) and table C have a Many-to-Many database relationship, while table B is a join table that construct the relationship. Table C and table D have a One-to-Many relationship. Finally, Table D and table E (Targeted Table) have a One-to-Many relationship. This algorithm filters the data in the Targeted Table E based on a number of query results obtained from table A to table D.

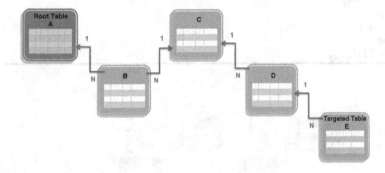

Fig. 5. Targeted Tables example

Definition 8 (Targeted Tables Query Algorithm). TTQ_{tables} denotes a set of CTTs and/or VETs names. $TTQ_{tablesSize}$ denotes the size of TTQ_{tables}. TTQ_{PK} denotes a set of row matrix with 2 rows and n columns. The first row stores the column name of a table primary key. The second row stores the value of a table primary key. TTQ_{select} denotes a set of SELECT clauses, where each table in TTQ_{tables} may have a SELECT clause. TTQ_{where} denotes a set of WHERE clauses, where each table in TTQ_{tables} may have a SELECT clause. TTQ_{type} denotes a table type of a table in TTQ_{tables}. $TTQ_{tablesi}$ denotes a current root table. $TTQ_{tablesi+1}$ denotes a current targeted table. Figure 6 shows an example of current root table and current targeted table that this algorithm may reaches during iterating the targeted table sequence list. $TTQ_{relation}$ denotes a relationship between two tables. TTQ_{PKi} denotes a primary key set for a current root table in the TTQ_{tables}. This set has only primary key IDs without values that can be obtained while iterating the loop of the algorithm for the current root table. TTQ_{array} denotes a two dimensional array that stores the retrieved rows.

Algorithm 8. TargetedTablesQuery (TTQ)

Input: T, TTQ_{tables}, TTQ_{PK}, TTQ_{select}, TTQ_{where}, F, and M
Output: TTQ_{array}
1. **for** $i \leftarrow 0$ **to** $TTQ_{tablesSize}$ **do**
2.   **if** $TTQ_{tablesSize} = (i + 2)$ **then** /* TTQ_{tables} **has 2 table** */
3. $TTQ_{relation} \leftarrow$ get the relationship between $TTQ_{tables\ i}$ and $TTQ_{tables\ i+1}$
4.   **if** $TTQ_{relation}$ is One-to-Many **then**
5. $TTQ_{array} \leftarrow$ **OneToManyQuery**(T, $TTQ_{tables\ i}$, $TTQ_{tables\ i+1}$, $TTQ_{PK\ i}$,
            $TTQ_{select\ i}$, $TTQ_{where\ i}$, F, M, TTQ_{type}) /* Algorithm 5 */
6.   **else if** $TTQ_{relation}$ is Many-to-One **then**
7. $TTQ_{array} \leftarrow$ **OneToManyQuery**(T, $TTQ_{tables\ i+1}$, $TTQ_{tables\ i}$,
            $TTQ_{PK\ i}$, $TTQ_{select\ i}$, $TTQ_{where\ i}$, F, M, TTQ_{type}) /* Algorithm 5 */
8.   **end if**
9.   **else if** $TTQ_{tablesSize} >= (i + 3)$ **then** /* TTQ_{tables} **has 3 or more tables** */
10. $TTQ_{PK\ i} \leftarrow$ **OneToManyPKQuery(...)** /* This algorithm is similar to Algorithm 5,
        but this algorithm returns only primary key IDs and does not store the results in an
        array */
11. **end if**
12. $i \leftarrow i + 1$
13.**end for**
14.**Return** TTQ_{array}

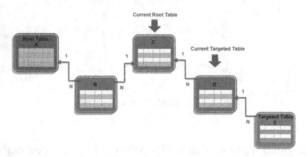

Fig. 6. Current Root Table and Current Targeted Table

6 Performance Evaluation

In [24] we have explored the potential of using EET multi-tenant database schema, and we performed several experiments to assess the effectiveness of EET by comparing it with Universal Table Schema Mapping (UTSM), which is one of the multi-tenant database schema techniques implemented commercially. Significant performance improvements were observed using EET when compared to UTSM, making EET schema a good candidate for the management of multi-tenant data in SaaS applications. In this paper, five types of experiments were performed to verify the practicability of

EETPS. These experiments are classified according to the complexity of the queries into five categories: simple, simple-to-medium, medium, medium-to-complex, and complex. These five experiments show comparisons between the response time of retrieving data from CTTs, VETs, or both CTTs and VETs. The response time of retrieving data from EET is evaluated by accessing EETPS functions.

6.1 Experimental Setup

EETPS was implemented in Java 1.6.0, Hibernate 4.0, and Spring 3.1.0. The database is PostgreSQL 8.4 and the application server is Jboss-5.0.0.CR2. Both, the database and the application server are deployed on the same PC. The operating system is Windows 7 Home Premium, with Intel Core i5 2.40 GHz CPU, 8 GB of RAM memory, and 500 GB of hard disk storage.

6.2 Experimental Data Set and Results

EETPS was developed to serve multiple tenants running in a single application instance, but the aim of the experiments is to evaluate the performance and show the differences between retrieving data of CTTs, VETs, or both CTTs and VETs together for a single tenant. As long as in the multi-tenant database, each tenant's data is isolated in a separate table partition, these experiments can evaluate the effectiveness of retrieving each single tenant's data from EET multi-tenant database. Furthermore, these experiments are performed using a single server instance, and we do not considered scale-up or scale-out multi-tenant database issues in this paper. In the five experiments, the test is performed on fourteen queries twice, the first test to retrieve only 1 row, and the second test to retrieve 100 rows by using the same queries. In order to produce accurate comparisons, the same data input is used for CTTs, VETs and CTT-and-VET to retrieve the same data output. The execution times of these query experiments are recorded based on six data sets for all the five types of experiments. These six data sets contain, (1) 500 rows, (2) 5,000 rows, (3) 10,000 rows, (4) 50,000 rows, (5) 100,000 rows, and (6) 200,000 rows. In this section, the average execution time is computed by executing ten tests on each of the six data sets to show accurate results. All of these data sets were for one tenant. In all the experimental diagrams, the vertical axis shows the execution time in milliseconds, and the horizontal axis shows the total number of rows that stored in a tenant's table. In the five experiments, the 'tenant_id' equals 1000. The CTTs that are used in the experiments, including 'product', 'sales_fact' and 'sales_details', and the corresponding 'db_table_id' of VETs for these tables are 16, 17, and 18 respectively. The data structures used for the queries in the various experiments are shown in Fig. 15, and listed below:

(1) **Simple Query Experiment – Single Table (Exp. 1):** In this experiment, the function of the Single Table Query Algorithm that retrieves data from a CTT is invoked by executing Query 1 (Q 1) that comprises of the Individual Query (IQ) 1, and retrieve the same data from a VET by executing Query 2 (Q 2) that comprises of IQ2 – IQ4. These experimental tests show how the Single Table

Algorithm retrieves physical rows from a CTT and virtual rows from a VET. The three cases that this algorithm is handling are described in Sect. 5. This experiment studies the third case that retrieves all rows of the 'product' CTT and the 'product' VET from the Single Table function without specifying any primary keys or row IDs; the structure of the 'product' table is shown in Fig. 7(a). The 'db_table_id' of the 'product' VET equals 16. The experimental results of Exp. 1 shows that the performance of the query execution time of a VET is faster than a CTT when 1 or 100 of table rows are retrieved. The details of the queries used in this experiment are shown in Tables 3 and 4, the output of these queries is shown in Fig. 8, and the throughputs of this experiment are depicted in Fig. 16(a) and (b).

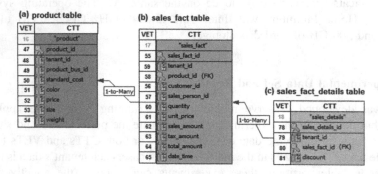

Fig. 7. The tables structures used in the experiments

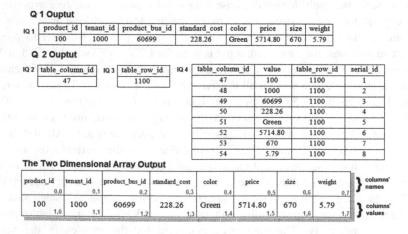

Fig. 8. The outputs of the Simple Query Experiment (Single Table)

(2) **Simple-to-Medium Query Experiment – One-to-Many (Exp. 2):** In this experiment, the function of One-to-Many Query Algorithm is invoked to retrieve data from two CTTs by executing Query 3 (Q 3) that comprises of IQ5, two VETs by executing Query 4 (Q 4) that comprises of IQ6 and IQ7, and CTT-and-VET by

executing Query 5 (Q 5) that comprises of IQ8 and IQ7 respectively. The focus of this experiment is to study each of these two table combinations that have a One-to-Many relationship between them. The master table of this relation is the 'product' table, and the details table is the 'sales_fact' table. The structure of these two tables is shown in Fig. 7(a) and (b). The value of the 'product_id' column that is used in this experiment equals 100 for both the 'product' CTT and VET. The 'product_id' of the VET is represented as the number 58. The experimental results of Exp.2 show that there is an approximate symmetry in the performance of the query execution time of VET and CTT-and-VET and they are one time faster than CTT when 1 row is retrieved. On the other hand, when 100 rows are retrieved, the query execution time of CTT is faster than VET, and CTT-and-VET is the fastest of the three queries. Moreover, the experimental results show that the execution time of CTT is approximately the same when 1 row and 100 rows are retrieved, whereas it increases for VET and CTT-and-VET when 100 rows are retrieved. The details of the queries used in this experiment are shown in Tables 3 and 4, the output of these queries is shown in Fig. 9, and the throughputs of this experiment are depicted in Fig. 16(b) and (c).

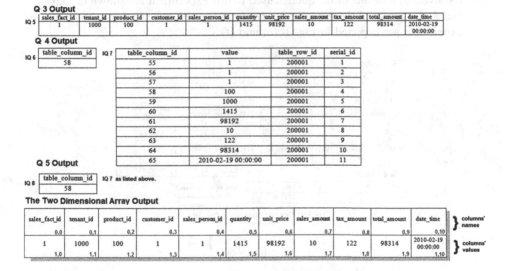

Q 3 Output

IQ 5

sales_fact_id	tenant_id	product_id	customer_id	sales_person_id	quantity	unit_price	sales_amount	tax_amount	total_amount	date_time
1	1000	100	1	1	1415	98192	10	122	98314	2010-02-19 00:00:00

Q 4 Output

IQ 6

table_column_id
58

IQ 7

table_column_id	value	table_row_id	serial_id
55	1	200001	1
56	1	200001	2
57	1	200001	3
58	100	200001	4
59	1000	200001	5
60	1415	200001	6
61	98192	200001	7
62	10	200001	8
63	122	200001	9
64	98314	200001	10
65	2010-02-19 00:00:00	200001	11

Q 5 Output

IQ 8

table_column_id
58

IQ 7 as listed above.

The Two Dimensional Array Output

sales_fact_id	tenant_id	product_id	customer_id	sales_person_id	quantity	unit_price	sales_amount	tax_amount	total_amount	date_time	
0,0	0,1	0,2	0,3	0,4	0,5	0,6	0,7	0,8	0,9	0,10	} columns' names
1	1000	100	1	1	1415	98192	10	122	98314	2010-02-19 00:00:00	} columns' values
1,0	1,1	1,2	1,3	1,4	1,5	1,6	1,7	1,8	1,9	1,10	

Fig. 9. The outputs of the Simple-to-Medium Query Experiment (One-to-Many)

(3) **Medium Query Experiment - Union (Exp. 3):** In this experiment, the function of the Union Query Algorithm that retrieve data from two tables is invoked by using a union operator for two CTTs by executing Query 6 (Q 6) that comprises of IQ9 and IQ10, for two VETs by executing Query 7 (Q 7) that comprises of IQ2, IQ3, IQ11, IQ12, IQ13, and IQ14, and for CTT-and-VET by executing Query 8 (Q 8) that comprises of IQ9, IQ12, IQ13, and IQ14 respectively. The aim of using this algorithm is to study, retrieving data from two tables. The first table is the 'product' table, and the second table is the 'sales_fact' table. The structures of

these two tables are shown in Fig. 7(a) and (b). In Q 6, in the SELECT clause two physical columns 'product_id' and 'price' are specified for the 'product' CTT, and two physical columns 'sales_fact_id' and 'unit_price' are specified for the 'sales_fact' CTT. In Q 7, in the SELECT clause two virtual columns are specified. The first column ID is 47, and the second column ID is 52 for the 'product' VET that equals 16. The column ID 47 corresponds to the 'product_id' column, and the column ID 52 corresponds to the 'price' column of the 'product' VET. In addition, in the SELECT clause two virtual columns are specified for the 'sales_fact' VET that equals 17. The first column is 55, and the second column is 61. The column ID 55 corresponds to the 'sales_fact_id' and the column ID 61 corresponds to the 'unit_price' of the 'sales_fact' VET. Finally, in Q 8, in the SELECT clause two physical columns 'product_id' and 'price' are specified for the 'product' CTT, and two virtual columns for the 'sales_fact' VET. The first column is 55, and the second column is 61. The experimental results of Exp. 3 shows that the query execution time of VET is faster than CTT, and CTT-and-VET is the fastest of the three queries when 1 and 100 rows are retrieved. Moreover, this experiment shows that the query execution times of the three types CTT, VET, and CTT-and-VET are approximately the same when 1 row, and 100 rows are retrieved. The details of the queries used in this experiment are shown in Tables 3 and 4, the output of these queries is shown in Fig. 10, and the throughputs of this experiment are depicted in Fig. 16(e) and (f).

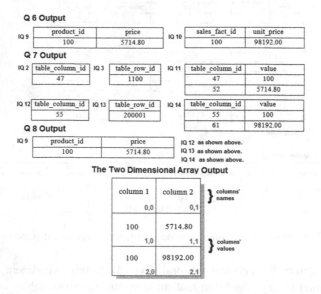

Fig. 10. The outputs of the Medium Query Experiment (Union)

(4) **Medium-to-Complex Query Experiment – Left Join (Exp. 4):** In this experiment, the function of the Left Join Query Algorithm is invoked to use a left join between three types of table combinations. First, two CTTs by executing Query 9 (Q 9) that comprises of IQ15 – IQ17. The two CTTs are the 'product' CTT and the

'sales_fact' CTT. Second, two VETs by executing Query 10 (Q 10) that comprises of IQ2, IQ18, IQ19, IQ4, and IQ21. The two VETs are the 'product VET that equals 16, and the 'sales_fact' VET that equals 17. Third, a CTT and a VET by executing Query 11 (Q 11) that comprises of IQ15, IQ8, IQ20, IQ1, and IQ21 respectively. These two tables are the 'product' CTT, and the 'sales_fact' VET that equals 17. Figure 11 shows the three Left Join operations that are used in this experiment. The experimental results of Exp. 4 shows that the query execution time of CTT-and-VET is faster than CTT, and the VET is the fastest of the three queries when 1 row and 100 rows are retrieved. The details of the queries used in this experiment are shown in Tables 3 and 4, the output of these queries is shown in Fig. 12, and the throughputs of this experiment are depicted in Fig. 16(g) and (h).

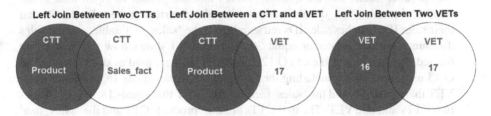

Fig. 11. The three left joins of the Left Join experiment

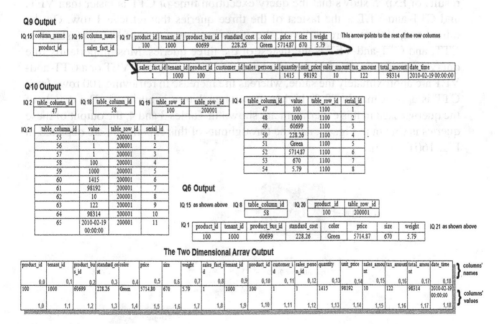

Fig. 12. The output of the Medium-to-Complex Query Experiment (Left Join)

(5) **Complex Query Experiment – Targeted Tables (Exp. 5):** In this experiment, the function of the Targeted Table Query Algorithm is invoked to join two CTTs by executing Query 12 (Q 12) that comprises of IQ22 and IQ23, two VETs by

executing Query 13 (Q 13) that comprises of IQ24 – IQ27, and CTT-and-VET by Query 14 (Q 14) that comprises of IQ28, IQ22, IQ29, and IQ27 respectively. This experiment is used to study, retrieving data from three targeted tables. The first table is the 'product' table, the second table is the 'sales_fact' table, and the third table is 'sales_fact_details'. The structure of these three tables is shown in Fig. 7(a), (b) and (c). These tables have relationships between them, and multiple query filters are used in each of these tables to filter data based on the results of subqueries, starting from the 'product' table (Root Table) until the 'sales_fact_details' table (Targeted Table). The 'product' table is filtered by retrieving only products with product IDs equal to 100. Then the 'sales_fact' table is filtered by retrieving the sales transactions that their product IDs match the sales IDs that are retrieved from the 'product' table, and the quantity values that are greater or equal than 9000. Finally, the 'sales_fact_details' table is filtered by retrieving the sales details that their sales IDs matches sales IDs retrieved from the 'sales_fact' table, and the sales discounts that are greater or equal 30 %. Figure 13 shows how the queries are filtered from the three tables. In Q 12, the three CTTs are used as stated above. The Q 13 uses three VETs, including the 'product VET that equals 16, the 'sales_fact' VET that equals 17, and the 'sales_fact_details' VET that equals 18. The Q 14 uses two CTTs and one VET. The two CTTs are the 'product' CTT and the 'sales_fact' CTT, and the VET is the 'sales_fact_details' that equals 18. The experimental results of Exp. 5 shows that the query execution time of CTT is faster than VET, and CTT-and-VET is the fastest of the three queries that retrieve 1 row. On the other hand, 100 rows are retrieved, the query execution time of VET is faster than CTT, and CTT-and-VET is the fastest of the three queries. Most importantly, the query execution times when retrieve 1 row or 100 rows from a VET or a CTT-and-VET are approximately the same, whereas the increase in retrieving 100 rows from CTT is approximately 70 % higher than when 1 row is retrieved. The details of the queries used in this experiment are shown in Tables 3 and 4, the output of these queries is shown in Fig. 14, and the throughputs of this experiment are depicted in Fig. 16(i) and (j).

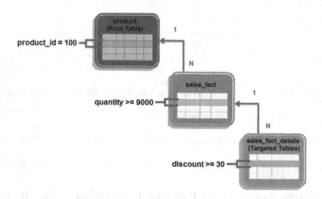

Fig. 13. The query filters of the Targeted Tables experiment

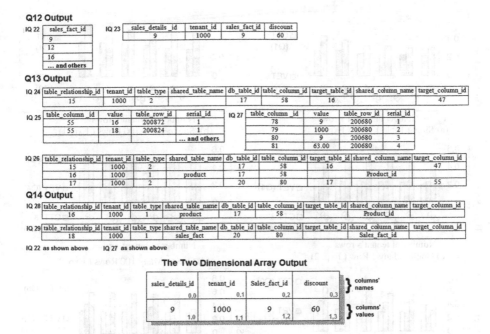

Q12 Output

IQ 22

sales_fact_id
9
12
16
... and others

IQ 23

sales_details _id	tenant_id	sales_fact_id	discount
9	1000	9	60

Q13 Output

IQ 24

table_relationship_id	tenant_id	table_type	shared_table_name	db_table_id	table_column_id	target_table_id	shared_column_name	target_column_id
15	1000	2		17	58	16		47

IQ 25

table_column _id	value	table_row_id	serial_id
55	16	200872	1
55	18	200824	1
		... and others	

IQ 27

table_column _id	value	table_row_id	serial_id
78	9	200680	1
79	1000	200680	2
80	9	200680	3
81	63.00	200680	4

IQ 26

table_relationship_id	tenant_id	table_type	shared_table_name	db_table_id	table_column_id	target_table_id	shared_column_name	target_column_id
15	1000	2		17	58	16		47
16	1000	1	product	17	58		Product_id	
17	1000	2		20	80	17		55

Q14 Output

IQ 28

table_relationship_id	tenant_id	table_type	shared_table_name	db_table_id	table_column_id	target_table_id	shared_column_name	target_column_id
16	1000	1	product	17	58		Product_id	

IQ 29

table_relationship_id	tenant_id	table_type	shared_table_name	db_table_id	table_column_id	target_table_id	shared_column_name	target_column_id
18	1000	1	sales_fact	20	80		Sales_fact_id	

IQ 22 as shown above   IQ 27 as shown above

The Two Dimensional Array Output

sales_details_id	tenant_id	Sales_fact_id	discount	} columns' names
0,0	0,1	0,2	0,3	
9	1000	9	60	} columns' values
1,0	1,1	1,2	1,3	

Fig. 14. The outputs of the Complex Query Experiment (Targeted Tables)

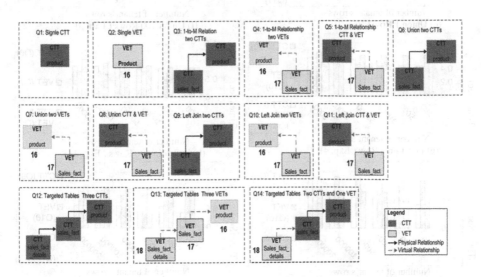

Fig. 15. The structures of the query used in the experiments

The above five experiments are summarized in Fig. 17 and Table 1 that show the average query execution times of the six data sets for each experiment when 1 row is retrieved, and in Fig. 18 and Table 2 that show the query execution times when 100 rows are retrieved. The results indicate that most of the experiments performed on

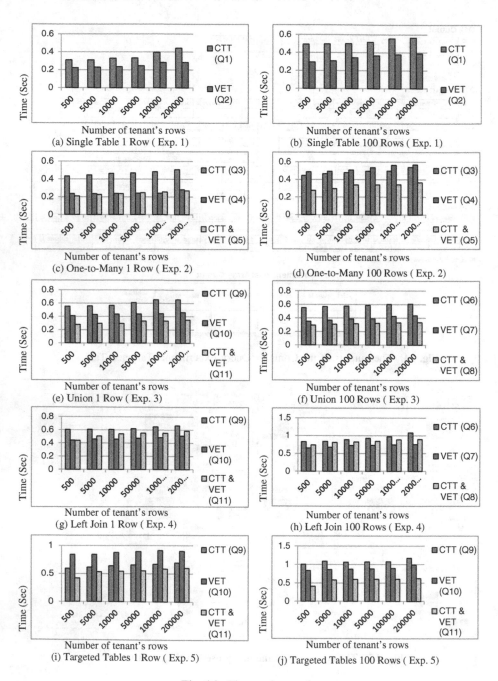

Fig. 16. The queries results

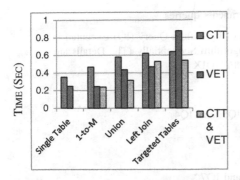

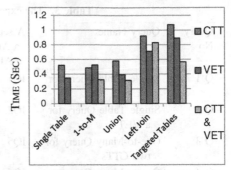

Fig. 17. The average experimental results of retrieving 1 row

Fig. 18. The average experimental results of retrieving 100 rows

Table 1. The average experimental results of retrieving 1 row in milliseconds

Retrieving 1 Row	CTT	VET	CTT-and-VET
Single Table (Exp. 1)	Q 1	Q 2	
	352	249	
One-to-Many (Exp. 2)	Q 3	Q 4	Q 5
	465	244	238
Union (Exp. 3)	Q 6	Q 7	Q 8
	579	435	313
Left Join (Exp. 4)	Q 9	Q 10	Q 11
	621	468	526
Targeted Tables (Exp. 5)	Q 12	Q 13	Q 14
	640	876	536

Table 2. The average experimental results of retrieving 100 rows in milliseconds.

Retrieving 100 Rows	CTT	VET	CTT-and-VET
Single Table (Exp. 1)	Q 1	Q 2	
	520	346	
One-to-Many (Exp. 2)	Q 3	Q 4	Q 5
	485	524	325
Union (Exp. 3)	Q 6	Q 7	Q 8
	580	391	316
Left Join (Exp. 4)	Q 9	Q 10	Q 11
	920	709	829
Targeted Tables (Exp. 5)	Q 12	Q 13	Q 14
	1075	889	566

Table 3. The experiments queries

Query No.	Query Name	A set of Individual Query (IQ) Executed in an Algorithm Sequentially (The Details are in APPENDIX II)
Q 1	Single Table Query for a CTT	IQ1
Q 2	Single Table Query for a VET	IQ2, IQ3, and IQ4
Q 3	One-to-Many Query for two CTTs	IQ5
Q 4	One-to-Many Query for two VETs	IQ6, and IQ7
Q 5	One-to-Many Query for a CTT and a VET.	IQ8, and IQ7.
Q 6	Union Query for Two CTTs	IQ9, and IQ10
Q 7	Union Query for Two VETs	IQ2, IQ3, IQ11, IQ12, IQ13, and IQ14
Q 8	Union Query for a CTT and a VET	IQ9, IQ12, IQ13, and IQ14
Q 9	Left Join Query for two CTTs	IQ15, IQ16, and IQ17
Q 10	Left Join Query for two VETs	IQ2, IQ18, IQ19, IQ4, and IQ21
Q 11	Left Join Query for a CTT and a VET	IQ15, IQ8, IQ20, IQ1, and IQ21
Q 12	Targeted Tables Query for two CTTs	IQ22, and IQ23
Q 13	Targeted Tables Query for two VETs	IQ24, IQ25, IQ26, and IQ27
Q 14	Targeted Tables Query for a CTT and a VET	IQ28, IQ22, IQ29, and IQ27

EETPS functions improved the query execution time for retrievals from VET and CTT-and-VET when compared to retrieval using CTT (traditional physical tables). Except in two cases the results show increase in execution times: first, when 100 rows are retrieved from the One-to-Many function, VET is slightly slower than CTT, and second, when 1 row is retrieved from the Targeted Tables function VET is slower than CTT and the average difference between them is 236 ms.

Table 4. The experiments queries details

Individual Query (IQ)	Query Details
IQ1	SELECT * FROM product p WHERE p.tenant_id = 1000 ORDER BY p.product_id LIMIT 1;
IQ2	SELECT tc.table_column_id FROM table_column tc WHERE tc. tenant_id = 1000 and tc.db_table_id = 16 and tc. is_primary_key_column = true ORDER BY tc.table_column_id;
IQ3	SELECT distinct ti.table_row_id FROM table_index ti WHERE ti. tenant_id = 1000 and ti.db_table_id = 16 and ti.table_column_id = 47 LIMIT 1;
IQ4	SELECT tr.table_column_id, tr.value, tr.table_row_id, tr.serial_id FROM table_row tr WHERE tr.tenant_id = 1000 and tr.db_table_id = 16 and tr.table_row_id IN (1100) ORDER BY 3,4 LIMIT 8 OFFSET 0;
IQ5	SELECT * FROM sales_fact sf WHERE sf.tenant_id = 1000 andsf. product_id = 100 ORDER BY sf.sales_fact_id LIMIT 1;
IQ6	SELECT trs.table_column_id FROM table_relationship trs WHERE trs. tenant_id = 1000 and trs.db_table_id = 17 and trs.table_type = 2 and trs.target_table_id = '16' and (trs.table_column_id = 58 or trs. target_column_id = 58) ORDER BY 1 ASC;
IQ7	SELECT tr.table_column_id, tr.value, tr.table_row_id, tr.serial_id FROM table_row tr WHERE tr.tenant_id = 1000 and tr.db_table_id = 17 and tr.table_row_id IN (SELECT distinct tr.table_row_id From table_index tr WHERE tr.tenant_id = 1000 and tr.db_table_id = 17 and ((tr. table_column_id = '58' and tr.value = '100')) LIMIT 1 OFFSET 0) ORDER BY 3,4 ASC LIMIT 11 OFFSET 0;
IQ8	SELECT trs.table_column_id FROM table_relationship trs WHERE trs. tenant_id = 1000 and trs.db_table_id = 17 and trs.table_type = 1 and trs.shared_table_name = 'product' and trs. shared_column_name = 'product_id' ORDER BY 1 ASC;
IQ9	SELECT p.product_id, p.price FROM product p WHERE p. tenant_id = 1000 ORDER BY p.product_id LIMIT 1;
IQ10	SELECT sf.sales_fact_id, sf.unit_price FROM sales_fact sf WHERE sf. tenant_id = 1000 ORDER BY sf.sales_fact_id LIMIT 1;
IQ11	SELECT tr.table_column_id, tr.value FROM table_row tr WHERE tr. tenant_id = 1000 and tr.db_table_id = 16 and tr.table_row_id IN (1100) and table_column_id in (47,52) ORDER BY tr.table_row_id, tr. serial_id LIMIT 2 OFFSET 0;
IQ12	SELECT tc.table_column_id FROM table_column tc WHERE tc. tenant_id = 1000 and tc.db_table_id = 17 and tc. is_primary_key_column = true ORDER BY tc.table_column_id;
IQ13	SELECT distinct ti.table_row_id FROM table_index ti WHERE ti. tenant_id = 1000 and ti.db_table_id = 17 and ti.table_column_id = 55 LIMIT 1;
IQ14	SELECT tr.table_column_id, tr.value FROM table_row tr WHERE tr. tenant_id = 1000 and tr.db_table_id = 17 and tr.table_row_id IN

(*Continued*)

Table 4. (*Continued*)

Individual Query (IQ)	Query Details
	(200001) and table_column_id in (55,61) ORDER BY tr.table_row_id, tr.serial_id LIMIT 2 OFFSET 0;
IQ15	SELECT c.COLUMN_NAME FROM INFORMATION_SCHEMA. TABLE_CONSTRAINTS pk,INFORMATION_SCHEMA. KEY_COLUMN_USAGE c WHERE pk.TABLE_NAME = 'product' and CONSTRAINT_TYPE = 'PRIMARY KEY' and c. TABLE_NAME = pk.TABLE_NAME and c. CONSTRAINT_NAME = pk.CONSTRAINT_NAME;
IQ16	SELECT c.COLUMN_NAME FROM INFORMATION_SCHEMA. TABLE_CONSTRAINTS pk,INFORMATION_SCHEMA. KEY_COLUMN_USAGE c WHERE pk. TABLE_NAME = 'sales_fact' and CONSTRAINT_TYPE = 'PRIMARY KEY' and c. TABLE_NAME = pk.TABLE_NAME and c. CONSTRAINT_NAME = pk.CONSTRAINT_NAME;
IQ17	SELECT * FROM product lt LEFT JOIN sales_fact rt ON lt. product_id = rt.product_id LIMIT 1 OFFSET 0;
IQ18	SELECT trs.table_column_id FROM table_relationship trs WHERE trs. tenant_id = 1000 and trs.db_table_id = 17 and trs.table_type = 2 and trs.target_table_id = '16' and (trs.table_column_id = 47 or trs. target_column_id = 47) ORDER BY 1 ASC;
IQ19	SELECT trl.table_row_id, trr.table_row_id FROM table_index trl, table_index trr WHERE trl.tenant_id = 1000 and trr.tenant_id = 1000 and(((trl.db_table_id = 16 and trl.table_column_id = 47) and(trr. db_table_id = 17 and trr.table_column_id = 58) and trl.value = trr. value)) LIMIT 1 OFFSET 0;
IQ20	SELECT cttl.product_id, trr.table_row_id as right_row_id FROM product cttl, table_index trr WHERE cttl.tenant_id = 1000 and trr. tenant_id = 1000 and((trr.db_table_id = 17 and trr. table_column_id = 58 and trr.value = CAST(cttl.product_id AS TEXT))) LIMIT 1 OFFSET 0;
IQ21	SELECT tr.table_column_id, tr.value, tr.table_row_id, tr.serial_id FROM table_row tr WHERE tr.tenant_id = 1000 and tr.db_table_id = 17 and tr.table_row_id IN (200001) ORDER BY 3,4 LIMIT 11 OFFSET 0;
IQ22	SELECT sf.sales_fact_id FROM sales_fact sf WHERE sf. tenant_id = 1000 and sf.quantity > = 9000 and product_id = 100 ORDER BY sf.sales_fact_id;
IQ23	SELECT * FROM sales_details sd WHERE sd.tenant_id = 1000 and sd. discount > = 30 and (sales_fact_id in (9, 12, 16, … and other IDs)) ORDER BY sd.sales_details_id LIMIT 1;
IQ24	SELECT * FROM table_relationship trs WHERE trs.tenant_id = 1000 and trs.db_table_id = 16 or trs.target_table_id = 16 ORDER BY trs. table_relationship_id;

(*Continued*)

Table 4. (*Continued*)

Individual Query (IQ)	Query Details
IQ25	SELECT tr.table_column_id, tr.value, tr.table_row_id, tr.serial_id FROM table_row tr JOIN table_column tc ON tr.table_column_id = tc. table_column_id and tr.tenant_id = tc.tenant_id and tr.db_table_id = tc. db_table_id WHERE tc.is_primary_key_column = 't' and tr. tenant_id = 1000 and tr.db_table_id = 17 and tr.table_row_id IN (SELECT distinct tr.table_row_id FROM table_row tr WHERE tr. tenant_id = 1000 and tr.db_table_id = 17 and tr.table_column_id = 60 and(cast(value as numeric) > = '9000') and tr.table_row_id IN (SELECT tr.table_row_id FROM table_index tr WHERE tr. tenant_id = 1000 and tr.db_table_id = 17 and((tr. table_column_id = '58' and tr.value = '100')))) ORDER BY 3,4 ASC;
IQ26	SELECT * FROM table_relationship trs WHERE trs.tenant_id = 1000 and trs.db_table_id = 17 or trs.target_table_id = 17 ORDER BY trs. table_relationship_id;
IQ27	SELECT tr.table_column_id, tr.value, tr.table_row_id, tr.serial_id FROM table_row tr WHERE tr.tenant_id = 1000 and tr.db_table_id = 18 and tr.table_row_id IN (SELECT distinct tr.table_row_id FROM table_row tr WHERE tr.tenant_id = 1000 and tr.db_table_id = 18 and tr. table_column_id = 81 and(cast(value as numeric) > = '30') and tr. table_row_id IN (SELECT distinct tr.table_row_id From table_index tr WHERE tr.tenant_id = 1000 and tr.db_table_id = 18 and((tr. table_column_id = '80' and tr.value = '9') OR (tr. table_column_id = '80' and tr.value = '12') OR (… and other symetric query filters, but with different values)) LIMIT 1 OFFSET 0)) ORDER BY 3,4 ASC;
IQ28	SELECT * FROM table_relationship trs WHERE trs.tenant_id = 1000 and trs.shared_table_name = 'product' ORDER BY trs. table_relationship_id;
IQ29	SELECT * FROM table_relationship trs WHERE trs.tenant_id = 1000 and trs.shared_table_name = 'sales_fact' ORDER BY trs. table_relationship_id;

7   Conclusion

In this paper, we have proposed a multi-tenant proxy service for EET called EETPS, which integrates, generates, and executes tenants' queries by using a codebase solution that converts multi-tenant queries into traditional database queries and execute them in a RDBMS. This service has three objectives. Firstly, it allows the users to choose from three EET database models, including multi-tenant relational database, integrated multi-tenant relational database with virtual relational database, and virtual relational database. Secondly, it allows users to extend their database schemas, by extending a single schema of a business domain database based on a traditional RDBMS during the application's runtime. Thirdly, it avoids programming effort associated with writing

SQL queries and backend data management code by utilizing the EETPS functions. EETPS functions execute simple and complex queries including join operations, filtering on multiple properties, and filtering of data based on subqueries results. Additionally, we have presented five sample algorithms for EETPS functions, and carried out five experiments for these functions to verify the effectiveness of EETPS. We classified these experiments according to the complexity of the queries. The five experiments show comparisons between the response time of retrieving data from CTTs, VETs, and both CTTs and VETs. The results of most of the experiments indicate improved performance of queries from VET and CTT-and-VET using EETPS functions when compared to queries using CTT (traditional physical tables). These results confirm the effectiveness of using EETPS and EET multi-tenant database and the associated three types of database models, making the EET multi-tenant schema and EETPS suitable for the software applications in general and SaaS applications in particular.

Our future work will focus on extending EETPS queries by adding GROUP BY and ORDER BY query clauses, and applying join operations to more than two tables. In addition, we plan to optimize data retrieval of EET by adding methods to determine the optimal query execution plans, and caching the frequently used queries to reduce the EETPS processing time and to minimize the use of EET database resources. We also plan to perform experiments to evaluate the applicability of EETPS to unstructured and semi-structured data. Furthermore, we plan to build the API for EETPS that will allow the users to retrieve data from EET. We also plan to focus on the scalability of EET and EETPS, and evaluate the performance in a scalable environment.

Acknowledgments. All authors wish to acknowledge UTS FEIT Research Seed Fund 2014 for financial support, and George Feuerlicht wishes to acknowledge the support of GAČR grant No. P403/11/0574.

References

1. Aulbach, S., Grust, T., Jacobs, D., Kemper, A., Rittinger, J.: Multitenant databases for software as a service: schema mapping techniques. In: Proceedings of the 34th SIGMOD International Conference on Management of Data, pp. 1195–1206. ACM, Vancouver (2008)
2. Aulbach, S., Grust, T., Jacobs, D., Kemper, A., Seibold, M.: A comparison of flexible schemas for software as a service. In: Proceedings of the 35th SIGMOD International Conference on Management of Data, pp. 881–888. ACM, Rhode Island (2009)
3. Bezemer, C., Zaidman, A.: Multi-tenant SaaS applications: maintenance dream or nightmare? In: Proceedings of the Joint Workshop on Software Evolution and International Workshop on Principles of Software Evolution, pp. 88–92. ACM, Antwerp (2010)
4. Bobrowski, S.: Optimal multitenant designs for cloud apps. In: 4th International Conference on Cloud Computing, pp. 654–659. IEEE Press, Washington (2012)
5. Demchenko, Y., Grosso, P., de Laat, C., Membrey, P.: Addressing big data issues in scientific data infrastructure. In: International Conference on Collaboration Technologies and Systems, pp. 48–55. IEEE, California (2013)
6. Domingo, E.J., Nino, J.T., Lemos, A.L., Lemos, M.L., Palacios, R.C., Berbís, J.M.G.: CLOUDIO: A cloud computing-oriented multi-tenant architecture for business information systems. In: 3rd International Conference on Cloud Computing, pp. 532–533. IEEE Press, Madrid (2010)

7. Dimovski, D.: Database management as a cloud-based service for small and medium organizations. Master Thesis, Masaryk University Brno (2013)
8. Du, J., Wen, H.Y., Yang, Z.J.: Research on data layer structure of multi-tenant e-commerce system. In: International Conference on Industrial Engineering and Engineering Management, Xiamen, pp. 362–365 (2010)
9. Foping, F.S., Dokas, I.M., Feehan, J., Imran, S.: A new hybrid schema-sharing technique for multitenant applications. In: Fourth International Conference on Digital Information Management, pp. 1–6. IEEE Press, Michigan (2009)
10. Force.com. http://www.salesforce.com/us/developer/docs/soql_sosl/salesforce_soql_sosl.pdf
11. Google Developers. https://developers.google.com/appengine/docs/python/datastore/overview#Comparison_with_Traditional_Databases
12. Heng, L., Dan, Y., Xiaohong, Z.: Survey on multi-tenant data architecture for SaaS. Int. J. Comput. Sci. Issues(IJCSI) **9**(6) (2012)
13. Indrawan-Santiago, M.: Database research: are we at a crossroad? Reflection on NoSQL. In: 15th International Conference on Network-Based Information Systems, pp. 45–51. IEEE Press, Melbourne (2012)
14. Kwok, T., Nguyen, T., Lam, L.: A software as a service with multi-tenancy support for an electronic contract management application. In: International Conference on Services Computing, pp. 179–186. IEEE, Hawaii (2008)
15. Liao, C.F., Chen, K., Chen, J.J.: Toward a tenant-aware query rewriting engine for universal table schema-mapping. In: Cloud Computing Technology and Science, pp. 833–838. IEEE, Taipei (2012)
16. Liu, G.: Research on independent SaaS platform. In: Information Management and Engineering, pp. 110–113. IEEE, Chengdu (2010)
17. Martinez, C.G.: Study of Resource Management for Multitenant Database Systems in Cloud Computing. Doctoral Thesis, University of Colorado (2012)
18. Mietzner, R., Unger, T., Titze, R., Leymann, F.: Combining different multi-tenancy patterns in service-oriented applications. In: Enterprise Distributed Object Computing Conference, pp. 131–140. IEEE, Auckland (2009)
19. Mietzner, R., Metzger, A., Leymann, F., Pohl, K.: Variability modeling to support customization and deployment of multi-tenant-aware software as a service applications. In: ICSE Workshop on Principles of Engineering Service Oriented Systems, pp. 18–25. IEEE, Vancouver (2009)
20. Weissman C.D., Bobrowski S.: The design of the force.com multitenant internet application development platform. In: Proceedings of the 35th SIGMOD International Conference on Management of Data, pp. 889–896. ACM, Rhode Island (2009)
21. Yaish, H., Goyal, M., Feuerlicht, G.: An elastic multi-tenant database schema for software as a service. In: Ninth IEEE International Conference on Dependable, Autonomic and Secure Computing, pp. 737–743. IEEE, Sydney (2011)
22. Yaish, H., Goyal, M., Feuerlicht, G.: Multi-tenant database access control. In: International Conference on Computational Science and Engineering, pp. 870–877. IEEE, Sydney (2013)
23. Yaish, H., Goyal, M., Feuerlicht, G.: Evaluating the performance of multi-tenant elastic extension tables. In: The International Conference on Computational Science, pp. 614–626. Elsevier, Cairns (2014)
24. Yaish, H., Goyal, M., Feuerlicht, G.: Multi-tenant elastic extension tables data management. In: The International Conference on Computational Science, pp. 2168–2181. Elsevier, Cairns (2014)

Boosting Streaming Video Delivery
with WiseReplica

Guthemberg Silvestre[1]([⊠]), David Buffoni[2], Karine Pires[2],
Sébastien Monnet[2], and Pierre Sens[2]

[1] CNRS, LAAS, 7 Avenue du Colonel Roche, 31400 Toulouse, France
gdasilva@laas.fr
[2] UPMC Sorbonne Universités, LIP6, CNRS, INRIA, 4 Place Jussieu, Paris, France
{david.buffoni,karine.pires,sebastien.monnet,pierre.sens}@lip6.fr

Abstract. Streaming video consumption has risen sharply over the last
years. It has not only reshaped the Internet traffic, it has also changed
the manner of watching videos. Users are progressively moving from
the old-fashioned scheduled television to video-on-demand (VoD) services. As broadcasting future seems to be online, customers have become
more sensitive to VoD quality, expecting ever-higher bitrates and lower
rebuffering. In this context, average bitrate is a key quality of service
(QoS) metric. Therefore, content delivery networks (CDNs) and content providers must be committed to enforce average bitrate through
service-level agreement (SLA) contracts. Adaptive content replication
is a promising technique towards this goal. However, this still offers a
major challenge for CDN providers, particularly as they aim to avoid
waste of resources. In this work, we introduce WiseReplica, an adaptive
replication scheme for peer-assisted VoD systems that enforces the average bitrate for Internet videos. Using an accurate machine-learned ranking, WiseReplica saves storage and bandwidth from the vast majority
of non-popular contents for the most watched videos. Simulations using
YouTube traces suggest that our approach meets users expectations efficiently. Compared to caching, WiseReplica reduces the required replication degree for the most-watched videos by two orders of magnitude, and
under heavy load, it increases the average bitrate by roughly 85 %.

Keywords: Peer-to-peer (P2P) · Video on-demand (VoD) · Caching ·
Replication · Service-level agreement (SLA) · Prediction

1 Introduction

The increasing consumption of Internet videos has made fundamental changes
in the Internet traffic and consumers' behaviour. Cisco System, Inc[1] forecasts
that the sum of all forms of video traffic will be in the range of 80 to 90 percent of

---

[1] Cisco Visual Networking Index: Forecast and Methodology, 2013–2018. www.cisco.
com, 2014.

© Springer-Verlag Berlin Heidelberg 2015
A. Hameurlain et al. (Eds.): TLDKS XX, LNCS 9070, pp. 34–58, 2015.
DOI: 10.1007/978-3-662-46703-9_2

global consumer traffic by 2018, including video on-demand (VoD), live streaming, and peer-to-peer (P2P) file sharing. In fact, as the Internet access has become ubiquitous, continuously faster, and cheaper, streaming video has become mainstream. Users are progressively moving from the old-fashioned scheduled television to VoD services. This contributes to increase the expectations of consumers on Internet video delivery.

Since broadcasting future seems to be online, customers have become more sensitive to VoD quality, expecting ever-higher bitrates and lower rebuffering. Contrary to many traditional workloads, e.g. social network messaging or search engines, specifying just latency as quality of service (QoS) metric does not suffice. Instead, streaming traffic requires proper average bitrate to avoid rebuffering and improve user experience. For example, Dobrain *et al.* [13] found that a 1 % increase in buffering ratio can reduce the consumer's expected viewing time by more than three minutes. Balachandran *et al.*, observe that increased average bitrate in Internet video delivery leads to a better user experience for viewers with mobile devices [3]. This suggests that service-level agreement (SLA) contracts must include average bitrate as a key QoS metric.

Yet, current Content Delivery Networks (CDN) platforms are not ready to fulfil the requirements of the increasing demand for VoD services and meet consumers' expectations. Through fine-grained client-side measurements from over 200 million client viewing sessions, Liu *et al.* [21] showed that 20 % of these sessions experience a rebuffering ratio of at least 10 %, 14 % of users have to wait more than 10 s for video to start up, more than 28 % of sessions have an average bitrate less than 500 Kbps, and 10 % of users fail to see any video at all.

To deal with these issues, CDN providers have started to combine datacenters and edge network resources in hybrid designs[2]. This includes *peer-assisted VoD systems* [17] whose deployment requires hybrid CDN platforms. The aim of peer-assisted VoD systems is to take advantage of both infrastructure-based resources and P2P communication facilities. Huang *et al.* [17] suggest the use of peer-assisted VoD systems to improve resource allocation for Internet video delivery. They argue that devices on edge networks, e.g. set-top-boxes, contribute with storage and bandwidth to video delivery, reducing dramatically the burden on infrastructure-based servers, and cutting operations costs. Many recent studies [10,18,25] confirm that exploring peer-assisted VoD system permits enhancing resource allocation for streaming videos, but none has properly evaluated the performance of video delivery regarding SLA enforcement.

In fact, there exists an increasing need for more research in easy-to-deploy, self-adapting techniques for ensuring tough QoS guarantees brought by the cloud paradigm. However, efficient resource allocation on hybrid CDNs to meet user expectations imposes big challenges, particularly for resource-hungry services as VoD. This paper identifies *adaptive content replication* as one of such challenges. Adaptive replication plays an important role on the content availability of distributed systems, contributing directly to both storage and bandwidth provision.

---

[2] Akamai acquires Red Swoosh. http://www.akamai.com/html/about/press/releases/ 2007/press_041207.html, April 2007.

As the popularity of a video varies, the number of replicas, or peers serving that video, must be adapted accordingly. Generally speaking, the faster and more precise the replication scheme reacts to changes on videos demand, the better is the resource allocation and content availability.

Considering average bitrate as target QoS metric, we make a case for a SLA-driven replication scheme named WiseReplica that allows us to meet users' expectations in peer-assisted VoD system properly. We assume the system must enforce the right average bitrate for each video through SLA contracts. Our ultimate goal is two-fold: (i) to prevent SLA violations and (ii) to reduce the number of video replicas. To perform efficient Internet video replication, WiseReplica relies on a novel, accurate machine-learned ranking of Internet videos. To rank video in order of demand, our prediction model encompasses multiple measurements of Internet video activity in peer-assisted VoD system, including active viewers, video duration, average serving time, and mean time between requests view. The use of this prediction model in WiseReplica provides the ability to adapt the replication degree of videos dynamically according to their encoding settings and popularity, reducing storage usage and enhancing network provision. We make two main contributions:

Investigate how predictable is a ranking of Internet videos. We design a learning model to capture the dynamic behaviour of streaming video demand. The model makes predictions based on lightweight measurements of the request arrival process. Using a novel machine-learned ranking, we predict demand of a video accurately. Thus, the higher the rank position, the higher the demand for fresh replicas. According to the video ranking position, VoD services operators can define and evaluate different replication policies. For instance, top-ranked Internet videos may be twice as much replicated as those ranked in the second position. This intuitive model allows us to decouple streaming demand from replication policy. Our model is flexible and can learn from different sources and big amounts of data, providing a robust framework for controlling VoD resource allocation. Simulations using YouTube traces, with non-stationary behaviours, suggest that our model is very accurate in predicting the ranking of Internet videos. Since our ranking of videos is based on random forests, a parallelizable, state-of-the-art machine learning method, it fits runtime requirements of large VoD systems.

Enforce average bitrate through SLA-based video replication. Based on our machine-learned ranking of Internet video, we designed and evaluated WiseReplica, an easy-to-deploy, SLA-based replication scheme that meets users' expectations for VoD services. WiseReplica is fully compliant with peer-assisted VoD systems in hybrid CDN platforms. It operates adaptive replication over sets of devices located close to each other in edge networks, namely *storage domains*. WiseReplica functioning per storage domain is straightforward. Gradually, it verifies the rank position of a video whenever a new local request arrives, and adapts the replication degree accordingly. Using a collaborative caching, video replicas are either pre-fetched or removed randomly. We show through simulations using YouTube traces that WiseReplica outperforms a non-collaborative caching approach by preventing violations, reducing storage usage, and enhancing network resources provision. Furthermore, our replication scheme is easy to adopt and flexible enough to offer interoperability with de facto approaches, including HTTP adaptive streaming technique and BitTorrent protocol [32].

This work is organized as follows. In Sect. 2, we present the context and challenges of this research. We describe in details our prediction model to rank Internet videos in order of demand in Sect. 3. Section 4 describes the approach of our adaptive replication scheme, WiseReplica. We explain our simulation methodology in Sect. 5. We then analyse the performance of WiseReplica in Sect. 6. Related works are discussed in Sect. 7, just before the conclusion in Sect. 8.

2   Context and Challenges

In this section, we describe the context and the challenges of this work.

2.1   Improving Content Availability to Better User Experience

Many studies have shown that quality of user experience while watching online videos is related to the good quality of content transmission. They presented many strategies to enhance the video content availability and its distribution. Most of these studies analyse in the field are focused on Youtube, being this the major player of video content distribution [1,5,6,14]. These studies include the analysis of crawled data from Youtube APIs and comparisons of caching strategies from collected data of users' point of view (HTTP logs from ISP or local networks).

Dobrian et al. [13] study has shown the correlation between the user engagement and the video quality, being the *Buffering Ratio* (fraction of the total session time spent in buffering) and *Rendering Rate* (frames per second) the most critical metric over the total played time for short videos, the current target of our method. This characterizes the relation between quality of service and user experience and endures the importance of avoidance of SLAs violations, which minimizes buffering ratio, confirming the main metric of evaluation in our work.

Furthermore, Finamore et al. [15] stated that the download bitrate of the video plays a fundamental role in video playback quality. They measured the smoothness of the playback by the bitrate ratio, defined as the ratio between the average session download bitrate and the video encoding bitrate. Considering different bitrates in the input dataset is a key aspect of the rendering rate metric in user engagement and playback quality.

Another important concern in studying the availability of Internet videos was to provide a SLA-based solution with the minimum constrains regarding deployment. However, recent studies [2,34] are based in substantial changes in the normally used stack of protocols and network infra-structure and they become hard to be considered as a feasible solution. Our solution takes in account a well-know and largely used infra-structure and have no changes in the stack protocol. Despite all these research efforts, enforcing video availability in large peer-assisted VoD systems remains a challenging issue.

2.2 On the Track of YouTube Popularity Growth Curves and High Quality Videos

A fair reproduction of user interactions to Internet videos is essential to evaluate peer-assisted VoD systems properly. Hence, we study in this work a workload that combines YouTube traces [14] to well-known videos' access patterns [33]. We are particularly interested in reproducing realistic popularity growth curves, considering advanced coding setting and common VoD demand patterns.

We study the data crawled by Figueiredo *et al.* [14], whose datasets are currently available online[3]. The dataset allows us to characterize the growth patterns of YouTube videos. In particular, they analysed three types of YouTube videos sets: videos that appear on YouTube top list, videos that were banned from YouTube due to copyrights violations, and videos that were randomly selected through API calls. They crawled once a number of videos' daily features. For each video, there are up to 100 daily measurements, or daily available samples, per feature. In this work, we are mostly interested in the measurements of *view data* feature, that depicts the popularity growth curve of a video through a array of cumulative number of daily views ranging from 0 to the total number of views.

In order to reproduce realistic, high quality videos encodings, we consider the YouTube advanced encoding settings[4]. Table 1 depicts the set of high definition (HD) video encodings that we use in this work.

Table 1. Advanced encoding settings for YouTube videos used in this work.

Type	Video bitrate	Mono audio bitrate	Stereo audio bitrate	5.1 Audio bitrate
1080p	50 Mbps	128 kbps	384 kbps	512 kbps
720p	30 Mbps	128 kbps	384 kbps	512 kbps
480p	15 Mbps	128 kbps	384 kbps	512 kbps
360p	5 Mbps	128 kbps	384 kbps	512 kbps

2.3 Investigating Network Resources Provision for Internet Videos

Replication schemes have become an important building block for Internet video providers to improve content availability and meet consumers' expectations. An

---

[3] The Tube over Time: Characterizing Popularity Growth of YouTube Videos. http://www.vod.dcc.ufmg.br/traces/youtime/data/, January 2013.

[4] Advanced encoding settings for YouTube videos. http://support.google.com/youtube/bin/answer.py?hl=en-GB&answer=1722171, June 2014.

adaptive replication scheme should offer content replica maintenance to handle popularity growth properly.

Non-collaborative caching remains the simplest approach to provide adaptive replication of web content [20]. They adapt the replication degree to the content popularity using cache replacement policies, and assuming fair-sharing as a key scheduling strategy. But, Internet videos' workloads on peer-assisted VoD systems bring major obstacles to non-collaborative caching, e.g. the resource imbalance in peers for replicas, and a growing need for high bitrate provision for meeting consumers' expectations. Therefore, relying just on cache replacement policies and fair-sharing scheduling can undermine the performance of the whole system.

Recent studies have sought an optimal solution to this problem. For instance, Chang and Pan [10] propose a modelling framework towards optimal caching strategies, including collaborative caching. They confirm that this problem is NP-hard, and only suboptimal solutions can be found.

2.4   Challenges

In order to meet increasing consumers' expectations on Internet videos, a *good* peer-assisted VoD system must overcome the following challenges:

1. It must cope with dramatic, unexpected variations in videos popularity.
2. It must avoid waste of resources, and reduce as much as possible storage and network usage on peers of edge networks.
3. It must prevent rebuffering of VoD streaming through a self-adaptive, easy-to-deploy technique.

Our simulations suggest that meeting consumers' expectations in terms of average bitrate is a difficult task, specially under heavy load. State-of-the-art approaches fail to handle these challenges mostly because they are not able (i) to capture VoD demand, and (ii) to define a metric to measure consumers' expectations. WiseReplica copes with these issues by inferring users' expectations for videos and predicting the amount of resources to fulfil the demand in a self-adaptive way. Our findings show that this approach produces a good balance between resource allocation and users' satisfaction.

3   A Machine-Learned Ranking of Internet Videos

We designed a prediction model for ranking Internet videos in order of demand. In this work, video demand involves both popularity and QoS requirements. Our main goal is to provide an intuitive, accurate method to capture requesting behaviours of streaming videos. In this section, we highlight the foundations of our statistical learning approach. First, we present a brief overview of statistical learning. Then we explain the model, describing our learning-to-rank problem. Finally, we describe our implementation and we present a framework for ranking predictions.

3.1   An Overview About How to Learn from Data

Statistical learning is about learning from seen data in order to predict unseen data with minimal error. Data comprise inputs $\mathbf{x}$ represented by a vector with a fixed number of dimensions p ($\mathbf{x} \in \mathcal{X} \subset \mathbb{R}^p$) from the input space $\mathcal{X}$. In our problem, $\mathbf{x}$ is a video, represented by a vector of measurements from video sessions' activity.

In supervised learning, each input measurement is coupled with a y, a label selected by an oracle, from the output space $\mathcal{Y}$. To learn, we take N pairs $(\mathbf{x}, y)$ drawn *independently and identically distributed* (i.i.d.) from a fixed but unknown joint probability density $Pr(X, Y)$. This is true for both training and testing datasets. For instance, we consider the training dataset $S = \{\mathbf{x}_i, y_i\}_{i=1}^{N}$ of N pairs $(\mathbf{x}, y)$. Using this dataset, the supervised learning algorithm searches for a function $f\colon \mathcal{X} \to \mathbb{R}$ in a fixed function class $\mathcal{F}$. State-of-the-art algorithms, such as *support vector machines* (SVM) [11] or *ensemble methods* [16], aim to find $f^\star$ in $\mathcal{F}$ with the lowest empirical risk defined as:

$$f^\star \in \arg\min_{f \in \mathcal{F}} \mathbf{r}_{emp}(f) \tag{1}$$

where $\mathbf{r}_{emp}(f) = \frac{1}{N}\sum_{i=1}^{N} I_{\{f(\mathbf{x}) \neq y_i\}}$ is computed over the training set, and $I_{\{.\}}$ is the indicator function which returns 1 if the predicate $\{.\}$ is true and 0 otherwise. In other terms, $\mathbf{r}_{emp}$ is a quality measure relating the label to the prediction provided by the function f on the training dataset S.

To model our prediction problem, we use a statistical learning approach called learning-to-rank. This approach has been a hot topic in Machine Learning community for the last 10 years. It combines properties of two well-known other approaches: regression, where $y \in \mathcal{Y} \subset \mathbb{R}$; classification where $y \in \mathcal{Y} \subset \{0, 1, ..., K\}$ with $K \geq 1$. In learning-to-rank approach, y gives an indication on the target order (formally represented by a permutation $\sigma \in \Sigma$).

3.2   A Ranking Model for Internet Videos

The main purpose of our learning model is to capture popularity growth dynamics and system resources availability of peer-assisted VoD systems. Therefore, we assume that prediction model must allow us to rank Internet videos in order of demand. This can be modelled as a learning-to-rank problem.

Given an i.i.d. sample $(\mathbf{x}, y)$ such as described in Subsect. 3.1, we model inputs and outputs as follows.

Inputs. We represent the input space $\mathbf{x}$ is a video described as 10 lightweight measurements from the request arrival process. These measurements are video size, network availability, network usage (load), current number of viewers and replicas, inter-arrival time between requests (delta), aggregate number of views, mean of time between requests (mtbr), life time, and average bitrate. We compute averages and means from up to the five last requests. Our goal is to gather as much information about users' interactions as possible in an easy manner to make accurate predictions about the ranking of videos. To extend our model, one can easily add further features or measurements such as geographical location, social network interactions data, buffering ratio, rate of buffering events, session join time, rendering quality, rate of bitrate switch, *etc.*

Outputs. The supervision y associated to each input video $\mathbf{x}$ is based on four possible ordered values which gives an indication for the final target ranking. In our model, $\mathcal{Y} \in \{0, 1, 2, 3\}$, whose labels are $\{$*non-popular, popular, very popular, viral*$\}$ respectively. It represents a natural ranking for Internet videos. Using this ranking model, we intend to provide a measure of video demand, which is closely related not only to the popularity, but also to the consumption of system resources.

Finally, the learning-to-rank module finds a function f from Eq. (1) with the constraint of maintaining the prediction order: $\forall i, j, i \neq j, y_i > y_j$ then $f(\mathbf{x}_i) > f(\mathbf{x}_j)$ explained in [7]. In that case, theoretical performance guarantees are provided. Practically, the use of the mean square error $(y - f(\mathbf{x}))^2$ instead of the indicator function $I_{\{.\}}$ (which is hard to optimize because it is non-differentiable) allows us to ensure a calibrated learning to rank algorithm. A calibrated algorithm means there is a theoretical link between the approximation of the empirical risk, that is easier to optimize, and its non-differentiable version [7,9,31,35].

3.3   Framework for Learning and Predicting, and Implementation

We implement our model using *ensemble methods*. According to Friedman *et al.*, ensemble learning consists of a set of very popular supervised methods, that are robust, simple to train and tune, and have a remarkable prediction performance. Our implementation is based on SCIKIT-LEARN, a general-purpose machine learning library [26].

We designed a simple framework to use our learning module, depicted in Fig. 1. Our framework has two phases: (i) learning and (ii) predicting. Each phase has its own YouTube-like workload. Learning is a preliminary phase that commonly runs offline in a batch mode, while the prediction can go online. In this work, both phases are performed with data from simulations. In the learning phase, we first generate the training dataset, described in Subsect. 5.4. Then we feed this training dataset to our learning model, represented here as module of

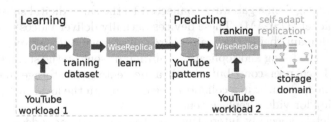

Fig. 1. Framework for learning and predicting ranking of Internet videos.

WiseReplica, in order to identify YouTube ranking patterns. Once the learning phase has been accomplished, WiseReplica can use its learning module in a predicting phase, as indicated in the left-hand side of Fig. 1. In this phase, inputs come for measurements of the request arrival process of workload 2, that permit accurately ranking Internet videos in order of *hotness* and instrumenting replication accordingly inside storage domains. We highlight WiseReplica functioning, including storage domains, in the next section.

4   Boosting VoD Delivery: The WiseReplica Approach

In this section, we describe WiseReplica replication scheme. First, we highlight how WiseReplica operates in edge networks, by in introducing the concept of storage domains. Then, we explain its replication strategy based on predictions of ranking of video demand.

4.1   Distributing VoD with Storage Domains

We assume that WiseReplica operates in peer-assisted VoD systems deployed on hybrid CDN platforms. We consider the hybrid CDN design called Caju, that is detailed in our previous work [30] as our target platform. It is based on sets of devices located close to customers, named storage domain. A storage domain is a logical entity that combines resources from both datacenters and edge networks in the last mile of the content delivery chain. As Fig. 2 shows, devices in a storage domain can play either a coordinator or peer role.

Coordinator is a server or a small-sized cluster of servers deployed in the nearby datacenter. We assume that the coordinator performs scheduling of video requests for the local storage domains. Therefore, it runs the main instance of WiseReplica, and keeps information about resources consumption. Its main goal is to maintain the right number of replicas per video in the local peers, by prefetching or deleting sources. Instead of always contacting the content providers, coordinators might interoperate in logically centralized way to fetch videos that have been vanished from a storage domain. They store the most recent videos in their own cache for replication purposes. Whenever a new replica is necessary, the coordinator pushes it to a randomly, uniformly selected peer. Similarly, coordinators send video deletion requests to local peers.

Peers is a set of devices located close to each other through which customers get network access, e.g. home gateways connected to the same digital subscriber line access multiplexer (DSLAM). These devices actually deliver videos to customers in a storage domain, being the main source of storage and network resources. They execute scheduling and replication commands sent by the storage domain's coordinator. Each peer contributes with a percentage of storage and network resources to the system, as in a collaborative caching. In the local cache is applied the LRU policy for videos replacement.

This model is specially interesting for the problem of videos delivery as it takes advantage of nodes geographical position [6]. It provides two main

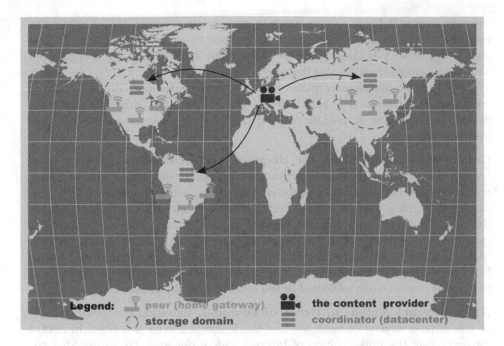

Fig. 2. Storage domains.

infrastructure properties to WiseReplica: replication group and hop limit. The replication group allows WiseReplica to adapt video replication for smaller sets of peers, most likely connecting customers with similar content interests. By enforcing a hop limit, storage domains avoid jitter, ensure low latencies, and permit WiseReplica improving the efficiency of network resource provision.

In addition, we assume that a storage domain enforces an initial placement policy. This policy defines the minimum replication degree m for initial copies for any new, just fetched Internet video. Request scheduling is simple. A view request is served by at most R nodes with uniform load. Available sources come from $r = min(n, R)$, where n is the number of current replicas. In this work, we consider m equals to two and R equals to five as default settings. For requests scheduling, this approach enforces well-known policies for peers in edge networks, including nearest source selection and multi-sourcing.

4.2 Self-Adapting Replication According to the Ranking of Internet Videos

Our utmost goal is to contribute to meet increasing customers expectation on Internet videos using peer-assisted VoD systems. To enhance VoD delivery, we assume that rebuffering is a major issue to be addressed. We propose to cope with this issue by enforcing minimum average bitrate of each streaming as the main QoS metric. In this scenario, content and CDN providers must be committed to enforce minimum average bitrate for videos through SLA contracts. Since

Internet videos delivery is a resource-hungry service, we must also adapt the network provision and storage usage as we aim to prevent violations. To this end, we propose WiseReplica, an adaptive replication scheme for peer-assisted VoD systems based on storage domains.

WiseReplica maintains replicas inside a storage domain. Running on the coordinator, it adapts the replication degree of Internet videos of a storage domain according to a machine-learned ranking. Our scheme follows a three-part procedure:

Collect Information from the Request Arrival Process. For each video request, WiseReplica collects 10 lightweight measurements. The goal is to gather comprehensive information for measuring the video demand and accurately predicting the raking. As described in Sect. 3, they are video size, network availability, network usage (load), current number of viewers and replicas, inter-arrival time between requests (delta), aggregate number of views, mean of time between requests (mtbr), life time, and average bitrate. We compute averages and means from the last up to five requests. It is important to notice that all these measurements can be easily collected in the storage domain's coordinator.

Rank Internet Videos in Order of Demand. Based on the measurements of the request arrival process, we use the learning model described in Sect. 3 for predicting the rank position of Internet videos demand. We can predict the video rank for each view from the second request. The ranking comprises information about demand and QoS requirements. Predictions are quite essential for enhancing VoD delivery. Since our learning model make predictions on a request basis, WiseReplica can react to the video demand as promptly as the rank position evolves. Indeed, ranking is an intuitive way to capture the demand of videos in peer-assisted VoD systems. The higher is the demand rank position of an Internet video, the higher is the demand for it. There are four positions on our machine-learned ranking: *non-popular, popular, very popular,* and *viral.* WiseReplica has a straightforward strategy to perform replication according to hotness rank positions. Videos that fall into the lowest rank position can have their replication degree reduced, otherwise they need more replicas. Thus, the maintenance of replication degree of Internet video, including video creations and deletions in peers, relies on replication policies.

Enforce Replication Policy Accordingly and in Time. The goal of replication policies is two-fold: first (i) ensure consumers' expectations in time and (ii) reduce the total number of replicas as much as possible. For that, WiseReplica must adapt replication of videos according to the forecasts of their rank positions. Our replication scheme enforces two types of replica maintenance policies: deletion and creation policy. In this work, we enforce a single video deletion policy. Whenever the coordinator receives a request to a video in the non-popular rank, the deletion policy says that one replica is deleted until the minimum replication degree m is reached. Similarly, our scheme periodically runs a maintenance procedure (e.g. each five minutes) to smoothly enforce the deletion policy for inactive videos. This allows WiseReplica to reduce the total number of replicas. To cope with SLA violations and meet customers' expectations, we evaluate four quite simple policies, namely uniform, linear, quadratic, and exponential. They are respectively defined as follows: B, Br, Br^2, and B^r, where B is a constant that represents the target number of replicas, and $r \in \{1, 2, 3\}$ the rank positions. We report on creation policies' performances in Sect. 6.

Our findings show that this approach produces a good balance between resource usage and consumers' satisfaction. It is important to note, however, WideReplica does not cover video durability, neither does fault-tolerant mechanisms (e.g. failure detection/recovery procedures). Rather, our goal is to improve VoD availability, boosting network provision, meeting consumers' expectations on VoD services, and reducing storage usage as much as possible. To this end, WiseReplica combines lightweight measurements, accurate predictions of Internet videos ranking, and replication policies enforcement in a particularly novel, flexible way. In peer-assisted VoD systems, it can easily interoperate with de facto approaches, including HTTP adaptive streaming technique and swarming protocols, such as BitTorrent.

5   Simulation Methodology

We simulate a peer-assisted VoD system based on a hybrid CDN design called Caju [30]. We evaluate WiseReplica using YouTube traces. We compare WiseReplica performance with other two adaptive replication schemes, namely non-collaborative caching and Oracle-like collaborative caching. The aim of our simulations is to study in details the variability of demand and resource allocation of VoD services on edge networks, and the performance of replication schemes in enforcing expected Internet video availability.

5.1   Workload from YouTube Traces and SLA Definition

The workload and SLA definitions are at the core of our evaluation. We define a workload that captures the main features of VoD services using YouTube traces, and a SLA contract that meets users' expectations.

In the workload definition, we are particularly interested in reproduce a realist request arrival process, placing the emphasis on popularity growth and video encodings. Thus, we use YouTube traces, presented in Subsect. 2.2. Before integrating YouTube traces to our workload, we first preprocessed their YouTube datasets to remove inconsistent measurements, such as videos with no views. Basically, we got rid of videos with small number of total views (those smaller than the first quartile) and videos with few daily measurements (those smaller than the third quartile). That allowed us to pick off 20 % most representative YouTube growth patterns, accounting for 21827 distinct curves. Then, we randomly selected, with a uniform distribution, curves from this preprocessed data to be assigned to videos of our workload. Similarly, we assigned high quality YoutTube video encodings to our workload videos, based on advanced settings depicted in Table 1. To summarize, Table 2 lists default values for workload

Table 2. Default values for workload parameters.

Workload	
Requests per user	uniform
Experiment duration	4 h
Mean requests per second	100
Requests fractions	5 % of creations, 95 % of views
Video size (follows Pareto)	shape = 3, between 13 MB and 1.6 GB
Video popularity (Zipf-Mandelbrot)	shape = 0.8, cutoff = number of videos
Videos' creation (Poisson)	λ = creations per second
Popularity growth from YouTube traces	21827 distinct patterns
YouTube encoding settings (bitrates)	5 Mbps, 15 Mbps, 30 Mbps, 50 Mbps

parameters. Finally, videos are always divided and distributed in chunks or segments of fixed size, 2 MB.

In terms of SLA definition, we assume that content and content delivery providers are committed to improving the Internet video availability for customers in a content-oriented approach. In our case, a *good* peer-assisted VoD system must ensure videos availability by avoiding rebuffering. Therefore, we consider a global, simple SLA contract drawn up to provide a minimal average bitrate according to each Internet video encoding setting. A SLA violation happens whenever the system fails to enforce the minimal average bitrate for any viewer session.

5.2   Evaluation Scenario

Our evaluation scenario (Fig. 3) includes 4002 nodes, arranged across two storage domains. There are one coordinator and 2000 peers per storage domain. Storage and network capacities differ according to the device role. Coordinators have 20 TB of storage capacity and full-duplex access link of 4 Gbps. Peers contribute 200 GB each, equipped with 100 Mbps full-duplex links. Note that the two coordinators contribute with a small fraction of aggregate edge resources, i.e. 5 % of the storage capacity and only 2 % of the total network capacity. This draws our attention to the performance of replication schemes towards peers resource allocation. We assume only 1 % peers' storage is available for caching additional replicas, namely 2 GB.

We implemented and evaluate this work using simulation. To this end, we developed a simulation tool on top of PeerSim [24] to implement storage domains in edge network and bandwidth scheduling.Our design focus on network's resource allocation accuracy for simulating bitrate enforcement and concurrent videos views properly. Design and implementations details of our tools to simulate network resource scheduling are available in our previous work [28]. We have performed our simulations using servers equipped with Intel Xeon E5450 3.00 GHz, and a RAM of 4 GB.

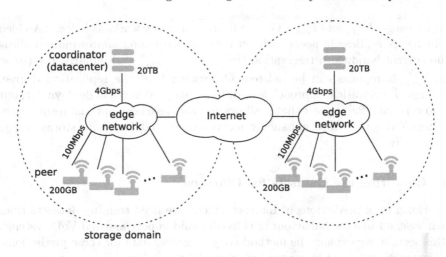

Fig. 3. Evaluation scenario.

5.3   Comparable Replication Schemes

We compare WiseReplica with two other schemes.

Non-collaborative Caching. Adaptive replication schemes based on non-collaborative caching, such as those that uses Least Recent Used (LRU) algorithm, are easy to implement and deploy. A new replica is created in a peer whenever a user requests to view a video. LRU replacement is enforced regarding the static percentage of the local storage capacity for caching of 1%.

Oracle-Like Collaborative Caching. This is an idealized benchmark case. Here, we assume a peer-assisted VoD system deployed in a network that runs a deadline-aware transport protocol, similar to Wilson *et al.* [34] work. Based on our previous work with AREN [29], an adaptive replication scheme for edge networks, we implemented a benchmark replication scheme that relies on bandwidth reservation and collaborative caching to provide an adaptive number of replicas for videos. We replicate videos according to aggregate network usage by enforcing a low and high thresholds. This makes the video replication a function of bandwidth reservation, and ensures that network and storage provision follows video demand properly, as depicted in Fig. 4. Per video, we consider two percentage thresholds for aggregate

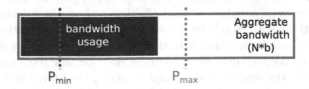

Fig. 4. Oracle-like bandwidth management for a video, illustrating aggregate bandwidth for N replicas and b available bandwidth, bandwidth reservation (bandwidth usage) and thresholds (P_{min} and P_{max}).

network usage: P_{min} and P_{max}. Our replication strategy works as follows. A video v that has N replicas in peers with network capacity of b requires more replicas if the current bandwidth reservation $U(v) > P_{max} \sum_{i=1}^{N} b$. Similarly, if $U(v) < P_{min} \sum_{i=1}^{N} b$, replicas can be deleted. Otherwise, keep the replication degree. Although this empirical approach is hard to be adopted in a real deployment, our previous results [29] suggest that it allows us to achieve near-optimal results, preventing *all* SLA violations, enhancing network usage and decreasing storage usage dramatically.

5.4   Collecting the Datasets for Learning

To perform rank predictions of Internet videos, we need training datasets from which we can learn the behaviour of video demand in peer-assisted VoD systems. In this section, we explain the methodology to gather data for these predictions.

The training dataset of our prediction model comes from measurements of the request arrival process on per-assisted VoD systems, as described in Subsect. 3.2. Each line of our training dataset has 11 values, 10 input measurements about a video current state, and a rank position. Although, the datasets evaluated in this work were synthetically collected by performing simulations with the Oracle-like benchmark replication approach (detailed in Subsect. 5.3), similar datasets can be collected from monitoring systems of running CDN systems.

In this work, Oracle-like benchmark replication approach (Subsect. 5.3) represents the near-optimal way to serve VoD service according to video encodings and popularity, whose functioning we are very interested in learning. In this empirical approach, a video requires additional replicas only if there exists a certain number of concurrent accesses, where concurrence is measured by checking a high threshold of the current reserved bandwidth, as detailed in Subsect. 5.3. We assume that popular videos are those that have additional replicas during its lifetime. Since Internet videos popularity distribution follows a Zipf-like distribution [33], concurrent access are rare events as well as popular videos classified by this approach, thus it provides a quite fair approach to identify popular videos.

Raw data from Oracle-like technique permits easily distinguishing between two ranking positions only, non-popular and popular videos, i.e. requests to non-popular videos are all those that do not trigger any replica creation, or those that resulted in deletions. However, there is a lack of information about different ranking positions of popular videos. Hence, depending on the frequency of replica creation, we add information to requests to popular videos classifying them in popular, very popular, or viral. To define these three levels of *hotness*, we run simulations with YouTube traces, collected the distribution of replicas creation in milliseconds, and split it in three nearly equal parts by observing the 66-percentile and 33-percentile inter-creation time for new replicas. This means that the higher is the frequency of replica creation, the hotter is the video, and the higher is the ranking position. Now, collected data suit model's definitions well.

6 Evaluation

The utmost goal of our performance evaluation is two-fold: (i) measure the accuracy of our learning model in ranking Internet videos in order of *hotness*, and (ii) evaluate the performance of our replication scheme in meeting viewers' expectations in peer-assisted VoD systems. Further details about evaluation set-up are available in Sect. 5.

6.1 Performance Evaluation Metrics

We aim to evaluate the performance of two main WiseReplica modules: machine-learned ranking and replication strategy. Hence we group evaluation metrics as follows:

Machine-Learned Ranking Accuracy. We adopt the normalized Discounted Cumulative Gain (nDCG) criterion as the main evaluation metric for our learning model. nDCG is a standard quality measure in information retrieval, especially for Web search [19,22]. We implement DCG measure proposed by Burges *et al.* [8]. Therefore, DCG is defined as $DCG_L = \sum_{i=1}^{L} \frac{2^{F(i)}-1}{\log_2(1+i)}$, where L is the global set of ranked videos, and $F(i)$ is the rank position of ith video. To compute nDCG, we divide DCG measure by the idealized DCG with perfect order of the set L. Thus, the perfect model scores 1. Unlike typical information retrieval problems, as a ranking of web content, our model does not have the notion of *query*. Instead, we rely on nDCG robustness to measure the performance of our learning model as a global ranking problem. Since the ranking problem shares properties with both classification and regression problems, we compare nDCG to other three popular machine learning metrics: the mean square error, a standard metric for regressions; precision, for classification; and a less robust, well-known variant of nDCG, namely in this work nDCG(2), described by Croft *et al.* in [12]. We evaluate three different state-of-the-art ensemble learning methods available in SCIKIT-LEARN library: RANDOM FOREST, EXTREMELY RANDOMIZED TREES, and GRADIENT TREE BOOSTING. Moreover, we report briefly on the sample size for learning, number of estimators or learners of ensemble methods, measurements or features importance, and the computational overhead of our model, including memory usage and computation time for prediction.

Metrics for Replication Strategies in Peer-Assisted VoD Systems. Assuming that content and CDN providers are committed to enforcing bitrate as main QoS metric through SLA contracts, we consider SLA violation as the primary performance metric. Thus, a SLA violation happens whenever the peer-assisted VoD system does not provide the minimum average bitrate for preventing rebuffering. This measures the WiseReplica capacity of meeting consumers' expectations. We also investigate the impact of our replication scheme using storage domains in peer-assisted VoD systems. To this end, our evaluation metrics are network and storage usage. Finally, we compare WiseReplica results with a non-collaborative caching and the Oracle-like assumption, described in Subsect. 5.3.

6.2 Fitting and Measuring the Accuracy of Our Ranking Model

The evaluation of our learning model comprises: ensemble method selection, number of *estimators*, sample size for learning, and inputs' relative importance. In this subsection, we aim to evaluate the most important settings and tune our model towards higher accuracy, using the learning framework described in Subsect. 3.3.

Selecting and Fitting an Ensemble Method. Ensemble methods have become very popular in statistical learning. Their algorithms combine several *estimators* or *week learners* to provide robust learning models and prevent overfitting. We fit and evaluate our model with three methods from SCIKIT-LEARN library: RANDOM FOREST(RF), EXTREMELY RANDOMIZED TREES(ET), and GRADIENT TREE BOOSTING(GB). We consider two distinct samples with 124,000 lines each, one for training and other for testing. We set to 10 the number of estimators as a common setting. All other parameters have default settings. Based on four metrics detailed on Subsect. 6.1, RANDOM FOREST fits our model better. Figure 5 depicts three of these metrics. RANDOM FOREST performs particularly well in nDCG score, the main metric for ranking problems. While EXTREMELY RANDOMIZED TREES and GRADIENT TREE BOOSTING score 0.9126 and 0.4128 respectively, RANDOM FOREST scores 0.9594. In terms of precision, RANDOM FOREST slightly better, with a score of 0.9922. EXTREMELY RANDOMIZED TREES scores 0.9899, and GRADIENT TREE BOOSTING scores 0.9502. It also outperforms the other two methods regarding the mean square error metric, scoring 0.0094 compared to 0.0122 with EXTREMELY RANDOMIZED TREES and 0.1021 with GRADIENT TREE BOOSTING. nDCG(2) metric

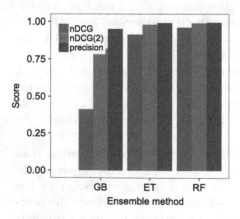
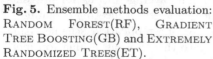
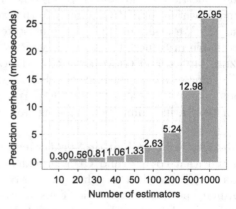

Fig. 5. Ensemble methods evaluation: RANDOM FOREST(RF), GRADIENT TREE BOOSTING(GB) and EXTREMELY RANDOMIZED TREES(ET).

Fig. 6. Overhead for different number of estimators of RANDOM FOREST.

confirms these results. Therefore, we select RANDOM FOREST method for implementing our prediction model and nDCG as the key accuracy metric for ranking predictions.

Adjusting the Number of *Estimators* to Learn. According to Friedman *et al.*, RANDOM FOREST performs predictions by building a collection of *decorrelated* trees, namely estimators, and then averages them. We investigated the impact of the number of estimators in ranking accuracy, memory and computation time. We varied the number of estimators progressively from 10 to 1000, with the same previous samples. Results show that the number of estimators has a negligible impact in the accuracy of our model. While a model with 10 estimators scores 0.9594, 1000 scores 0.9569, slightly worse. One reason for this might be the number of inputs, relatively small, that is likely to require a small number of estimators. Yet, the number of estimators impacts on the model overhead, specially for computation time. As depicted in Fig. 6, the computation time ranges from 0.3 ms with 10 estimators to almost 26 ms with 1000 ones. Although the worst case still represents low overhead, the lower the better. Memory overhead is rather negligible, ranging from 30 to 32 MB. Overall, our model has a quite low overhead, suitable for going online in large peer-assisted VoD systems. Since there is no evidence to increase the number of estimators, we keep 10 estimators as a default, fair setting.

Evaluating Bigger Samples for Fitting the Model. Towards a higher accuracy, we evaluated bigger samples for fitting our prediction model in its learning phase, described in Subsect. 3.3. We collected more information by running longer simulations. As expected, Fig. 7 confirms that we improve accuracy through bigger samples. The improvement in accuracy was slight, about 0.03 as we use a sample size almost six times bigger, i.e. 683,000. It is quite important to highlight, though, that this has no impact on computation time of predictions. Thus, we use the biggest sample for the remaining evaluations.

Analysing the Relative Importance of Model's Inputs. We were particularly interested in evaluating the contribution of each input of our model, described in Subsect. 3.2. SCIKIT-LEARN library allows us to measure the relative importance of each input for predicting the ranking position using the RANDOM FOREST method. Figure 8 highlights the relative importance for all 10 inputs of our ranking model. The two most relevant inputs are the current number of viewers and network availability. These inputs alone account for 99.6 % of the all model's accuracy. It seems quite reasonable, since the former measures the demand for a video and the later depicts the offer of network resources, the main system feature for enforcing average bitrate. Based on the analysis of the current datasets, the remaining eight inputs are less important to the ranking model's accuracy. Surprisingly, the number of replicas, current network load, and video

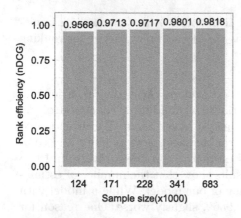
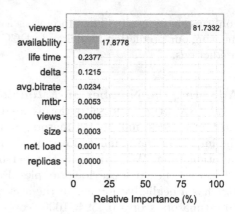

Fig. 7. Accuracy with different sample sizes.

Fig. 8. Relative importance to ranking of the 10 model's inputs.

size seem to be useless to our model. It is likely that network availability is a particularly good measurement, making these eight inputs rather redundant. For simplicity, we include all inputs in the rest of the work. This is harmless for the model's accuracy.

6.3 Evaluating Replication Strategies in Peer-Assisted VoD Systems

In this subsection we analyse the replication strategy used in WiseReplica. First, we evaluate four simple replication policies. Then, we compare WiseReplica with a non-collaborative caching and Oracle-like benchmark replication approach, both described in Subsect. 5.3. We evaluate their capacity to meet consumers' expectation by observing the number of violations. In addition, we compare their resource allocation performance regarding network and storage usage.

Enforcing Simple Replication Policies on Ranked VoD. For the three highest rank position, WiseReplica enforces a replica creation policy, described in Subsect. 4.2. It defines the replication degree growth factor. Considering the smallest evaluated system load (with mean video size of 20 MB), we analyse four simple creation policies, namely uniform, linear, quadratic, and exponential. Table 3 shows the number of violations by varying B from 2 to 6. Overall, creation policies that take into account the rank positions, i.e. linear, quadratic, and exponential, performed better. Results show that there is relatively small difference for $B \geq 3$, suggesting that our ranking model reacts promptly to modifications on network availability, preventing over-replication. However, for $B \geq 5$, it appears that replication increases the network load system load, causing few more violations. We selected the linear policy with $B = 4$ that seems to be the most resilient towards proper resource allocation, providing a fair replication degree growth factor.

Table 3. Replication policies.

Policy	Parameter c				
	2	3	4	5	6
Uniform	867	567	44	28	23
Linear	123	77	6	9	16
Quadratic	102	21	42	46	58
Exponential	118	32	19	27	28

Load Resiliency. A good replication strategy must cope with changes on the system load. We vary the global load of the system by changing the mean video size, described in Subsect. 5.1. Assuming the three mean video sizes, namely 20 MB, 30 MB and 40 MB, caching had 1814, 3864, and 7049 violations respectively, while WiseReplica had only 6, 77, and 106. Figure 9 compares the number of violations using WiseReplica and a non-collaborative caching. As the load of the system increases, concurrency in bitrate allocation also increases, causing more violations. WiseReplica outperforms caching mostly because it predicts and prevents useless replication. Therefore, we set to the highest evaluated system load, 40 MB, as the default mean video size workload setting.

Benefits of Prediction on Storage Usage. We aim to adapt the number of replicas to the number of views of a video, especially for the most popular ones. Figure 10 plots the maximum number of replicas for the 1 % most popular videos. Using caching, the maximum number of replicas is high, ranging from 816 to 1367. The Oracle-like assumption allows to decrease significantly the lower and upper limits, to 10 and 190. WiseReplica also reduces the maximum replica range, which is from 19 to 160. More interestingly, the shape of the replication

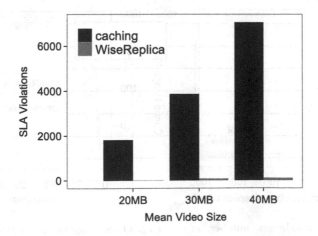

Fig. 9. Mean video size. Higher loads increase the concurrence in network resources, as a result, more violations.

curves of WiseReplica and Oracle-like are quite similar indeed. It confirms that
our predictions are accurate, and that a simple replication policy works properly.

Reducing the number of replicas implies that the systems requires less storage
for replication. Figure 11 shows storage usage for replicas by replication scheme.
Although WiseReplica utilizes more storage than Oracle-like, its usage remains
two orders of magnitude smaller than a non-collaborative caching. The maximum
storage usage for Oracle-like, WiseReplica, and a non-collaborative caching were
34, 85, and 7921 GB respectively. WiseReplica creates more replicas than Oracle-
like because it does not rely on bandwidth reservation to prevent violations. Yet,
WiseReplica maintains replicas efficiently, keeping storage usage very low, and
making cache replacement policies unnecessary. This suggests that the LRU
policy, which would eventually be enforced in peers cache, has no impact on the
WiseReplica performance.

Enhancing Bitrate Provision for Meeting Consumers' Expectation.
WiseReplica performance is also quite similar to Oracle-like regarding preventing
violations. Each point of the Fig. 12 represents the number of SLA violations for
intervals of five minutes. Overall, caching caused 7049 violations affecting 86 %
of all viewers, WiseReplica had just 106 violations, and Oracle-like, evidently,
none. Compared to caching, WiseReplica prevents nearly 99 % of violations.
It copes with violations by (i) creating new replicas for hot videos only, and
(ii) adapting the number of replicas according to the rank position. Vertical
lines in Fig. 12 represent the first access to the 10 videos with the worst content
provision through caching. They account for 80.62 % of all caching violations.
The appearance of these videos puts the system under heavy load, which makes
caching fail to prevent violations.

Figure 13 depicts the average bitrate for viewers of the 10 videos with the
worst content provision using caching. When caching was under heavy load,

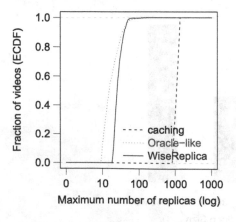

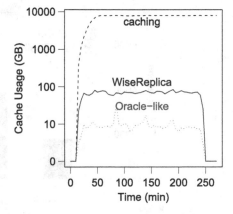

Fig. 10. The maximum number of replicas for the 1 % most popular videos.

Fig. 11. Storage usage for replication.

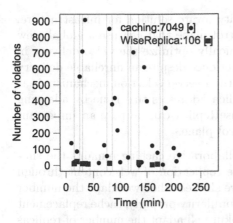

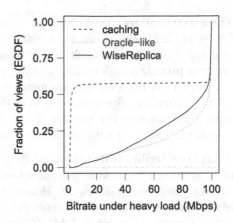

Fig. 12. SLA violations. Vertical lines highlight the first view to 10 videos with the worst content provision using caching.

Fig. 13. Bitrate for viewers of the 10 most popular videos under heavy load.

half of viewers experienced a very low bitrate, ranging between 230 Kbps and 2575 Kbps. The mean bitrate with caching was 43 Mbps. On average, WiseReplica improved this bitrate by roughly 85 % under heavy load. Actually it performs almost as well as the Oracle-like assumption, that improved bitrate provision by 93 %. These finds suggest that WiseReplica largely outperforms caching, fairly meeting consumers' expectations under heavy load conditions.

7 Related Work

Our related work is two-fold: Internet videos and adaptive replication schemes.

Internet videos: Recent studies [14,33] have drawn attention to reach a better understanding of Internet videos properties, such as popularity growth. They point out that well-known popularity characteristics are applicable to multimedia content. For instance, Internet videos popularity distribution follows power law, and popularity bursts have a short duration and are quite likely to happen just after the content publication. Dobrian *et al.* [13] shed some light on the performance of Internet videos provision on CDNs. They show that average bitrate plays an important role in videos availability. A hybrid solution between CDNs and P2P is presented by Mansy *et al.* [23]. Their purpose is to model and analyze a live video system and one of their main concerns is to adapt bitrate for guarantee user satisfaction. Adhikari *et al.* [1] work described the YouTube video delivery system through measurements of DNS resolutions and video playback traces. One of their findings is that over a globally distributed network (PlanetLab) most part of the nodes have a nearby Youtube video cache server to delivery the video data. Moreover, Brodersen *et al.* [6] presented a detailed study over the strong connection between popularity and geographic locality of Youtube videos.

These facts endure our decision of a locality aware solution for infrastructure. Liu *et al.* [21] make a case for a video control plane that can use a global view of client and network conditions to dynamically optimize the video delivery in order to provide a high quality viewing experience despite an unreliable delivery infrastructure. However, the granularity of their server selection mechanism is at a CDN, ignoring edge resources. WiseReplica addresses this issue by adapting replication close to the viewers. Thus, WiseReplica can be play an important role in collaborating with an Internet control plane.

Adaptive replication schemes: Non-collaborative caching remains the simplest approach to provide popularity-aware replication of web content through cache replacement policies [20]. However, we showed when we adapt the number of replicas according to the Internet video popularity properly, cache replacement policy becomes redundant. EAD [27] and Skute [4] adapt the number of replicas by using a cost-benefit approach over decentralized and structured P2P systems. EAD creates and deletes replicas throughout the query path with regard to object hit rate using an exponential moving average technique. Similarly, Skute provides a replication management scheme that evaluates replicas price and revenue across different geographic locations. Despite presenting an efficient framework for replication, they provide an inaccurate bitrate provision, hence inappropriate for high-quality video delivery. WiseReplica copes with this issue by analysing the request arrival process, performing accurate predictions about the ranking of Internet videos, and maintaining replication degree accordingly.

8   Conclusions

In this work, we presented WiseReplica, a SLA-based, adaptive replication scheme for meeting customers' expectations and enhancing resource allocation in peer-assisted VoD systems. To adapt replication, WiseReplica relies on a prediction model for ranking Internet videos in order of demand. Our intuitive model is flexible, and can learn from different sources and big amounts of data, providing a robust framework for controlling VoD resource allocation. Simulations using You Tube traces suggest that our ranking predictions of videos are important to enhance video delivery in peer-assisted VoD systems, allowing us to self-adapt replication degree to video demand properly. WiseReplica increases the average bitrate provision by roughly 85 %, contributing decisively to enhance viewing experience of users. Our future work will mainly cover a proof-of-concept prototype for evaluating WiseReplica in a real testbed.

References

1. Adhikari, V.K., Jain, S., Chen, Y., Zhang, Z.-L.: Vivisecting youtube: an active measurement study. In: INFOCOM (2012)
2. Alizadeh, M., Greenberg, A., Maltz, D.A., Padhye, J., Patel, P., Prabhakar, B., Sengupta, S., Sridharan, M.: Data center TCP (DCTCP). In: SIGCOMM (2010)

3. Balachandran, A., Sekar, V., Akella, A., Seshan, S., Stoica, I., Zhang, H.: Developing a predictive model of quality of experience for internet video. In: SIGCOMM (2013)
4. Bonvin, N., Papaioannou, T.G., Aberer, K.: A self-organized, fault-tolerant and scalable replication scheme for cloud storage. In: SOCC (2010)
5. Braun, L., Klein, A., Carle, G., Reiser, H., Eisl, J.: Analyzing caching benefits for youtube traffic in edge networks - a measurement-based evaluation. In: NOMS (2012)
6. Brodersen, A., Scellato, S., Wattenhofer, M.: Youtube around the world: geographic popularity of videos. In: WWW (2012)
7. Buffoni, D., Calauzenes, C., Gallinari, P., Usunier, N.: Learning scoring functions with order-preserving losses and standardized supervision. In: ICML (2011)
8. Burges, C., Shaked, T., Renshaw, E., Lazier, A., Deeds, M., Hamilton, N., Hullender, G.: Learning to rank using gradient descent. In: Proceedings of the 22nd International Conference on Machine Learning (2005)
9. Calauzenes, C., Usunier, N., Gallinari, P., et al.: On the (non-) existence of convex, calibrated surrogate losses for ranking. In: Neural Information Processing Systems (2012)
10. Chang, L., Pan, J.: Towards the optimal caching strategies of peer-assisted VoD systems with HD channels. In: ICNP (2012)
11. Cortes, C., Vapnik, V.: Support-vector networks. Mach. Learn. **20**, 273–297 (1995)
12. Croft, W.B., Metzler, D., Strohman, T.: Search Engines: Information Retrieval in Practice. Addison-Wesley, Reading (2010)
13. Dobrian, F., Sekar, V., Awan, A., Stoica, I., Joseph, D., Ganjam, A., Zhan, J., Zhang, H.: Understanding the impact of video quality on user engagement. In: SIGCOMM (2011)
14. Figueiredo, F., Benevenuto, F., Almeida, J.M.: The tube over time: characterizing popularity growth of youtube videos. In: WSDM (2011)
15. Finamore, A., Mellia, M., Munafò, M.M., Torres, R., Rao, S.G.: Youtube everywhere: impact of device and infrastructure synergies on user experience. In: IMC (2011)
16. Hastie, T., Tibshirani, R., Friedman, J.H.: The Elements of Statistical Learning: Data Mining, Inference, and Prediction: With 200 Full-Color Illustrations. Springer, New York (2001)
17. Huang, C., Li, J., Ross, K.W.: Can internet video-on-demand be profitable? In: SIGCOMM (2007)
18. Huang, Y., Fu, T.Z., Chiu, D.-M., Lui, J.C., Huang, C.: Challenges, design and analysis of a large-scale P2P VoD system. In: Sigcomm (2008)
19. Järvelin, K., Kekäläinen, J.: Cumulated gain-based evaluation of IR techniques. ACM TOIS **20**, 422–446 (2002)
20. Jin, S., Bestavros, A.: Popularity-aware greedy-dual-size web proxy caching algorithms. In: ICDCS (1999)
21. Liu, X., Dobrian, F., Milner, H., Jiang, J., Sekar, V., Stoica, I., Zhang, H.: A case for a coordinated internet video control plane. In: SIGCOMM (2012)
22. Manning, C.D., Raghavan, P., Schütze, H.: Introduction to Information Retrieval. Cambridge University Press, Cambridge (2008)
23. Mansy, A., Ammar, M.H.: Analysis of adaptive streaming for hybrid CDN/P2P live video systems. In: ICNP (2011)
24. Montresor, A., Jelasity, M.: PeerSim: a scalable P2P simulator. In: P2P (2009)
25. Parvez, N., Williamson, C., Mahanti, A., Carlsson, N.: Analysis of bittorrent-like protocols for on-demand stored media streaming. In: SIGMETRICS (2008)

26. Pedregosa, F., Varoquaux, G., Gramfort, A., Michel, V., Thirion, B., Grisel, O., Blondel, M., Prettenhofer, P., Weiss, R., Dubourg, V., Vanderplas, J., Passos, A., Cournapeau, D., Brucher, M., Perrot, M., Duchesnay, E.: Scikit-learn: machine learning in Python. JMLR **12**, 2825–2830 (2011)
27. Shen, H.: An efficient and adaptive decentralized file replication algorithm in P2P file sharing systems. IEEE Trans. Parallel Distrib. Syst. **21**, 827–840 (2010)
28. Silvestre, G., Fernandes, S., Kamienski, C., Sadok, D.: Most wanted internet applications: a framework for P2P identification. In: CNSR (2010)
29. Silvestre, G., Monnet, S., Krishnaswamy, R., Sens, P.: Aren: a popularity aware replication scheme for cloud storage. In: ICPADS (2012)
30. Silvestre, G., Monnet, S., Krishnaswamy, R., Sens, P.: Caju: a content distribution system for edge networks. Technical report, UPMC Sorbone Universités (2012)
31. Steinwart, I.: How to Compare different loss functions and their risks. Constr. Approx. **26**, 225–287 (2007)
32. Bittorrent. http://bittorrent.com
33. Szabo, G., Huberman, B.A.: Predicting the popularity of online content. Commun. ACM **53**, 80–88 (2010)
34. Wilson, C., Ballani, H., Karagiannis, T., Rowstron, A.: Better never than late: meeting deadlines in datacenter networks. In: SIGCOMM (2011)
35. Zhang, T.: Statistical behavior and consistency of classification methods based on convex risk minimization. Ann. Stat. **32**(1), 56–134 (2004)

A Cloud-Based, Geospatial Linked Data Management System

Kyriakos Kritikos[1]([✉]), Yannis Rousakis[1], and Dimitris Kotzinos[1,2]

[1] Information Systems Laboratory, Institute of Computer Science,
Foundation of Research and Technology - Hellas (FORTH),
N. Plastira 100, 700 13 Heraklion, Crete, Greece
{kritikos,rousakis,kotzino}@ics.forth.gr
[2] Lab. ETIS (ENSEA/UCP/CNRS UMR 8051),
Department of Computer Science, University of Cergy-Pontoise,
2 av. Adolphe Chauvin, 95000 Pontoise, France

Abstract. The Web has been evolving to a sink of disparate information sources which are totally isolated from each other. The technology
of Linked Data (LD) promises to connect such information sources in
order to enable their better exploitation by humans or automated programs. While various LD management systems have been proposed, only
few of them are able to handle geospatial data which are becoming quite
popular nowadays and lead to the creation of large geospatial footprints.
However, none of the few systems that support Linked Open Geospatial Data is able to scale well to handle the increasing load from user
queries. In addition, the publishing of geospatial LD also becomes quite
advantageous due to complexity reasons. To this end, this article proposes a novel, cloud-based geospatial LD management system which can
scale out or scale in according to the incoming load in order to serve
the respective user requests with the appropriate service level. On top
of this system lies a LD-as-a-service offering which abstracts away the
user from any LD publishing complexities and provides all the appropriate functionality for enabling a full LD management. We also study
and propose architectural solutions for the distributed update problem.
The proposed system is evaluated under heavy load scenarios and the
results show that the respective improvement in performance incurred
is quite satisfactory and that the scaling actions are performed at the
appropriate time points.

1 Introduction

While the Web is evolving extremely in many aspects and gets evens bigger, it
still lacks mechanisms through which disparate but related information sources
can be queried to obtain particular data for the current user task at hand. In fact,
this is one of the major disadvantages of the Web which leads to user frustration
as well as to many isolated islands of information which although related cannot
be easily connected.

© Springer-Verlag Berlin Heidelberg 2015
A. Hameurlain et al. (Eds.): TLDKS XX, LNCS 9070, pp. 59–89, 2015.
DOI: 10.1007/978-3-662-46703-9_3

The technology of Linked Data (LD) promises to remedy the above problem by enabling data to reference other data and be linked to them. In this sense, a user query targeting different information islands can be able to discover all needed information by exploiting the links between these islands. However, the big problem with LD technology is that it has not reached the performance levels and maturity of the traditional database technology. In addition, by also considering that users are increasingly providing a geospatial aspect to the description of the information that they publish (e.g., consider that images taken by various devices are now tagged with geospatial information), another problem is raised concerning the efficient evaluation of respective geospatial queries by exploiting the LD technology.

The current LD management systems are making good progress towards solving the above problems with commercial LD engines such as Virtuoso[1] reaching a good level of performance by exploiting different storing techniques at the physical level (e.g., no-sql-like solutions). However, such systems are not able to handle all possible cases in geospatial information management. In addition, they cannot reach good performance levels for all possible types of queries. They are also not very scalable unless the user pays a great amount of money so that particular clustered or cloud-based versions of these systems is exploited to guarantee a certain scalability level. Finally, usually such systems enforce the user to handle low-level details inherent to the LD technologies used.

In the context of the InGeoCloudS project (www.ingeoclouds.eu), a LD Management System (LDMS) has been developed which provides satisfactory query performance levels and supplies a Linked Data Management API/service which is language independent and hides the complexities of the LD technology from the end-user. This API also provides particular functionality which is able to manage not only normal but also geospatial LD in terms of storing, updating, querying and exporting them. Moreover, this API also provides the functionality of exporting INSPIRE-compliant data which is a feature highly important for geospatial data providers if we consider the current and future INSPIRE[2] directives. In this paper, apart from analysing the functionality of the API and its most important features, we will also describe in detail the cloud-based architecture of the LDMS which enables it to be quite scalable and able to supply appropriate quality levels to the normal or geospatial queries posed. The latter is proven through a thorough empirical evaluation which also partially justified particular features of the architecture proposed as well as the scalability policies enforced.

The rest of the article is structured as follows. Section 2 reviews related work. Section 3 provides background knowledge useful for the proper comprehension of the article and its proposed system. Sections 4 and 5 analyse the proposed system and in particular the functional and architectural extensions made to its previous and more limited version. Section 5 presents and discusses empirical evaluation results with respect to the query performance of the proposed system. Finally, Sect. 6 concludes the article and draws directions for further research.

---

[1] http://virtuoso.openlinksw.com/.

[2] http://inspire.jrc.ec.europa.eu/.

2   Related Work

To the best of our knowledge, there is no geospatial data management system that is scalable, supplies high performance levels and provides all appropriate management functionality in a LD technology-independent way. Our claim is backed up by the following table which classifies and compares the related approaches with respect to particular comparison criteria. These criteria include:

- *distribution:* a characterization of whether the approach is *centralized, clustered* or *cloud-based* which is related to the approach capability to scale in order to exhibit better performance levels.
- *store type:* the type of store (i.e., *research (and open)* or *proprietary*) which can have an influence on the cost of the respective approach based on the required capabilities.
- *geospatial support:* indicates the level of geospatial support provided by the approach (i.e., *none, basic* and *advanced*), where the difference between a basic and advanced support is that the second enables the use of more advanced geospatial operators, such as (feature) aggregation operators.
- *service level:* indicates the level of the services offered (i.e., RDF *query* or full *management* services). Obviously, a full management service level is preferred as the additional effort in adapting a particular approach selected will be minimal.
- *input mapping:* indicates the capability of the approach to map input data of a different form to RDF ones (i.e., *none, relational* and *multiple* input formats). This is a very interesting and important aspect, especially if we consider the current form of the Web and the need for transforming data from various formats into RDF ones. Thus, a data mapping approach supporting multiple input formats will be preferred. Please note that as the relational mapping is the most involved one, especially in terms of realization, an approach is evaluated as supporting multiple input formats when it supports at least relational mapping along with the mapping from one or more additional formats. Please consider that such kind of mapping might also be used for doing on the fly SPARQL to SQL rewritings so that we can query the original data sources.

As it can be seen from Table 1, our approach is the sole approach evaluated with the best possible choice for each criterion. Next comes Oracle with two particular disadvantages with respect to our approach: (a) it is a proprietary solution and (b) does not support the mapping of data from various formats to RDF. Virtuoso is another good alternative, which apart from being proprietary has the disadvantage of providing only basic geospatial support. Another possibility is the Strabon RDF store which however does not offer a data input mapping functionality. The worst approaches seem to be the cloud/clustered research ones which do not provide geospatial and full RDF management support as well as input mapping functionality. This seems quite reasonable if we consider the fact that such approaches have been developed to showcase how Cloud-based technologies can be exploited to boost the query answering time.

Table 1. Comparison analysis of related work

Approach	Distribution	Store type	Geospatial support	Service level	Input mapping
Hausenblas [13]	cloud	research	none	query	none
Stein and Zacharias [20]	cloud	research	none	query	none
Bugiotti et al. [2]	cloud	research	none	query	none
Ladwig and Harth [12]	cloud	research	none	query	none
Guéret et al. [6]	clustered/cloud	research	none	query	none
Yars2 [7]	clustered	research	none	query	none
Mika and Tummarello [14]	clustered	research	none	query	none
Tanimura et al. [22]	clustered	research	none	query	none
Husain et al. [9]	clustered	research	none	query	none
Sun and Jin [21]	clustered	research	none	query	none
Papailiou et al. [17]	clustered	research	none	query	none
Franke et al. [4]	clustered	research	none	query	none
Ravindra et al. [18]	clustered	research	none	query	none
Newman et al. [16]	clustered	research	none	query	none
Dydra	cloud	proprietary	none	management	none
AllegroGraph	clustered/cloud	proprietary	basic	management	none
BigData	clustered	proprietary	none	management	none
OWLIM	clustered/cloud	proprietary	basic	management	none
Virtuoso	clustered/cloud	proprietary	basic	management	multiple
Oracle	clustered/cloud	proprietary	advanced	management	relational
Strabon [11]	centralized	research	advanced	management	none
RDF-3X [15]	centralized	research	basic	management	none
Parliament [1]	centralized	research	basic	management	none
Yago2 [8]	centralized	research	basic	management	none
TDB	centralized	research	none	management	none
Our approach	cloud	research	advanced	management	multiple

In the following, we analyze the related work by also clustering it according to its distribution capability into different groups mapping to separate subsections. We should also highlight Geoknow (http://www.geoknow.eu/project) as an interesting project focusing on addressing the whole management life-cycle of open geo-spatial LD and supporting the respective SDI standards. However, this project does not focus on scalability, elasticity and reliability issues.

2.1   Distributed Approaches

In this category, the related work relies on a distributed approach which is either realized in a cluster of machines or exploits cloud resources. In either type of realization, the approaches attempt to split the data and computation across the available machines or resources. However, the cloud-based approaches are better as they can automatically scale indefinitely through the triggering of scaling rules while the clustered-based approaches are limited based on the size of the underlying data centre (if it really exists) as well as they need additional effort in terms of development of the respective tools to enable automated scaling. Moreover, Cloud-based approaches exhibit good query performance levels which are far better than those exhibited by clustered approaches. In both types of realization, we also see either the use of well-known proprietary RDF management systems or customed and special-purpose (research-based) RDF Stores with, however, limited capabilities, such as the partial support of the standard LD query language SPARQL[3]. All research approaches do not offer any geo-spatial support. They also do not provide web or REST [3] services [19] through which a user can exploit the functionality provided. The well-known proprietary RDF stores do provide basic geo-spatial functionality as well as SPARQL end-points along with other services and APIs to enable the appropriate LD management. However, they do not usually enable the automatic mapping between relational and RDF data which is a critical feature for enabling the benefits that LD technology brings about by transforming data in their original, relational form to LD.

Research Approaches. BigQuery[4] is a web service running on the Google Cloud that enables performing SQL-like queries and interactive analysis on massive data sets typically using a small number of very large, append-only tables. To enable the semantic aspect, Dr. Hausenblas [13] has extended BigQuery with the capability to load RDF/N-Triples content and query this content using BigQuery's syntax.

Stein and Zacharias [20] have developed the Stratustore prototype system which acts as a back end for the Jena semantic framework and stores LD in SimpleDB. The queries are realized through TripleMatch objects and exploit a particular entity-oriented mapping where one item represents the data known for a particular subject and the attributes map to the subject URI and to the predicates which are related to this subject.

Bugiotti et al. [2] have implemented a research prototype in the Amazon Cloud where RDF files are stored in the Amazon Simple Storage Service and SimpleDB is used for indexing purposes. Four different indexing strategies have been realized which were evaluated for different types of queries to assess the most prevailing one.

Ladwig and Harth [12] have developed a research LD storage and querying prototype which exploits distributed key-value stores and especially Cassandra. This prototype has realized two alternative storage schemes: (a) a hierarchical layout scheme based on supercolumns and (b) a flat layout scheme. The flat scheme was empirically assessed to lead to a better triple pattern query time.

The TripleCloud RDF management system [6] can exploit two cloud-based key value stores: (a) HBase[5] and (b) Google App Engine Datastore as the data layer on top of the eRDF framework [5] by relying on the fact that these stores provide common methods which map directly to the primitives required by eRDF.

---

[3] http://www.w3.org/TR/2013/REC-sparql11-query-20130321/.

[4] https://cloud.google.com/bigquery/.

[5] http://hbase.apache.org/.

Yars2 [7] is a federated semantic search engine for performing interactive query answering over heterogeneous LD collected from many disparate Web sources. The local indexing scheme adopted comprises: (a) keyword indices based on Apache Lucene to enable keyword lookups, (b) full quad sparse indices, and (c) join indices to speed up queries. For global-based indexing, three partitioning methods are employed to decide on the node where a particular quad will be indexed.

Mika and Tummarello [14] have produced a research prototype in the form of a back-end for the Sesame Triple Store which exploits Pig to load and query RDF data, where RDF loading is performed by converting RDF to Pig's data model.

Tanimura et al. [22] have implemented a scalable RDF data processing framework which exploits parallel database processing over the Google File System (GFS). Hadoop is used as the basic infrastructure based on GFS and MapReduce while Pig is used as the data processing platform. For efficient RDF querying, a particular RDF storage scheme which combines vertical partitioning with the Hadoops key-value data format was adopted.

Husain et al. [9] have developed a scalable and fault-tolerant framework which exploits a particular scheme for storing RDF Data in the Hadoop File System and supports data intensive query processing.

A RDF storage and querying prototype system has been implemented in [21] based on MapReduce and HBase. The realized storage scheme employs six HBase tables to cover all RDF triple pattern combinations, while triples are indexed through the HBase index structure on row key.

A distributed RDF prototype store is presented in [17] based on MapReduce and HBase. The storage scheme employs three indices to cover particular triple pattern combinations stored in HBase tables in the form of key-value pairs.

Franke et al. [4] have implemented a prototype with two different distributed RDF storage schemes based on HBase and MySQL Cluster, respectively. The HBase database schema relies on creating two tables for storing RDF triples, while the MySQL-based scheme relies on a simple table which has as columns the triple subjects, predicates and objects, respectively.

An extension of the RAPID prototype system is proposed in [18] which relies on Pig and Hadoop and exploits PigLatin as the high-level language to support ad-hoc processing and querying over large data-sets.

An RDF molecule-based store has been realized in [16] by exploiting Hadoop to scale-out the distributed query processing. A number of extensions with respect to molecule hierarchy and structure are proposed to the initial molecule definition to resolve particular query performance issues.

Proprietary Approaches. Dydra[6] is a multi-tenant, cloud-based graph database deployed on the Amazon Cloud, which exhibits various features, such as versioning and disaster recovery. RDF data are stored as a property graph which directly represents the relationships between them.

---

[6] www.dydra.com.

AllegroGraph[7] is a high-performance, persistent graph database which efficiently utilizes memory in conjunction to disk-based storage to scale to billions of quads without compromising performance. It is offered via standalone, clustered and cloud-based versions. It fully supports SPARQL, exploits 7 indices for triple storage and exhibits advanced text indexing per predicate, while a column-based compression of indices is also imposed for reduced paging and better performance. Concerning the geo-spatial support, it provides a novel mechanism for efficient storage and retrieval of 2D geo-spatial data by also supporting both Cartesian and spherical coordinate systems.

BigData[8] is a horizontally scaled storage and computing fabric featuring high concurrency and high aggregate I/O rates. It is offered in a standalone or clustered mode. It includes a RDF database which supports RDFS and performs distributed operations on a cluster with dynamic key-range sharding of indices. This database also supports full-text indexing suitable for entity matching and integration hooks for full text search and indexing using Lucene. Basic geospatial support has been recently advertized through the creation of a new geospatial index and the use of one and many Z-values for points and regions, respectively.

OWLIM[9] is a family of semantic repositories which exploit native RDF engines developed in Java as well as Sesame and Jena for RDF management and guaranteeing high-performance levels. It is offered via different versions: a standalone, a clustered and a cloud-based one. The clustered version of OWLIM (OWLIM-SE) exploits file-based indices in order to scale to billions of statements. A literal index is also built for faster lookups of numeric and date/time object values, while index compression can also be switched on. OWLIM-SE supports 2D spatial data which use the WGS84 Geo Positioning RDF Vocabulary, while R-Tree indices are created for these data to allow the evaluation of particular query types which exploit particular topological relation functions. Only spherical Coordinate Reference Systems (CRSs) are supported.

Virtuoso[10] is a middleware and database engine hybrid combining the functionality of R/ODBMS, RDF Stores, and Web Application and File Servers. It is offered via three variants: (a) standalone, (b) clustered, and (c) cloud-based. The current version of Virtuoso employs a column-based indexing scheme. Two main indices are created on RDF data as well as three partial indices. Strings are given a unique Integer ID to save space but also to keep a full text index of them. Geometries are represented as object values in an RDF quad conforming to the WKT vocabulary and are indexed through R-Trees. Only 2D geometries are currently supported.

Oracle[11] provides an open, scalable, secure and reliable RDF management platform called Oracle Spatial and Graph RDF Semantic Graph. Oracle performs

---

[7] www.franz.com/agraph/allegrograph/.
[8] www.systap.com/bigdata.htm.
[9] www.ontotext.com/owlim&www.ontotext.com/owlim/geo-spatial.
[10] http://virtuoso.openlinksw.com.
[11] http://www.oracle.com/technetwork/database-options/spatialandgraph/overview/rdfsemantic-graph-1902016.html.

semantic indexing by exploiting a particular index type which makes use of information extractors and annotators to semantically index documents in relational tables. Oracle exhibits advanced data manipulation and spatial analysis features including a whole portfolio of functions for spatial data mining, geometric unions and intersections, and linear inferencing. It also includes a GeoRaster datatype to store and manage image and gridded raster data and meta-data. 3D geo-spatial data are supported to enable the storage and management of lines, surfaces, triangulated irregular networks, point clouds, and terrain models. Such data are indexed through R-Tree indices. Oracle considers the Whole Earth geometry model to take into account the curvature of Earths surface when performing calculations on geodetic data, supports over 30 of most commonly used distance and area units, and provides comprehensive tools for managing CRSs and respective projections based on the European Petroleum Survey Group model and data set.

2.2 Centralized Approaches

Some centralized approaches, such as Strabon [11], offer good geo-spatial support in terms of: (a) geo-spatial operators that can be used in GeoSPARQL (http://www.opengeospatial.org/standards/geosparql) queries and (b) specialized indices as well as query evaluation/optimization methods. Such approaches also provide a SPARQL end-point to be used for basic RDF data management. Moreover, they have shown good performance in evaluating particular types of geo-spatial queries. We should highlight here that no thorough performance evaluation of geo-spatial queries has been conducted in the cloud. This could be utilized to assess whether cloud capabilities are indeed exploited by RDF Stores which adopt a cloud-based architecture to become more scalable.

Strabon [11] is an open-source, geo-spatial RDF store prototype which exploits Sesame and PostGIS. It is able to exploit both the WKT and GML vocabularies for the representation of 2D geometries and offers functions from the OpenGIS Simple Feature Access for SQL OGC standard to manipulate spatial literals and provide support for multiple CRSs. The RDF triples are stored using the one table per predicate scheme of Sesame and dictionary encoding. The spatial literals are stored in a table with a particular schema accommodating for an id column, which represents the unique encoding of a spatial literal based on the mapping dictionary, as well as a value column with a PostGIS geometry data type for storing the geometry determined by the spatial literal and a srid column to store the original CRS of the geometry.

Parliament [1] is an open-source RDF triple store which exploits a particular storage and indexing scheme based on linked lists and memory-mapped files. A particular extension to Parliament has been developed to enable the indexing of geospatial data and the evaluation of GeoSPARQL queries. Three indices are employed for geo-spatial data: (a) a R-Tree index, (b) a temporal index, and (c) a basic numeric index for optimizing range queries on numeric data types. Both WKT and GML are supported for representing geometries.

RDF-3X [15] is a complete, open-source RDF management system based on three key principles: (a) physical design is workload independent, (b) query processor is RISC-style relying on merge joins, and (c) the query optimizer focuses on join order for the generation of plans. RDF-3X stores all triples in a clustered B+-tree. RDF-3X models 2D spatial data through WKT and indexes them via R-Trees.

YAGO2 [8][12] is an extension of the YAGO Knowledge Base enabling the modeling of entities, facts and events according to the additional aspects of time and space. Time is represented via the *yagoDate* data type typically with a resolution of days or sometimes in years. All entities with a permanent spatial extent on Earth are subsumed by the *yagoGeoEntity* class. The position of such entities is described via geographical coordinates expressed via a special data type called *yagoGeoCoordinates* which is a pair of latitude and longitude values. As this is quite restricting for locations with a physical extent, particular rules are exploited in order to assign a specific position for particular location types, such as cities or military and industrial establishments. Special types of spatial relations are exploited to express a permanent location of an entity, to associate facts with the location they concern, and to express relations between time and location.

TDB[13] is part of Jena for RDF storage and querying and can be used as a high performance store on a single machine which can be accessed either through scripts or programmatically via the Jena API. The indexing scheme of TDB comprises: (a) a node table (dictionary) storing the representation of RDF terms, (b) three full triple and quad indexes for unnamed and named graphs, respectively and (c) the prefixes table which uses a node table and a index for GPU.

3   Background

In our previous work [10], we have developed a similar system to the one being proposed in this article for which the basic components were analysed. The added-value and advancement of this article lies on the fact that a better system architecture has been adopted which takes into account the current and prospective usage of the system and is able to scale appropriately in such a way that the query performance remains at satisfactory levels while the updating of LD is carried out in a lazy fashion by considering the fact that such updating does not jeopardise the integrity of the application running on top of the system as well as does not deteriorate the system's performance. In addition, the exposed functionality of the system has been extended to also handle geospatial LD as well as different publishing and exporting ways. Moreover, in comparison to previous work, the system has been heavily tested and evaluated to indicate that it exhibits the desired performance under the most extreme situations.

---

[12] www.mpi-inf.mpg.de/yago-naga/yago/.
[13] http://jena.apache.org/documentation/tdb.

In order to acquaint the prospective user with our previous work and corresponding system version, the next subsections analyse the previous system architecture and its main basic components.

3.1 Previous System Architecture

The architecture of the previous version of the system, shown in Fig. 1, comprised a component called *Distributor* responsible for processing user requests in terms of Linked Data Management Service (LMS) methods and then forwarding each request to one or more *Scaling Layers*. The latter components were responsible for the management of data pertaining to one or more data providers (and thus corresponding RDF graphs) such that data partitioning among different layers and replication at same layer was achieved in order to sustain a high-level of data reliability and integrity. Each scaling layer consisted of many image instances, called just instances from now on, each exposing the basic system functionality in terms of LD Management and containing a LMS implementation and an underlying Virtuoso Universal Server exploited by this service. Each scaling layer was responsible of forwarding a user query or export request to one instance, thus catering for load balancing, and all update requests to all instances to guarantee that all such instances were mapping to the same RDF data. As LMS and Virtuoso constitute the backbone of our system providing the basic LD management functionality exposed by it, they are analysed in the following two subsections.

3.2 LD Management Service

The two variants of our system rely on Virtuoso as the back-end triple store. While Virtuoso offers a SPARQL end-point, a REST-based Service called LMS was developed which exposes an API that provides all appropriate management functionality to be exploited by data providers and potential users of geo-spatial Linked Open Data (LOD). This service abstracts way from the particularities of any RDF Data Management API exposed by an underlying triple store and enables the simple and intuitive use of a specific set of LOD management methods. In fact, with little re-engineering effort (mostly concerning connection peculiarities), LMS could well function with a different underlying store. LMS allows a programmatic as well as a web-based access to its methods, where the web-based access can be facilitated through the development of particular forms accessible via a browser in a specific URL. Moreover, LMS exposes a querying capability that allows producing results in the following formats: "sparql-results/xml", "sparql-results/json", "sparql-results/tsv" and "sparql-results/csv"[14]. In addition, importing and

---

[14] xml → http://www.w3.org/TR/rdf-sparql-XMLres/.
json → http://www.w3.org/TR/2013/REC-sparql11-results-json-20130321/.
csv and tsv → http://www.w3.org/TR/2013/REC-sparql11-results-csv-tsv-20130
321/.

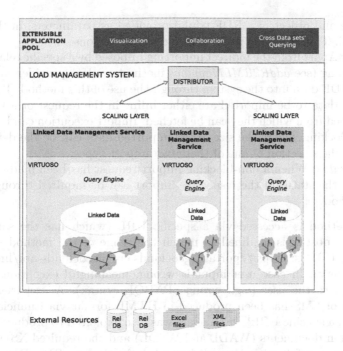

Fig. 1. The previous architecture of the LD Management System

exporting functionality is exposed which can handle a variety of LD formats, such as RDF/XML, NTriples[15], and Turtle[16].

LMS exposes the following methods:

- *ldquery:* It takes as input the SPARQL query as a String and optionally a timeout and row limit parameters and returns the result in the format requested by the user.
- *ldupdate:* Similarly to *ldquery*, this method takes as input a SPARUL (SPARQL 1.1 Update Language[17]) update statement (along with the same optional parameters) and applies/executes it.
- *addR2RMLMappings:* It takes as input the mapping specified as String in R2RML (RDB to RDF Mapping Language[18]), which is a W3C Recommendation that aims at enabling the description of customized mappings between a relational database and RDF datasets, as well as the name of the graph to be created and initiates the relational-to-linked data mapping procedure offered by Virtuoso Triple Store.
- *ldexport:* It exports either a complete graph or a set of statements, which involve from zero to at most three URIs (pertaining to the URIs of subject,

[15] http://www.w3.org/2001/sw/RDFCore/ntriples/.
[16] http://www.w3.org/TR/turtle/.
[17] http://www.w3.org/TR/sparql11-update/.
[18] http://www.w3.org/TR/r2rml/.

predicate and object in a RDF triple) provided as parameters, in the format requested. The exporting result is inline in the response.

– *ldimport:* Apart from the indirect importing imposed by a specific relational-to-LD mapping (see *addR2RMLMappings* method), a data provider can directly import RDF data into the system through the use of this method. To this end, the RDF data to be imported are either inline in the request or a URL must be provided from which they can be fetched. Import execution can be blocking or non-blocking, where the size of the imported data can be the determinant factor in the selection of one of these two import types.

– *import_status:* When a non-blocking import request has been made by a data provider, the status of the respective import can be inquired through calling this method.

Each method is accessed via a specific URL (which has the same prefix but just the postfix is modified to match the name of the method – e.g., for *ldquery*, the URL is: https://portal.ingeoclouds.eu/ingeoclouds-api/linkeddata/rest/ld/ldquery). In case user input is wrong, meaningful exception messages are returned to the user (e.g., wrong SPARQL syntax). A user-friendly documentation of LMS has been produced in HTML format via Enunciate and is accessible in a specific URL[19]. Enunciate was also exploited to produce the interface definition documents (WADL and WSDL) and the required XSD schemas. LMS exploits the following java modules: (a) the Sesame RDF Data Management API which provides bridge methods between a user application (which is LMS in this case) and an underlying Triple Store, (b) the Virtuoso's JDBC driver (for properly exploiting Virtuoso via the Sesame API), and (c) Jersey (for REST-based realization of LSM).

3.3   Virtuoso Universal Server

Virtuoso Universal Server is a hybrid of a database engine and a middleware which combines the functionality of a traditional RDBMS, an ORDBMS, a RDF-Store, a virtual database, a web application server and a file server. It maps to a single-threaded server process supporting multiple Web and Internet protocols, such as HTTP, HTTPs, WebDav, SOAP, UDDI, SPARQL and SPARUL. Moreover, for enabling the development of database-based applications and system integration, Virtuoso has implemented a wide variety of industry standard data access APIs, such as ODBC, JDBC, OLE DB, and ADO .NET. Virtuoso Universal Server can be exploited either in a standalone, clustered or cloud-based manner. As the latter two exploitation ways are not free, we have relied on the first one to build our system and have realized update synchronization mechanisms to enable its transformation into a clustered set of Triple Stores via also exploiting cloud-based technologies.

Virtuoso supports not only the querying and updating of LD through the SPARQL language but also their complete management by offering various low-level SQL functions that can be exploited. In addition, from version 7 and on,

---

[19] https://portal.ingeoclouds.eu/ingeoclouds-api/linkeddata/.

Virtuoso enables the representation of features in a two-dimensional space, by realizing a new geometry data type (virtrdf:Geometry) and a corresponding R-Tree index, and in this way allows the use of spatial operators (actuall SQL MM functions) in SQL and SPARQL queries[20]. This feature was proprietary in the version 6 of Virtuoso that was exploited by our previous work but it can now be fully exploited in our new version of the LD Management system proposed in this article. As it will be seen in the next section, through this new feature, the user has now the capability to perform geospatial queries in two different ways, where the inline Virtuoso way has a better performance but lacks particular geospatial functionality. In this way, the user has the ability to choose one of these two ways depending on the desired geospatial functionality to be exploited in the respective queries and his/her query performance requirements.

Fully supporting a set of geospatial functions is not common in the corresponding systems. The available standards like GeoSPARQL are rather young and the respective systems offer limited support, as discussed also in the previous sections. Virtuoso on the other hand provides a very good infrastructure to extend and build our own functionalities.

4 LD Management Service Extensions

While the initial functionality of LMS focused mainly on providing basic LD management functionality, it became apparent that there was a need for also appropriately handling the special LD type of geospatial data. Apart from this, additional importing requirements were set based on the feedback from particular data providers in the InGeoCloudS project, while some performance problems were identified due to the use of Strings as the main representations of the LMS methods' input and output (I/O). Moreover, due to the fact that it is imposed that the INSPIRE directives should be embraced by data providers until 2020, it was also decided to realize INSPIRE exporting functionality for the LD stored. To this end, LMS was extended according to the following aspects: (a) additional methods were introduced which enable the management of geospatial LD, (b) an additional import method was introduced, (c) methods for exporting LD in INSPIRE format were implemented and (d) the handling of I/O now occurs via java streams. The additional methods realized are the following:

- *geoldquery:* This method is similar to *ldquery* but allows the issuing of GeoSPARQL queries instead of SPARQL ones. The realization of this method relied on the exploitation of the USeekM framework[21].
- *geoldtransform:* This method can be used to transform (Geo)SPARQL results of any format into a feature collection representation format, such as GML[22] and KML[23]. As some of these formats enable a direct representation of the

---

[20] http://docs.openlinksw.com/virtuoso/rdfsparqlgeospat.html.
[21] https://dev.opensahara.com/projects/useekm.
[22] http://www.opengeospatial.org/standards/gml.
[23] http://www.opengeospatial.org/standards/kml.

results in a map-based GUI, this along with the previous method constitute added-value functionality useful for building geospatial applications.

- *INSPIRE_export:* This method can be used to export the LD stored in INSPIRE. The input required for this method is the geospatial theme for which the data need to be exported as well as a set of SPARQL FILTER constraints which impose filtering conditions on the data to be returned. Internally, each theme is mapped to a particular SPARQL query which is first joined with the FILTER constraints and then issued to the underlying store. The results obtained are mapped to INSPIRE based on a particular mapping from the geo-scientific spatial observation model (GSOM) [10] to INSPIRE. GSOM has been proposed at the conceptual level as a means to integrate the various information sources involved in the InGeoCloudS project and as well as an information model that complements INSPIRE in particular aspects, such as the complete modelling of events and geo-scientific activities. To this end, the GSOM-to-INSPIRE mapping involved in the realization of this method is incomplete due to the fact that some GSOM information is not included in INSPIRE.
- *inspire_query_export:* This method is also able to export LD in INSPIRE format. The difference with respect to the previous method lies on the fact that a direct (Geo)SPARQL query is provided by the user which is used to fetch the SPARQL results and then transform them into the INSPIRE format. Internally, the method is able to recognize the theme(s) involved in the query as well as the mappings from SPARQL variables to GSOM entities and based on these to perform the LD to INSPIRE transformation.
- *theme_query_info:* This method takes as input the name of one theme and returns to the user useful information that can be used to invoke one of the previous INSPIRE export methods. The information returned includes the exact SPARQL query issued as well as the names of the variables that can be filtered along with a short description of their semantics and their domain of values. Through this information, the user can understand which filtering conditions suit his/her needs and then use them either to invoke the *inspire_export* along with the theme name or the *inspire_query_export* method via joining the theme's SPARQL query with the desired filtering conditions and using the result as input to this method.
- *addXSLMappings:* this method can be used to indirectly import the data of a provider into the underlying triple store through exploiting as input an XSLT specification which indicates the way the provider's XML-based data can be transformed into RDF ones.

The last method completes the import capabilities of the LMS which relieve the user from the peculiarities of the publishing process by also enabling him/her to provide the less possible input and can cater for different LD publishing cases: (a) the provider directly imports the LD him/herself and has the direct control of what is imported. If his/her data are not in LD form, then obviously a transformation is needed. This publishing way is appropriate when the provider's original data are in LD form or when he/she desires to transform a portion of his/her original data and have it published in the system (e.g., for privacy reasons does not desire to publish all of his/her data); (b) the provider has relational data and desires to import them into the system. An R2RML specification is then defined and fed to the system which initiates the unidirectional relational-to-LD mapping process that also caters for keeping the two different forms of data synchronized. This automated publishing way is appropriate when the provider's data are in relational form and the provider has the capability to define an R2RML specification. The data provider can control which data are transformed and imported via the R2RML specification; (c) the provider has XML-based data and needs to transform and store them in the system. This publishing way is similar to the previous one with the following exceptions: not relational but XML data are concerned, the XML data need to be provided inline in the respective method request and the synchronization is not fully automated as new data need to indirectly imported into the system by calling again the *addXSLMappings* method.

5   Linked Data Management Architecture

5.1   Previous Architecture Drawbacks and Current Solutions

While the previous architecture is able to address well the need of storing a huge amount of data as well as of performing load balancing in order to guarantee a certain level of LD query/export performance, it suffers from the following drawbacks: (a) it is quite costly as it includes many load balancing components and even more image instances, (b) the query performance was not adequate in the case of queries not targeting a particular RDF graph, as query results from all scaling layers had to be collected and joined before being returned to the user and (c) updating was performed across all instances of a particular scaling layer, thus creating increased traffic in the system as well as increasing the update execution time (which could also deteriorate query performance in cases or domains where the update frequency is higher).

To resolve the above drawbacks, it was decided to rely on a more simplified architecture which is less costly and draws additional resources only when really needed. On the other hand, such an architecture provides the necessary sophistication to adequately handle the challenges of distributed operations. This decision also relied on the current and forthcoming patterns of system usage where it is expected that the majority of user requests will require querying and exporting functionality and not updating one. In fact, in all of the applications currently supported by the system, the updating was performed sparsely and only in some cases a little bit more frequent in terms of a few times per day (e.g., consider that a set of earthquakes occurring at the same day in a certain country cannot lead to a frequent and enormous updating of the data stored in the system). By also considering that through testing it was observed that the performance of Virtuoso was stable even for an increasing and huge amount of LD stored, it was then decided that there was no need for partitioning the data into different RDF Stores scattered in different instances.

However, before sketching and then realizing the new architecture, it had to be decided how to deal with the issue of updating as this was creating traffic to the system if all Virtuoso servers involved in the instances had to be updated. Furthermore, the problem of updating new instances to the most up-to-date RDF content had to be resolved. To this end, it was decided: (a) to directly update a Virtuoso server only in one instance, from now on called the *master instance*, via LMS and propagate the changes only to the current instances running, from now on called *slave instances*, in the load balancing component (which are of course less than those used in the previous architecture) and (b) lazy update the image used to create new slave instances, from now on called *slave image*, in a timely fashion (e.g., every half an hour) and only when updates have previously occurred after the previous image updating. While the first decision does not totally remedy the first problem, we followed it by having in mind the fact that the current (master and slave) instances should be up-to-date with respect to the RDF content while new slave instances can be allowed to be a little bit out of date as this does not jeopardize the proper functioning of the applications supported by the system. Such lazy updating was rather a necessity by considering the fact that image updating can take minutes and is costly so it cannot be performed each time a single update is performed in the system.

The above decisions had to be properly backed up by the respective technologies exploited. On one hand, the free and latest version of Virtuoso does not allow the updating of many Virtuoso servers that might form a certain cluster in an automated way. Such an updating is a proprietary feature of all Virtuoso versions. To this end, we proceeded in developing our own mechanism for updating the current running Virtuoso servers by exploiting the underlying SQL functionality of Virtuoso. In the first place, we created triggers on the master instance that were used when the main RDF table of the respective Virtuoso server was updated (i.e., the one named RDF_QUAD) to update the Virtuoso servers in the (running) slave instances. However, this ended up becoming quite slow as the update was finished only when all Virtuoso servers were updated. To solve this, we decided to follow a log-based approach where the triggers write into a specific file what is updated (in the form of actual SQL statements) and then a Java program consumes the entries of this log file and is responsible for updating the remaining Virtuoso servers. This component, which is named as *Updater*, is also responsible for updating the slave image only every half an hour and only when an update has occurred after the last slave image updating. It exploits the Amazon Web Services SDK for java (http://aws.amazon.com/documentation/sdk-for-java/) to find out the IPs of the remaining Virtuoso instances as well as perform the slave image updating. Through this solution, the LD updating ends when the Virtuoso instance receiving the update request finishes processing it; the Virtuoso servers of the slave instances are updated subsequently via the Updater. As such, there is no actual delay in performing LD updating and we allow for a small inconsistency until LD updating is propagated to the remaining Virtuoso servers which, as already stated, is acceptable.

On the other hand, the (basic) load balancer (LB) offered by the currently exploited cloud (Amazon EC2) does not offer the capability to route an update request to just one instance. On the contrary, each request is propagated in a round-robin manner to only one instance belonging to the load balanced group. Moreover, through experiments, we have also noticed that co-locating LMS with Virtuoso created memory issues in cases of demanding queries and increased query load as the container in which LMS was deployed required at least 2 GB of main memory. To solve this problem, it was decided to use LMS as a first entrance of user requests which will process them and then decide to connect: (a) either to the Virtuoso residing at the master instance in case of update requests or (b) to the Amazon Load Balancer which will redirect the connection request to the next instance in the load balancing group in case of query or export requests. This solution has the advantage that LMS can base its decision upon the respective LMS method called and thus it is easy to implement the connection policy to the appropriate Virtuoso instance. To not consume many resources which are not actively exploited (i.e., in the case of infrequent updates to the master instance), it was decided to include the master instance in the load balancing group of Amazon LB which of course also includes one or more slave instances that are inserted or removed from it in terms of particular scale-in and scale-out policies/rules. As such, query/export requests are also answered by the master instance. The LB group was set to have at least one instance and to remove the newest instances developed when they are no more needed so that the master instance is always present even when one instance has been left in the group.

Based on the above analysis, the following sub-section provides an insight on the new architecture proposed and its main advantages.

5.2   Architecture

Figure 2 shows the new architecture of our LD Management System. As it can be seen, the topmost component is LMS which is regarded as a first level of user-request processing and which issues connection requests to either the master instance or to Amazon LB depending on the type of method requested. Amazon LB is regarded as the second level of user-request processing and routes each incoming connection to that Virtuoso engine running in the appropriate instance from its group. Then the respective instance selected constitutes the final processing level for user requests where low level RDF management commands are executed in the underlying Virtuoso server. In case of updates, only the master instance is selected and after the update of respective Virtuoso server, the triggers produce the respective entries in the log file which are consumed by the *Updater* in order to update the Virtuoso servers of the slave instances. The *Updater* also updates the slave image every half an hour only when updates have occurred in the meantime between the latest image update.

To further enhance the availability of the system, each instance (slave or master) includes a small script which checks the availability of the respective component implementations included in it: (a) the Virtuoso server and (b) *Updater* in case of a master instance, and reboots them if needed. In addition, the master instance is backed up via LMS by a back-up instance which temporarily takes

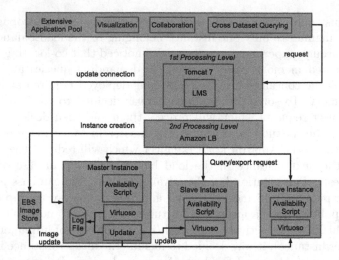

Fig. 2. The new architecture of the LD management system

over until the master instance is up again. As the master instance is a vital component of the system, there is also a script in the instance hosting LMS which is informed when the master instance is down and attempts to reboot it.

As it can be easily understood, the difference between a master and a slave instance is that a master instance has triggers associated to the *RDF_QUAD* table of Virtuoso server and also includes the *Updater* component.

The image updating relies on the EBS-back up mechanism of Amazon which enables to create snapshots of image volumes and then the respective AMIs out of them which can then be used to create new instances in a rapid manner. This also ensures that: (a) system data become reliable as they are stored across many places in the Amazon Cloud and (b) as snapshots are incremental, the system cost is increased only in terms of what is updated. When back-up takes place, the master instance is shut down to ensure that image creation does not lead to any file integrity issues. In this case, query and export requests are served by the slave instances in the Amazon LB group while update requests are served by the backup master instance. When the master instance is up again, it is updated by the backup instance based on the RDF updating mechanism mentioned above.

The advantages of the proposed architecture are the following: (a) it is not very costly: LMS can be hosted in a small-sized instance and new slave instances are created only when the load is assessed to be heavy for the current instances running while one or more created instances are deleted when the load is not so heavy any more but after a particular period passed by such that we avoid any circular scale-in and scale-out effect which can become quite costly, (b) updating is eventually propagated to all instances running and to those instances that will be created, (c) load balancing can guarantee a satisfactory performance level for query/export requests which represent the majority of the user requests incurred, and (d) the system reliability level has been increased as the availability of most components is checked and controlled.

The obvious disadvantage of this architecture is the one concerning the handling of updates. LD updates lead to applications that might not be well informed for a particular amount of time. This does not constitute a major limitation for the current applications supported but certainly limits the application of the system in terms of reaching out real-time (emergency) applications. Another limitation is that LMS is the only component in the system that constitutes a single point of failure as when it fails, user requests cannot be processed any more. However, the load on this component is minimal and the processing effort is also quite minimal as it is actually moved to the respective Virtuoso instance. In addition, another script runs in the instance hosting LMS which can take care of rebooting it when it goes down. This means that it is not very probable that the component can really reach its limits such that it can fail and when it fails, it can be rebooted rapidly. Obviously, a fatal failure cannot always be neglected so one small extension to the current system architecture would be to add an Amazon LB on top of LMS, fixed to have just one instance, such that when it permanently goes down a new instance hosting it can be created. Amazon LB is not a single point of failure as it is replicated so in this sense there would not be any single point of failure in the system any more. However, this will add some small latency in handling user requests as well as an additional operating cost to the system.

The advantages of the proposed architecture can have an effect only when the system is properly configured. This means that the image updating and scaling policies should be specified in such way that the system functions as desired without raising any significant issue, such as very frequent image updating that leads to system performance deterioration or circular scaling actions that raise the system cost in terms of the resources used. The next section identifies the experiments that have been performed to determine the correct content of these policies as well as for evaluating the query/export performance of the proposed system.

6   Evaluation and Implementation

6.1   Experiment Set-Up

Two main experiments were performed each having the goal to measure the average query performance and cpu load in the course of time when a particular number of concurrent users is issuing a specific number of queries for a standalone and a load-balancing based configuration. In the first experiment, 100 concurrent users were created and each was able to issue 50 requests, while in the second experiment, the respective numbers were 50 and 50, respectively, for the concurrent user and request numbers. In the standalone configuration, depending on whether we desire to evaluate the old or the new LMS system, the LMS either connects only to the Virtuoso engine of the master instance or to the respective scaling layers which are related to the content of the queries to be performed, while in the load-balancing configuration (LB for short), which reflects our proposed system architecture, LMS connects to the Amazon LB which redirects the connection to the next instance in the LB group.

As it can be understood, we are attempting to evaluate not only the new LMS system but also the old one. In order to be fair in the comparison of the two LMS systems, we regard that there are two scaling layers in the old system that are obviously related to the content of cross-layer queries. This is the minimum and meaningful configuration of the LMS system which can be used for the comparison as in the minimalistic case where just one scaling layer is involved, then the performance of the old LMS system will be either better (if many nodes are involved) or equivalent (if just one node is involved in the layer) to the one of the new LMS system configured in standalone mode.

We should also note that we have decided that it is not meaningful to compare the performance of the two versions of the system in the distributed case. This decision relied on the results of the standalone configuration where it was apparent that the old system has a worse performance with respect to the new one for cross-queries (which span different scaling layers). It is actually expected that in the distributed case, again the new system will have an even better performance than the old one.

Each experiment focused on a particular type of query (both are shown in the paper's appendix):

- *geospatial query:* the first query focuses on providing particular information (e.g., latitude, longitude, depth, magnitude and date) for all earthquakes that have occurred in the region of the Crete island (main land and surrounding sea with a particular radius). Apart from checking a huge amount of RDF data (around 2 million triples), this query imposes a geospatial filter on the area where the earthquake to be returned has occurred. Thus, apart from requiring the existence of normal RDF indices, it also requires exploiting a geospatial index. To this end, this query is quite demanding in processing effort and when a particular query load is imposed on just one Virtuoso engine, it is expected that the respective hosting VM will reach a high CPU load leading to a continuous deterioration of query response time.

- *complex normal query:* the second query is more complex than the first as it includes optional clauses while it also involves processing a bigger amount of data with respect to the first query. In fact, the respective data set over which the query is posed comprises of 253 millions triples which as an amount is of course more than hundred times greater than the previous query one. This query involves obtaining all lithostratigraphy analysis samples related to various areas in Europe along with additional information, such as the drilling depth, the elevation, the reliability of the sample as well as the minimum and maximum depth involved in the respective sampling activity. While not requiring a geospatial index, due to the huge amount of data that has to be processed and the use of the optional clause, this query is expected to be more demanding that the first both in terms of main memory and CPU load.

We should note here that these two queries represent the minimum and maximum complexity of queries that are posed in the LSM system. In this way, these queries are expected to map to the exact load range that is imposed to the system. Thus, all other queries have a complexity between the complexity range of these two queries and respective load that is expected to be between the load imposed by these two queries.

To conduct the experiments, Apache JMeter was used which enabled us not only to automate the issuing of the queries but also to store information about all the requests issued by all clients and especially the requests' response time. The standalone experiments involved measuring the CPU every 10 s and the respective measurement values were collected via the assistance of the 'sar' tool. All this information was then processed to produce the respective graphs.

The VM hosting Virtuoso was a m1-large Amazon VM with the following characteristics: 2 vCPUs, 7.5 GB of main memory and a 200 GB of storage, while a m3-medium Amazon VM (1 vCPU, 3,75 GB main memory and 20GB storage) was used to host Tomcat (version 7) on which the LMS was deployed. As the requirements on the VM hosting LMS were not so strict, we have decided to have a differentiation and assign a VM with less capabilities on LMS. As it has already been observed, the Tomcat container on which LMS was deployed did not need more than 3 GB of main memory at all cases. On the other hand, Virtuoso did require a VM with very good characteristics due to the load developed when processing RDF management requests. An even stronger VM could be exploited but the cost budget is quite limited and restricted based on the amount of funding for the sort of activities performed which is attributed to the InGeoCloudS project. The Amazon LB was configured to have a minimum and desired capacity of 1 instance with the maximum capacity reaching 3 instances again due to reasons of cost.

6.2   Analysis

Standalone Experiment Results. We start the presentation and analysis of the results by concentrating on the standalone experiment configurations in order to also highlight why particular scalability policies were finally followed.

Figures 3(a), (b) show the results of the first experiment for the standalone configuration. Figure 3(a) shows the progress in average query time for every 50 requests that get served by the system for the first query. Figure 3(b) shows the progress in average CPU time per 10 s (which was the measurement frequency for 'sar').

We should highlight here that each line in all graphs presented is named in a particular way to denote the configuration and the version of the system evaluated. In this way, "standalone_new" means new system with standalone configuration, "standalone_old" means old system with standalone configuration and "lb_new" means new system with LB configuration.

As it can be seen, Virtuoso's behaviour with respect to query time seems to be polynomial with a small increase pace for the new LMS system while for the old LMS system the behaviour is almost opposite with high query times in the

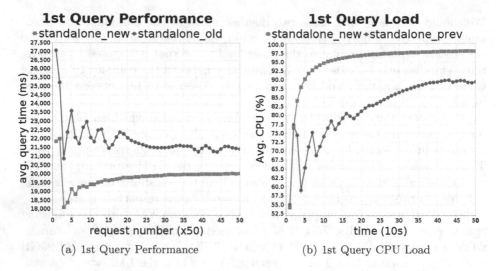

(a) 1st Query Performance   (b) 1st Query CPU Load

Fig. 3. 1st Experiment results for the system's standalone configuration

beginning which drop and become stabilized at some time point. In this way, it is apparent that the new LMS system is better than the old one and more cost effective as it uses just one instance instead of two. The query time decrease in the old system is due to the distribution of the respective data in two instances, thus requiring less processing per instance to be performed for each user query request. We should also indicate that the initial high query time observed in both system versions is due to a main memory effect where Virtuoso realizes that its currently allocated main memory is not sufficient and attempts to gain more resources, thus further delaying the servicing of the current requests. After the main memory allocated reaches a particular value, then the query addressing gets improved which subsequently leads to a good reduction in query time.

On the other hand, the CPU load follows a clear course on all system versions where it sharply increases in the beginning and then increases in a very small pace until a specific point (97.5 % and 90 % for the new and old LMS system, respectively). This means that throughout the time where all requests are made, the VMs/instances reach quite high numbers of usage. So, if the load was shared between two or more VMs, then obviously the query service time would decrease more sharply. Indeed, by lowering the number of concurrent users from 100 to 50, then the CPU load gets decreased and the respective query time becomes quite small. Thus, the results of the first query indicate that there is an opportunity here for obtaining more resources in order to better serve the incoming requests to the system.

We need to note here that the CPU load on the old system version is lower than that imposed on the new one due to the rationale provided above for query response time: less (related) data are stored in each VM which leads to a smaller amount of processing.

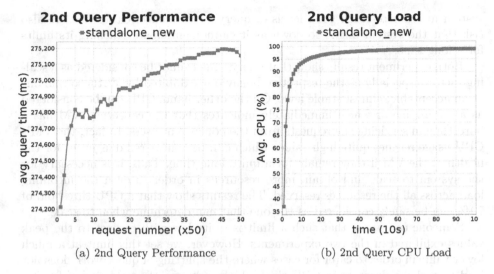

(a) 2nd Query Performance   (b) 2nd Query CPU Load

Fig. 4. 2nd Experiment results for the system's standalone configuration

Similarly to the above case, Figs. 4(a), (b) show the results of the second experiment for the standalone configuration, where Fig. 4(a) shows the progress in average query time for every 50 requests for the second query, while Fig. 4(b) shows the progress in average CPU time per 10 s for the same query. It should be noted here that based on the results of the 1st experiment, it was decided that it is pointless in further checking the performance of the old system as it is expected that this performance will be even worse for a query with a higher complexity.

The depicted results indicate that the second query is indeed more complex and leads to even worse results than the first, something that is expected based on the nature of the second query and its characteristics. Concerning the average query time, the behaviour of Virtuoso is similar (while the query time increase pace is even smaller) to the first experiment case but the query times anticipated are much worse ranging between 274 and 275 s (i.e., they are 9 times greater) which is quite unacceptable for users especially in real world environments. We should highlight at this point that although Virtuoso has a hard time in servicing the requests, its behaviour is almost stable, which means that the system exhibits a good reliability level.

As far as the CPU is concerned, the behaviour is again similar with respect to the first experiment where we see a sharp increase in the beginning and then an increase with a very small pace until a specific point (around 99 %). However, the peak point is higher than that of the first query. This means that the VM has a harder time than in the case of the first experiment and in both cases it reaches its limits in terms of CPU usage. These two facts, i.e., sharper increase and higher CPU peak values, also highlight the complexity difference between the queries considered. Based on these results, there is a great need of scaling the system in order to reach good levels of query performance. Otherwise, we also risk that the system might go down as it cannot anticipate reaching its limits for a long time.

Both experiment results show that query time cannot be considered as a scaling factor, especially as the respective behaviour exhibited by Virtuoso remains at an acceptable, almost stable level. On the other hand, CPU can be considered as a scaling factor which immediately indicates that the concerned VM has a hard time in servicing the requests from the concurrent users. In fact, the VM's CPU usage reaches quite high values which can be considered dangerous for the health of the VM if they remain for a quite long time. Thus, it is necessary for the system to scale and obtain more resources in order to even the incoming load across all the resources reserved. The results show that a CPU threshold of 70 % can be safely considered as the one that can determine when to scale.

Someone can argue that such a limit is quite low with respect to the peak values exhibited in the two experiments. However, we set this limit at a much lower value in order to cater for cases where the splitting of query work does not lead to a sharp decrease in CPU time which indicates the necessity of further increasing the resources to be utilized. This has been checked through other experiments with the rest of the queries which show that this threshold really discriminates when Virtuoso has a hard time in servicing the user requests. These other experiments, by assessing the performance of queries whose complexity lies in between those of the two queries considered, have shown that indeed a similar behaviour is observed which lies in between the one exhibited by the addressing of the two queries considered. To this end, we have considered not showing these experiment results in this article. Based on the above analysis, the CPU threshold determination method can be considered as rather complete by taking an exhaustive approach to guarantee that the choice made has been correct.

The main question would then be for how long to wait until to scale by considering that the average CPU value constantly remains above the threshold obtained. The experiments show that the checking period should be as minimum as possible in order to offload the current number of VMs for the current load that is anticipated by them. To this end, it was decided that the checking period should be 2 min so that we are confident that a temporal spike in load is not experienced but a high load that is more or less constant. This period length is appropriate to cater for both experiment cases where the higher need of more instant reactiveness for the first experiment case is also covered (see smaller response times for this case with respect to the second). By also considering that it takes time (some minutes) to create a new instance, the considered period length seems appropriate. In case of a higher value we run into the danger of reserving more resources when it is already too late with respect to the load incurred for the current instance. Again, this choice is guaranteed through following an exhaustive approach both at real time as well as in extreme synthetic cases for all types of queries issued by the respective applications. Thus, it seems as the most appropriate solution for the current situation as well as for forthcoming ones, once our system is exposed to an additional number of end-user applications.

Apart from scaling-out when more resources are needed, the system should scale-in when there is no need to spend too much resources for the current load. As the charging of VMs is hour-based, it is better to scale in nearly when one hour of usage has been spent for a new resource/instance. This can be translated to a scale-in policy which attempts to scale-in the system when the lower threshold of 30 % on average CPU is passed for two consecutive periods of 20 min. In this way, by also assuming that a new VM is required for at most 20 min, we speculate that it will be no longer needed for the next period of 40 min as long as the average CPU is below 30 %. Via the use of two consecutive periods we also cater for the case that we might have again increased load inside the one hour-space of new VM usage, so we should retain it in this case as long as it is needed.

LB Experiment Results. The experiments conducted where repeated with the LB configuration of the system based on the previously mentioned characteristics of the LB as well as the scale-in and -out conditions and checking periods proposed. The number of concurrent users and of requests per user did not change. We have considered meaningful to also present the results for the CPU in order to highlight the way the CPU load drops once additional resources are reserved.

Concerning the first experiment, the results, which are shown in Figs. 5(a) and (b), indicate that after 50 rounds (i.e., 2500 requests), the system scales-out and its performance gets improved (almost 3 s gain which can be considered even higher if we examine the respective raw query times). However, by also inspecting the CPU load, it rather stays around high values (around 70 %) which necessitates performing another scale out action. Indeed, the second scale-out action (around 70th round) further improves the performance (less than 2.5 s from the beginning) while the CPU load continuously drops until 40 %. It could be argued that the performance is not significantly improved through the reservation of additional resources. However, we should keep in mind that we present the current average value whose calculation includes the values obtained from the very beginning of the experiment. This means that the raw query times experienced by the users will be even better. Moreover, if we had left the experiment to continue for further rounds, then the performance improvement would have been even better, especially if we consider the significant drop in CPU (after 1250 s) and the way the query time drops in the second scale-out.

The results for the 2nd experiment, which are shown in Fig. 6 indicate that two scale-out actions have been performed at the 4th and 9th round. This highlights that the load created by 50 concurrent users with respect to the second query cannot be tolerated alone by 2 VMs and a third one is also needed. Each scale-out action has lead to a significant reduction of query time from 200 s to 160 s and further down to 100 s. By comparing the maximum and minimum query time anticipated, we can clearly see that the final query time is one third of the initial one. We should also note that while it might be seen that in the 1st experiment, the scale-out is performed with a delay, this is not the actual case as the query times in the involved experiments are of a different scale.

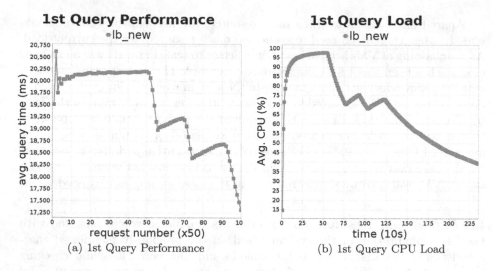

(a) 1st Query Performance   (b) 1st Query CPU Load

Fig. 5. 1st Experiment results for the system's LB configuration

Concerning the CPU load, we certainly see some improvement, as CPU load initially drops to 95 % and then to almost 92 %. However, this means that still the VMs exploited reach high CPU load values and there is a risk for VMs health deterioration. Unfortunately, the budget restrictions do not allow us to scale out for reserving more resources. Furthermore, this is a sign that the query issued is quite complex and even if the load on a particular VM is reduced, the CPU processing load is not reduced in a high degree as Virtuoso seems to attempt to exploit as much resources as possible in order to address the reduced load incurred. In addition, the current number of users that exploit the respective application does not mandate for actually exploiting such additional resources.

Actually, with this query, we needed to indicate the worst possible scenario where a big number of concurrent users issue the most complex query to the LMS system and to highlight the cost-effectiveness as well as the scalability of the system in terms of query processing time. The results obtained indicate that our goals have been achieved for both queries and thus for any other query having a complexity in between the complexity exhibited by these two queries.

To summarize, we can clearly see that in both experiments, the scale-out activities occur as soon as possible. In addition, the high limit on instance number to be reserved is indeed the most appropriate as the less complex query obtains both a great reduction in CPU load, which does not require reserving additional resources, and a query time speed-up while for the second query there is a significant speed-up but due to its high complexity, the CPU load is not highly decreased, which mandates for spoiling cost-effectiveness if additional resources are reserved. The low limit has been posed based on the current application usage which does not go over more than ten concurrent users. If this changes in the near future, then we will certainly attempt to raise this limit to better handle the new and increased query traffic.

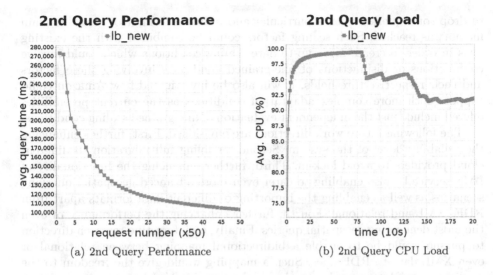

(a) 2nd Query Performance   (b) 2nd Query CPU Load

Fig. 6. 2nd Experiment results for the proposed system's LB configuration

7 Conclusions and Future Work

This article has presented a cloud-based geospatial LD Management System which is scalable, cost-effective and sustains good levels of (geospatial) query performance. Apart from its performance and cost-effective capabilities, the system offers a particular Service called Linked Data Management Service (LMS) which exposes added-value functionality in terms of different ways of publishing, exporting and querying geospatial LD. LMS relieves the application developer from the peculiarities of the underlying triple store and as it is REST-based enables the developer to use any programming language of his/her choice. Moreover, LMS caters for different LD publishing scenarios which vary in terms of provider data format and publishing control and which require from the provider the provisioning of the least possible amount of information. LMS also supports standards, such as GeoSPARQL, SPARQL and INSPIRE. In fact, the support of INSPIRE can be considered as a fundamental feature of LMS as it enables the potential data providers exploiting it to follow the strict forthcoming INSPIRE directive which dictates an INSPIRE-complianet form of data published and exported by them. LMS finally supports simple and more advanced forms of geospatial queries which require the use of sophisticated geospatial operators and functions.

The evaluation conducted on the proposed system reveals its benefits in terms of increased performance and scalability as well as justified the content of the particular scalability policies followed. What remains to be performed is a more thorough evaluation which includes highly demanding scenarios involving both LD updating and querying. In addition, we will investigate additional scaling factors which could be exploited towards performing the scaling activities of our system. The VM's main memory seems a very good candidate as Virtuoso tends to drop some queries when a particular and quite small limit of available main memory is reached. Such scaling factors could be combined with the existing ones in order to create more up-to-date scaling conditions which could involve conjunctions or disjunctions of fine-grained conditions involving these factors and their respective thresholds. It will also be investigated how Amazon could support such more complex adaptation conditions as the current possibilities offered include just the independent evaluation of fine-grained scaling conditions.

The following future work directions are envisioned. First, further enhancing the reliability level of the system. Second, enabling full migration to different cloud providers to avoid lock-in. Third, further enhancing the functionality of LMS service by also enabling to cater even more advanced geospatial querying scenarios as well as enabling the importing of different data formats apart from RDF, XML and relational. Fourth, further enhancing the performance of even the most demanding geospatial queries. Finally, an interesting research direction to pursue would be to enable a bidirectional mapping between relational or even XML data to RDF ones. Such a mapping would give the freedom to the application or data provider to choose the way his/her data can be updated. For instance, the provider might already have existing programs which update a particular portion of his/her data in their original form but could also develop new programs which, after moving towards LD, enable the updating of a different data portion. As such, different updates on different data formats will be possible with the capability to synchronize between them without also having to make any modifications to existing data update programs.

Appendix A - Experiment SPARQL Queries

1st query

```
select ?earthquake ?id ?date ?asGML ?asWKT ?latitude ?longitude
?locstring ?doc ?docName ?depth ?magnitude where {
?earthquake a sci:S23_Earthquake;
            crm:P7_took_place_at ?place;
            crm:P1_is_identified_by ?id;
    crm:P4_has_time-span ?date;
    sci:O17_has_dimension ?dd;
            crm:P70_is_documented_in ?doc.
?doc crm:P1_is_identified_by ?docName.
?place geo:hasGeometry ?point;
    crm:P87_is_identified_by ?d;
crm:P87_is_identified_by ?long;
crm:P87_is_identified_by ?lat;
        crm:P3_has_note ?locstring.
?d sci:O20_has_value ?depth.
?point geo:asGML ?asGML;
       geo:asWKT ?asWKT.
filter(regex(?d,"/Depth/")).
filter(regex(?long,"/Longitude/")).
filter(regex(?lat,"/Latitude/")).
?dd crm:P90_has_value ?magnitude.
```

```
?lat sci:020_has_value ?latitude.
?long sci:020_has_value ?longitude.

filter (bif:st_within(bif:st_geomfromtext(?asWKT),
bif:st_geomfromtext('POLYGON((33 24, 33 26, 35 26, 35 24, 33 24))'))).
}
```

2nd query

```
select ?bhole ?bcode ?bname ?depth ?asGML ?elev ?top ?topVal ?bottom ?bottomVal
?layer ?LITHOSTRA1 ?RELIABILITY where {
?bhole a sci:S16_Borehole;
    crm:P1_is_identified_by ?bcode;
    crm:P1_is_identified_by ?bname;
    sci:07_consists_of ?bcollar;
    crm:P43_has_dimension ?d;
    sci:09_contains_or_confines ?place.
OPTIONAL {
?place sci:012_upper_vertical_limit ?top;
    sci:013_lower_vertical_limit ?bottom.
?top sci:020_has_value ?topVal.
?bottom sci:020_has_value ?bottomVal.
}
?d crm:P2_has_type "DEPTH";
    crm:P90_has_value ?depth.
?bcollar geo:hasGeometry ?point;
        crm:P87_is_identified_by ?el.
filter(regex(?el,"Elevation")).
?el sci:020_has_value ?elev.
?point geo:asGML ?asGML.
filter(regex(?asGML,"EPSG:4326")).
?bname a crm:E41_Appelation.
?bcode a crm:E42_Identifier.
filter(regex(?bcode, "/ID/")).

?layer crm:P53_has_former_or_current_location ?place;
        a crm:E26_Physical_Feature;
        sci:019_has_preferred_type ?l1;
        crm:P2_has_type ?rel.
filter(regex(?rel, "Reliability/")).
?rel crm:P3_has_note ?RELIABILITY.
?l2 crm:P3_has_note ?LITHOSTRA1.

}
```

References

1. Battle, R., Kolas, D.: Enabling the geospatial semantic web with parliament and geosparql. Semantic Web **3**(4), 355–370 (2012)
2. Bugiotti, F., Goasdoué, F., Kaoudi, Z., Manolescu, I.: RDF data management in the amazon cloud. In: Proceedings of 2012 Joined EDBT/ICDT Workshops, pp. 61–72. ACM, Berlin (2012)

3. Fielding, R.T., Taylor, R.N.: Principled design of the modern web architecture. ACM Trans. Internet Technol. **2**(2), 115–150 (2002). http://doi.acm.org/10.1145/514183.514185

4. Franke, C., Morin, S., Chebotko, A., Abraham, J., Brazier, P.: Distributed semantic web data management in hbase and mysql cluster. In: Proceedings of the 2011 IEEE 4th International Conference on Cloud Computing, pp. 105–112. CLOUD 2011. IEEE Computer Society, Washington, DC (2011), http://dx.doi.org/10.1109/CLOUD.2011.19

5. Guéret, C., Groth, P., Oren, E., Schlobach, S.: eRDF: A Scalable architecture for querying the Web of Data. http://bit.ly/eRDF_tr

6. Guéret, C., Kotoulas, S., Groth, P.: TripleCloud: An infrastructure for exploratory querying over Web-Scale RDF Data. In: Proceedings of the 2011 IEEE/WIC/ACM International Conferences on Web Intelligence and Intelligent Agent Technology (WI-IAT 2011), pp. 245–248. IEEE Computer Society, Washington, DC (2011)

7. Harth, A., Umbrich, J., Hogan, A., Decker, S.: YARS2: a federated repository for querying graph structured data from the web. In: Aberer, K., et al. (eds.) ASWC 2007 and ISWC 2007. LNCS, vol. 4825, pp. 211–224. Springer, Heidelberg (2007)

8. Hoffart, J., Suchanek, F.M., Berberich, K., Weikum, G.: Yago2: a spatially and temporally enhanced knowledge base from wikipedia. Artif. Intell. **194**, 28–61 (2013). http://dx.doi.org/10.1016/j.artint.2012.06.001

9. Husain, M.F., Khan, L., Kantarcioglu, M., Thuraisingham, B.M.: Data intensive query processing for large rdf graphs using cloud computing tools. In: IEEE CLOUD, pp. 1–10. IEEE (2010). http://dblp.uni-trier.de/db/conf/IEEEcloud/IEEEcloud2010.html#HusainKKT10

10. Kritikos, K., Roussakis, Y., Kotzinos, D.: Linked open GeoData management in the cloud. In: 2nd International Workshop on Open Data (WOD 2013), Paris, France (2013)

11. Kyzirakos, K., Karpathiotakis, M., Koubarakis, M.: Strabon: a semantic geospatial DBMS. In: Cudré-Mauroux, P., et al. (eds.) ISWC 2012, Part I. LNCS, vol. 7649, pp. 295–311. Springer, Heidelberg (2012)

12. Ladwig, G., Harth, A.: CumulusRDF: linked data management on nested key-value stores. In: Proceedings of the 7th International Workshop on Scalable Semantic Web Knowledge Base Systems (SSWS 2011) (2011)

13. Le-Phuoc, D., Parreira, J.X., Hausenblas, M., Han, Y., Hauswirth, M.: Live linked open sensor database. In: Proceedings of the 6th International Conference on Semantic Systems, I-SEMANTICS 2010, pp. 46:1–46:4. ACM, New York (2010). http://doi.acm.org/10.1145/1839707.1839763

14. Mika, P., Tummarello, G.: Web semantics in the clouds. IEEE Intell. Syst. **23**(5), 82–87 (2008). http://dx.doi.org/10.1109/MIS.2008.94

15. Neumann, T., Weikum, G.: The rdf-3x engine for scalable management of rdf data. VLDB J. **19**(1), 91–113 (2010)

16. Newman, A., Li, Y.F., Hunter, J.: Scalable semantics - the silver lining of cloud computing. In: Proceedings of the 2008 Fourth IEEE International Conference on eScience, ESCIENCE 2008, pp. 111–118, IEEE Computer Society, Washington, DC (2008). http://dx.doi.org/10.1109/eScience.2008.23

17. Papailiou, N., Konstantinou, I., Tsoumakos, D., Koziris, N.: H2rdf: Adaptive query processing on rdf data in the cloud. In: Proceedings of the 21st International Conference Companion on World Wide Web, WWW 2012 Companion, pp. 397–400. ACM, New York (2012). http://doi.acm.org/10.1145/2187980.2188058

18. Ravindra, P., Deshpande, V.V., Anyanwu, K.: Towards scalable rdf graph analytics on mapreduce. In: Proceedings of the 2010 Workshop on Massive Data Analytics on the Cloud, MDAC 2010, pp. 5:1–5:6. ACM, New York (2010). http://doi.acm.org/10.1145/1779599.1779604

19. Richardson, L., Ruby, S.: RESTful Web Services. O'Reilly Media, USA (2007)

20. Stein, R., Zacharias, V.: RDF on cloud number nine. In: 4th Workshop on New Forms of Reasoning for the Semantic Web: Scalable and Dynamic, pp. 11–23. CEUR (2010)

21. Sun, J., Jin, Q.: Scalable rdf store based on hbase and mapreduce. In: 3rd International Conference on Advanced Computer Theory and Engineering (ICACTE 2010), pp. 633–636. IEEE (2010)

22. Tanimura, Y., Matono, A., Lynden, S., Kojima, I.: Extensions to the pig data processing platform for scalable rdf data processing using hadoop. In: IEEE 30th International Conference on Data Engineering Workshops (ICDEW 2010), pp. 251–256. IEEE Computer Society, Los Alamitos (2010)

A Scalable Expressive Ensemble Learning Using Random Prism: A *MapReduce* Approach

Frederic Stahl[1], David May[2], Hugo Mills[1], Max Bramer[3],
and Mohamed Medhat Gaber[4]($\boxtimes$)

[1] School of Systems Engineering, University of Reading,
Whiteknights, Reading RG6 6AY, UK
f.t.stahl@reading.ac.uk, hugo@carfax.org.uk
[2] Real Time Information Systems Ltd,
1st and 2nd Floors, 8 South Street, Chichester PO19 1EH, UK
david.m@rtis.co.uk
[3] School of Computing, University of Portsmouth,
Buckingham Building, Lion Terrace, Portsmouth PO1 3HE, UK
max.bramer@port.ac.uk
[4] School of Computing Science and Digital Media, Robert Gordon University,
Riverside East Garthdee Road, Aberdeen AB10 7GJ, UK
m.gaber1@rgu.ac.uk

Abstract. The induction of classification rules from previously unseen examples is one of the most important data mining tasks in science as well as commercial applications. In order to reduce the influence of noise in the data, ensemble learners are often applied. However, most ensemble learners are based on decision tree classifiers which are affected by noise. The Random Prism classifier has recently been proposed as an alternative to the popular Random Forests classifier, which is based on decision trees. Random Prism is based on the Prism family of algorithms, which is more robust to noise. However, like most ensemble classification approaches, Random Prism also does not scale well on large training data. This paper presents a thorough discussion of Random Prism and a recently proposed parallel version of it called *Parallel Random Prism*. Parallel Random Prism is based on the MapReduce programming paradigm. The paper provides, for the first time, novel theoretical analysis of the proposed technique and in-depth experimental study that show that Parallel Random Prism scales well on a large number of training examples, a large number of data features and a large number of processors. Expressiveness of decision rules that our technique produces makes it a natural choice for *Big Data* applications where informed decision making increases the user's trust in the system.

1 Introduction

Big Data technologies have opened the door wide for researchers to re-engineer their data science products, allowing for unprecedented scalability. Scalability is key to the success of *cloud computing* hosted applications. An enabler approach providing scalability to a wide range of applications is the *MapReduce*

© Springer-Verlag Berlin Heidelberg 2015
A. Hameurlain et al. (Eds.): TLDKS XX, LNCS 9070, pp. 90–107, 2015.
DOI: 10.1007/978-3-662-46703-9_4

framework [10]. Motivated by the recent developments in this area, we scale up ensemble classification adopting rule-based classifiers, using *MapReduce* framework. Ensemble classification is the training of individual and diverse base classifiers and the integration of their predictive models into a combined classification model. The aim of ensemble classifiers is to increase the predictive accuracy compared with that of a single classifier. One of the best known ensemble learners is Breiman's Random Forests (RF) [7], which is based on Ho's Random Decision Forests (RDF) [14] ensemble classifier and Breiman's **B**ootstrap **agg**regat**ing** (Bagging) approach [6]. Bagging is used in RF to increase the ensemble classifier's stability and accuracy. In unstable classifiers small variations in the training data cause major variations in the classification. The aforementioned ensemble classifiers are based on decision trees. However, alternatives exist, such as Chan and Stolfo's *Meta-Learning* [9] which combines heterogeneous classifiers using a *Meta-Learning* that makes use of different classifier combining strategies such as *voting, arbitration* and *combining*.

Most rule based classifiers are either based on the 'divide and conquer' or the 'separate and conquer' rule induction approaches [24]. 'Divide and conquer' based classifiers produce a decision tree, such as Quinlan's C4.5 decision tree induction algorithm [18]; 'separate and conquer' based classifiers produce a set of IF...THEN classification rules, such as the Prism family of algorithms [4,5,8]. As pointed out in [20], most ensemble classifiers are based on the 'divide and conquer' approach even though Prism classifiers have shown to be less vulnerable to overfitting compared with decision tree based classifiers [4]. This is especially the case when confronted with noise and missing values in the data [4]. A recently developed ensemble classifier named *Random Prism* [20], which is inspired by RF and RDF, makes use of the Prism family of algorithms as base classifiers. An empirical evaluation of the Random Prism classifier shows that it outperforms its standalone base classifier in terms of a better classification accuracy [20]. Further empirical experiments [20] show that Random Prism also has a higher tolerance to noise compared with its base classifier.

However, also pointed out in [20] Random Prism's CPU time consumption is also considerably higher compared with that of a standalone Prism classifier. This is because Random Prism builds for each base classifier a bag of size N of the original training data [22], if N is the number of data instances in the original training data. Thus even modest sized training data impose a considerable computational challenge to ensemble learners using bagging, such as Random Prism. A bag is a collection of data instances in which each data instance may occur more than once. In order to tackle this problem of scalability to larger data a parallel version of the *Random Prism* classifier, called *Parallel Random Prism*, has been developed [22]. Parallel Random Prism is based on data parallelisation and makes use of Google's MapReduce programming paradigm [10]. In particular, Parallel Random Prism uses the Hadoop implementation of MapReduce in order to distribute the induction of each individual base classifier on its own bag to different machines in a computer cluster [1]. Thus the base classifiers are induced concurrently. In this paper we use the expression *parallel* and *distributed* in the context of algorithms interchangeably, both referring to the concurrent execution of base classifiers through distribution of the training data to multiple computer cluster nodes.

This paper provides a detailed and exhaustive description of Random Prism and Parallel Random Prism approaches. Additionally, it also provides, for the first time, a formal theoretical scalability analysis of Random Prism and Parallel Random Prism, which examines the scalability to much larger computer clusters. This contribution provides a theoretical underpinning that can be used for scalability of the *MapReduce* framework. It also presents a thorough experimental study of Parallel Random Prism's scalability. In particular we look into its scalability with respect to the number of training examples and number of features. It is worth noting that we use the terms 'feature' and 'attribute' interchangeably in this paper.

This paper's structure is as follows: Sect. 2 presents the Random Prism ensemble learner. The parallel version of Random Prism is outlined in Sect. 3. Section 4 provides a theoretical scalability analysis of a standalone Prism classifier, the Random Prism ensemble learner and then the Parallel Random Prism approach. This formal scalability analysis is then supported by an empirical evaluation in Sect. 5. Finally, Sect. 6 closes the paper with some concluding remarks.

2   Random Prism

As aforementioned Random Prism is inspired by RDF and RF. Ho's RDF approach induces multiple trees, each induced on a random subset of the feature space [14]. This is done in order to make the individual trees generalise better on the training data, which Ho evaluated empirically. RF similarly to RDF induces the trees on feature subsets. However, differently from RDF, RF uses a new random subset of the feature space for evaluating the possible splits of each node in the decision tree [7]. In addition, RF also uses 'Bagging' [6] in order to further increase the predictive accuracy of the ensemble classifier. This is according to [12] because the composite classifier model reduces the variance of the individual classifiers. However, the authors of [11] suggest that bagging not necessarily always reduces variance, but also equalises the influence of training examples and thus stabilises the classifier. Bagging builds for each base classifier a bootstrap sample D_i of a training dataset D using sampling with replacement [6]. Most commonly D_i is of size N where N is the number of training instances in D.

In this paper, we adopt PrismTCS which is a computationally efficient member of the Prism family, and also maintains a similar predictive accuracy compared with the original Prism classifier [5]. A good computational efficiency is needed as ensemble learners generally do not scale well to large datasets. Due to bagging even modest sized training data present a considerable computational challenge to ensemble learners. In addition, the implemented base classifier makes use of J-pruning as it not only generalises the induced classifier further, but also lowers its runtime [19]. This is because J-pruning will reduce the number of rule terms induced and thus lower the number of iterations of the base classifier [19].

The random feature subset selection of a random size is also implemented inside the base classifier. This takes place for each rule and for each term expansion of that rule. The resulting base classifier has been termed 'R-PrismTCS', where the 'R' stands for the 'Random' components in the base classifier (random feature subset selection for each rule term and bagging).

Algorithm 1 shows the steps of R-PrismTCS with the exception of J-pruning. F denotes the total number of features, D is the original training data and $rule\_set$ is an initially empty set of classification rules. The operation $rule.add$ $Term(A_x)$ adds attribute value pair A_x as a rule term to $rule$ and the operation $rule\_set.add(rule)$ adds $rule$ to $rule\_set$. In step 2 for each A_x the conditional probability $p(class = i|A_x)$ is calculated, which is the probability with which A_x covers the target class i.

Algorithm 1: R-PrismTCS Algorithm

$D' =$ build random sample with replacement from D;
$D'' = D'$;
Step 1: find class i that has the fewest instances in D'';
rule = new empty rule for target class i;

Step 2: generate a feature subset f of size m, where $(F > m > 0)$;
calculate for each A_x in f $p(class = i|A_x)$;

Step 3: select the A_x with the maximum $p(class = i|A_x)$;
$rule.addTerm(A_x)$;
delete all instances in D'' that do not cover rule;

Step 4: repeat 2 to 3 for D'' until D'' only contains instances of target class i;

Step 5: $rule\_set.add(rule)$;
create a new D'' that comprises all instances of D' except those that are covered by all rules induced so far;

Step 6: IF (number of instances $D'' > 1$){ repeat steps 1 to 6 };

Figure 1 shows the conceptual architecture of Random Prism. Each R-Prism TCS base classifier is induced on a training sample of size N from the training data, where N is also the size of the training data. This sample is drawn using random sampling with replacement. This statistically results in samples that contain 63.2 % of the original instances, some of them drawn multiple times. The remaining 36.8 % of the instances that have not been drawn are used as validation data to estimate the individual R-PrismTCS classifier's predictive accuracy ranging from 0 to 1. We call this accuracy the classifier's weight. The individual classifier's weights are then used to perform weighted majority voting on unlabelled data instances. The weights can also be used to filter base classifiers, i.e., retain the classifiers with high predictive accuracy and eliminate those with a poor one according to a user's predefined threshold.

Random Prism's predictive accuracy has been evaluated empirically on several datasets of the UCI repository [3,20]; and it has been found that Random

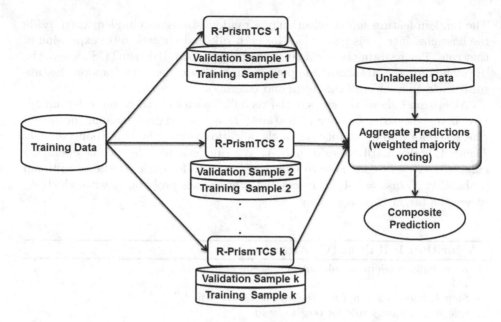

Fig. 1. The architecture of the Random Prism ensemble classifier.

Prism's classification accuracy is superior to that of RrismTCS's. Furthermore results published recently in [20], show that Random Prism's potential unfolds when there is noise in the training as well as in the test data. Here Random Prism clearly outperforms PrismTCS [20].

However, this paper is more concerned with the scalability of Random Prism to large datasets. One would expect that the runtime of Random Prism inducing 100 base classifiers is approximately 100 times longer, compared with PrismTCS, as Random Prism induces base classifiers with a bag of size N for each base classifier, where N is the total number of training instances. Yet, this is not the case according to the results published in [20]. The reason for this is the random component in R-PrismTCS, which only considers a random subset of the total feature space for the induction of each rule term. Thus the workload of each R-PrismTCS classifier for evaluating candidate features for rule term generation is reduced by the number of features not considered for each induced rule term.

3   The Parallel Random Prism Classifier

This section addresses our proposal to scale up Random Prism ensemble learner by introducing a parallel version of the algorithm. This will help to address the increased CPU time requirements, and also the increased memory requirements. The increased memory requirements are due to the fact that there are k data samples of size N required if k is the number of R-PrismTCS classifiers and N the number of total instances in the original training data. If k is 100, then the required memory would be 100 times larger compared with the memory requirements of the standalone PrismTCS classifier. The CPU requirements of Random Prism are high, but not 100 times higher due to the random feature subset selection. The parallelisation of the algorithm allows harvesting of the memory and CPU time of multiple workstations for inducing the Random Prism ensemble classifier.

In *data parallelism* smaller portions of the data are distributed to different computing nodes on which data mining tasks are executed concurrently [23]. Ensemble learning lends itself to data parallelism as it is composed of many different data mining tasks, the induction of base classifiers, which can be executed independently, and thus concurrently. Hence, a data parallel approach has been chosen for Random Prism. However, there are some limiting factors concerning scalability, which will be analysed in Sect. 4.

Section 3.1 highlights the MapReduce paradigm which has been adopted for the parallelisation of Random Prism, and Sect. 3.2 highlights the architecture of Parallel Random Prism.

3.1 Parallelisation Using the MapReduce Paradigm

A programming paradigm for parallel processing introduced by *Google* is *MapReduce* [10]. It provides a simple way of developing 'data' parallel data mining techniques and thus lends itself to the parallel development of ensemble learners [17]. In addition, MapReduce computer cluster implementations, such as the open source *Hadoop* implementation [1] provide fault tolerance and automatic workload balancing. Hadoop's MapReduce implementation is based on the Hadoop Distributed File System (HDFS), which distributes the data over the computer cluster and stores it redundantly in order to speed up the data access and establish fault tolerance.

Figure 2 illustrates a Hadoop computer cluster. MapReduce partitions an application into smaller parts implemented as *Mapper* components. Mappers can be processed by any computing node within a MapReduce cluster. The aggregation of the results produced by the Mappers is implemented in one or more *Reducer* components, which again can be processed by any computing node within a MapReduce cluster.

MapReduce's significance in the area of data mining is evident through its adoption for many data mining tasks and projects in science as well as in businesses. For example, by 2008 Google made use of MapReduce in over 900 projects [10], such as clustering of images for identifying duplicates [16]. In 2009 the authors of [17] used MapReduce in order to induce and assemble numerous ensemble trees in parallel.

Random Prism can be broken down into multiple R-PrismTCS classifiers induced on bagged samples of the training data. Loosely speaking, Random Prism can be parallelised using Hadoop through implementing R-PrismTCS classifiers as Mappers which can be executed concurrently in a MapReduce cluster. More details on the Parallel Random Prism architecture are highlighted next in Sect. 3.2.

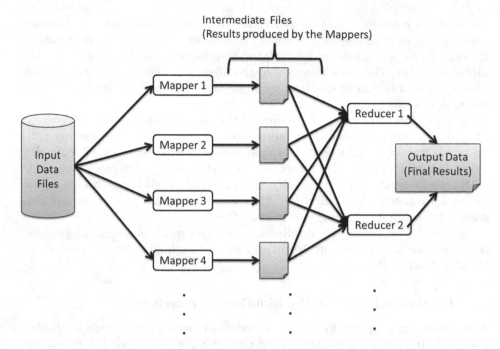

Fig. 2. A typical setup of a Hadoop computing cluster. A physical node in the computer cluster can execute more than one Mapper and Reducer.

3.2   Parallel Random Prism Classifier

Several aspects of the Random Prism algorithm have to be considered for the parallelisation through data parallelism with the MapReduce paradigm. These are the bagging procedure, the induction of R-PrismTCS classifiers and the combination of the individual classifiers into a composite classifier.

Induction of R-PrismTCS Classifiers. As mentioned in Sect. 3.1, Random Prism can be broken down into multiple R-PrismTCS classifiers induced on bagged samples of the training data. These R-PrismTCS classifiers can be induced independently. The only operation that requires the input of all classifiers is the aggregation of their individual sets of classification rules and their weights. Hence, the induction of a R-PrismTCS classifier is implemented directly in a Mapper. Multiple instances of this Mapper can be executed concurrently in a Hadoop cluster. If there are more instances of Mappers than computing nodes, then several Mappers queue to be executed on a node. Thus we keep the computational nodes utilised through pipelining. However, the execution of p Mappers at the same time is still concurrent, where p is the number of available computing nodes in the cluster. Once the last mappers are executed on the cluster there may be a small synchronisation overhead as some mappers may finish earlier than others, thus leaving some of the computational nodes idle, but only in the very last stage of the algorithm's execution.

Bagging Procedure. The building of a boot strap sample from the training data, using bagging, needs to be executed for each R-PrismTCS classifier in order to create as diverse samples as possible (as required by Random Prism). Thus bagging imposes a considerable computational overhead, which needs to be addressed as well. In the proposed Parallel Random Prism classifier implementation, multiple bagging procedures are executed concurrently. This is realised by integrating the bagging procedure in the Mapper that implements R-PrismTCS. Thus the execution of p bagging procedures at the same time is concurrent, if p is the number of available computing nodes in the cluster. The original training is distributed to each computing node in the Hadoop cluster at the beginning of Parallel Random Prism's execution. We have not taken influence on how Hadoop distributes the data. However, Hadoop typically distributes chunks and redundant copies of the training data across the cluster. This partition and redundancy reduces the communication overhead as well as provides more robustness in the case a cluster node fails. This is done in order to keep the communication overhead low. This way the original training data only needs to be communicated once, as the local Mappers on a computing node only need the local copy of the training data in order to build their individual samples.

Building of Composite Classifier. The aggregation of the individual R-PrismTCS classifiers and their associated weights is implemented in a single Reducer. Once the individual R-PrismTCS Mappers finish the induction of their rulesets, they send the rulesets and their associated weights to the Reducer. The Reducer simply holds a collection of classifiers with the weight. If a new unlabelled data instance is presented, then the Reducer applies a weighted majority voting of each classifier, or a subset of the best classifiers (according to their weight), in order to label the new data instance. The data that is transmitted from the Mapper to the Reducer is relatively small in size comprising all the rules of the induced R-PrismTCS base classifiers. Nevertheless, we have incorporated this communication in our analysis in Sect. 4. However, assuming that the number of R-PrismTCS classifiers is increasing, one may consider distributing the computational and communication overhead (associated with the aggregation of the classifiers) over several Reducers executed on different computational nodes.

Parallel Random Prism Architecture. Figure 3 shows the principal architecture of Parallel Random Prism using four Mappers, one Reducer and three cluster nodes.

The input data (training data) is sent to each computing node. A computing node can execute multiple Mappers. Each Mapper implements the R-PrismTCS base classifier outlined in Algorithm 1, creates a validation and a training set and then produces a set of rules using the training data and a weight using the validation data. Then each R-PrismTCS Mapper sends its ruleset and the associated weight (determined using the validation data) to the Reducer. The Reducer keeps a collection of the received classifiers and their weights and applies a weighted majority voting of each, or a subset of the best classifiers, to new

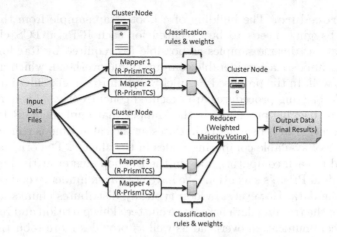

Fig. 3. The Parallel Random Prism Architecture on a Hadoop cluster with two computational nodes, four Mappers and one Reducer.

unlabelled data instances. The basic steps of Parallel Random Prism are outlined in Algorithm 2.

Algorithm 2: Parallel Random Prism Algorithm

Step 1: Distribute a copy of the training data to each node in the cluster using the Hadoop Distributed File System;

Step 2: Start k Mappers, where k is the number of R-PrismTCS classifiers desired. Each Mapper comprises, in the following order;
- Build a training and validation set using Bagging;
- Induce a ruleset by applying R-PrismTCS on the training data;
- Calculate the ruleset's weight using the validation data;
- Send the ruleset and its weight to the Reducer;

Step 3: Optionally the Reducer applies a filter to eliminate the worse and retrain the strongest rulesets according to their weights;

Step 4: The Reducer returns the final classifier, which is a set of R-PrismTCS rulesets, which perform weighted majority voting for each new unlabelled data instance;

---

4   Theoretical Analysis of Parallel Random Prism

The complexity of PrismTCS is based on the number of probability calculations for possible split values. In this paper this is denoted as the number of cutpoints. In the ideal case, there would be one feature that perfectly separates all the classes, or simply all data instances would belong to the same class. An average case is difficult to estimate, as the number of iterations of PrismTCS is dependent on the number of rules and rule terms induced, which in turn are dependent on the concept encoded in the training data. However, it is possible to estimate the worst case, assuming that N is the number of instances and M the number of features in the training data. Furthermore a categorical feature will occur at most in only one term per rule, whereas a continuous feature may occur in two terms per rule, as two rule terms can describe any value interval in a continuous feature. Thus in the worst case all features are continuous and all rules have $2M$ terms. Also in the worst case each (with the exception of 1) instance is encoded in a separate rule which will lead to $N - 1$ rules in total. The -1 is because if there is only one instance left in step 6 of the PrismTCS pseudocode, then there is no need to generate a further rule for it. The complexity (number of cutpoint calculations) of inducing the rth rule is $2M(N - r)$. The factor $(N - r)$ is the number of training instances not covered by the rules induced so far, as mentioned above, in the worst case each rule covers only one training instance. These uncovered instances are used for the induction of the next rule. For example, the number of cutpoint calculations for a term of the first rule $(r = 1)$, where the training data is still of size N, would be $2M(N - 1)$. The total number of cutpoint calculations for the whole rule in this case $(r-1)$ would be $2M(N-1)$ as there are $2M$ rule terms. This summed up for the whole number of rules leads to:

$$T_{PrismTCS} = \sum_{r=1}^{N-1} (2M) \cdot (N - r) = 2M \cdot \frac{N \cdot (N - 1)}{2}$$

Which is equivalent to a complexity of $O(N^2 \cdot M)$. Please note that this estimate for the worst case is very pessimistic and unlikely to happen. In reality larger datasets often contain many fewer rules than there are data instances [21]. This is because Random Prism is a stable classifier due to the usage of R-PrimTCS as base classifier and bagging. Also stated before in Sect. 2, Random Prism employs J-pruning which further reduces the number of rule terms per rule [19]. Hence, in this case linearity can be exhibited as N^2 is reduced to R^2 where R is the total number of rules. An empirical study presented in [21] suggests that the number of rules and rule terms induced does not increase linearly with the number of instances. Also results in [19] suggest a more linear scalability of PrismTCS.

Assuming on average a linear complexity $O(N \cdot M)$ for PrismTCS, the complexity with respect to N and M of Random Prism is a product of four factors. The factors are PismTCS's complexity $O(N \cdot M)$, the average percentage of features f considered by R-PrismTCS (this is a diminishing factor ranging between 0 and 1), the number of classifiers b (which is an increasing factor of a whole number of at least 1 or higher) and a further diminishing factor d which reflects the decrease of rules caused by having repeated instances in the training data for each R-PrismTCS classifier. This leads to $O(N \cdot M) \cdot f \cdot b \cdot d$. As pointed out in Sect. 2, one would intuitively expect the runtime of Random Prism to be 100 times longer, assuming 100 base classifiers are induced, compared with the serial PrismTCS classifier. Yet the results in [20] show that the runtimes are longer but not 100 times longer. In this particular case the increasing factor b would be 100. However, factors f and d are diminishing and thus have a shortening influence on the runtime. In general as none of these factors comprises an increasing dependence on N or M, this can be approximated to an overall linear complexity of $O(N \cdot M)$. Please note that the complexity of building the composite classifier is not dependent on the training data size but on the number of classifiers. Also building the composite classifier is a computationally relatively inexpensive operation. The bagging is also of linear complexity $O(N)$ assuming that the bag is of size N, as in Random Prism.

Stepping away from the complexity, the actual runtime T_{total}, which is needed to execute the serial version of Random Prism, can be described by:

$$T_{total} = \sum_{i=1}^{b} (T_{sam,i} + T_{cla,i} + T_{asm,i})$$

where T_{total} is the total serial runtime, b is the number of base classifiers, $T_{sam,i}$ is the time needed for sampling (using bagging) for classifier i; $T_{cla,i}$ is the execution time for classifier i and $T_{asm,i}$ is the time needed to integrate classifier $i's$ ruleset into the composite classifier. This description of T_{total} will be used as a base for describing Parallel Random Prism's runtime requirements.

As discussed, the basic Random Prism total runtime description T_{total} can be extended for describing the Parallel Random Prism runtime as shown in the equation below, where p is the number of computing nodes in the Hadoop cluster:

$$T_{total}(p) = T_{comdat} \cdot p + \frac{\sum_{i=1}^{b} T_{sam,i}}{p} + \frac{\sum_{i=1}^{b} T_{cla,i}}{p} + \frac{\sum_{i=1}^{b} T_{comres,i}}{p} + \frac{\sum_{i=1}^{b} T_{asm,i}}{r}$$

$T_{comdat} \cdot p$ is a new term that describes the time needed to communicate the training data to p mappers. p is defined as $p = n \cdot \delta$, where n is the number of computational nodes int the cluster and δ is the number of mappers hosted per n. T_{comres} is also a new term that describes the time needed to communicate the R-PrismTCS rulesets and weights to the Reducer. $T_{sam,i}$, $T_{cla,i}$ and $T_{asm,i}$ are the same terms as in the equation for the serial Random Prism algorithm. However, in the parallel version $T_{sam,i}$ (sampling using bagging) and $T_{cla,i}$ (R-PrismTCS induction) are executed concurrently using multiple Mappers on p processors and hence their runtime can be divided by p.

$T_{asm,i}$ (assembling of the composite classifier) is executed on r Reducers in the Hadoop cluster. Hence the division by r. However, in the setup used for the experiments in Sect. 5 only one reducer has been used, hence $r = 1$ in the empirical results. The reason for setting $r = 1$ is because the computational requirement for $T_{asm,i}$ is very low. The only two terms that are not parallelised are $T_{comdat} \cdot p$ and $T_{asm,i}$ and thus these present a computational bottleneck. However, for term $T_{comdat} \cdot p$, the data transmitted to each node is a copy of the original data and it is assumed that the time needed to perform the transmission to each node is the same. Further assume that a star topology network is used with a switch in the centre node, which is the actual setup we used for our empirical evaluation in Sect. 5. In this case a multicast can be used which transmits the training data from the original node only once to the switch, which then multiplies the data and distributes them to each computing node on a separate wire. Hence, in this case, we can ignore the multiplication of $T_{comdat,i}$ with p as in this case $p = 1$. $T_{asm,i}$ remains a computational bottleneck, which increases with the number of base classifiers. However, its computational requirements are relatively low even for large numbers of base classifiers and is not expected to have a large impact on $T_{total}(p)$. Nevertheless, it would be possible to parallelise $T_{asm,i}$, at least to a certain extent, by using multiple Reducers executed on different cluster nodes. One Reducer per two Mappers could combine the rule sets of these two mappers. The Reducers' outputs (again rules sets) could then be combined similarly using further Reducers executed on different cluster nodes. This may be beneficial for very large numbers of base classifiers. The speed-up factor is a standard metric to evaluate the scalability of parallel algorithms with respect to the number of computing nodes or processors p being used [13,15]. It shows how much a parallel version of an algorithm is faster compared with its single processor version. The generic formula for the speed-up $S(p)$ is:

$$S(p) = \frac{runtime\ T\ on\ 1\ processor}{runtime\ T\ on\ p\ processors}$$

For Parallel Random Prism the numerator of $S(p)$ can be substituted by $T_{total}(1)$ and the denominator of $S(p)$ can be substituted by $T_{total}(p)$. Thus the speed-up for Parallel Random Prism can be described by:

$$S(p) = \frac{T_{total}(1)}{T_{total}(p)} = \frac{T_{comdat} + \sum_{i=1}^{b} T_{sam,i} + \sum_{i=1}^{b} T_{cla,i} + \sum_{i=1}^{b} T_{comres,i} + \sum_{i=1}^{b} T_{asm,i}}{T_{comdat} \cdot p + \frac{\sum_{i=1}^{b} T_{sam,i}}{p} + \frac{\sum_{i=1}^{b} T_{cla,i}}{p} + \frac{\sum_{i=1}^{b} T_{comres,i}}{p} + \frac{\sum_{i=1}^{b} T_{asm,i}}{r}}$$

Again, what can be seen is that the only limiting factors are $T_{comdat} \cdot p$ and $\sum_{i=1}^{b} T_{asm,i}$ in the denominator of $S(p)$ as they are not parallelised. Yet, the time needed to execute $T_{asm,i}$ and $T_{comdat} \cdot p$ is neglectably small compared with the parallelised portions of Parallel Random Prism. Thus we can assume that the $S(p)$ will be close to the ideal case, which is $S(p) = p$. For example, if running Parallel Random Prism consumes 10000 ms on one node, then for using 4 nodes we would expect the runtime to be 2500 ms (4 times faster assuming the ideal case), hence $S(4) = \frac{10000\,ms}{2500\,ms} = 4$.

The formula for $S(p)$ above could also be used to determine the theoretical maximum speed-up, through building the derivative $S'(p)$, and calculating its x-axis intercepts and then determining subsequently its global maxima. However, we refrain from this step.

Next Sect. 5 will provide an empirical analysis of Parallel Random Prism supporting the theoretical analysis presented in this section.

5   Empirical Scalability Study

The empirical study comprises size-up and speed-up experiments on several benchmark datasets. Size-up experiments examine the algorithm's performance (runtime) with respect to the size of the training data; and speed-up experiments examine the algorithm's performance with respect to the number of computing nodes used, using speed-up factors as highlighted in the previous section. For the experiments we used two synthetic datasets from the infobiotics data repository [2]. We have chosen these datasets as they can still be run on a single computing node in our cluster, which can be used as a reference point. The datasets are outlined in Table 1. The Hadoop cluster is hosted on 10 identical off the shelf workstations, each comprising 1 GB memory, 2.8 GHz CPUs and a XUbuntu operating system. The Hadoop version installed on the cluster was 0.20.203.0rc1. All experiments highlighted in this section measure the total runtime from the loading of the data to the cluster, up to aggregating the results at the Reducer.

Table 1. Datasets used for evaluation. Attributes hold double values and class values are represented by a single character.

Test data	Number of data instances	Number of attributes	Number of classes
1	50000	5	5
2	30000	3	2

Again, size-up experiments examine the performance of Parallel Random Prism on a fixed number of cluster nodes with an increasing workload (training data size). In general a linear increase in the runtime with respect to the training data size is desired. We produced larger versions of the two datasets in Table 1 by appending the data to itself in vertical (multiplying instances) and horizontal directions (multiplying attributes). Please note that this appending of data does not introduce new concepts and hence does not take influence on the rulesets produced. This is important as altered rule sets may result in different runtimes of the system, and hence the size-up comparison would not be reliable.

The reasoning for this way of increasing the data size is that it will not change the concept encoded in the data. Simply taking different sized samples from the original training data will influence the concept and thus the runtime needed to find rules describing the concept. Appending the data to itself allows Parallel Random Prism's runtime to be examined more precisely. The calculation of the weight of the individual R-PrismTCS classifiers might be influenced by this way of building different sized samples as some instances may appear in both, the training and the test set. However, this is not relevant for these experiments, as this evaluation examines the computational performance and not the classification accuracy. For all experiments we used 100 R-PrismTCS base classifiers.

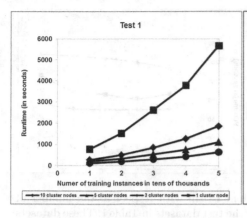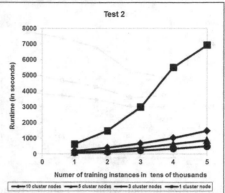

Fig. 4. Size up behaviour of Parallel Random Prism with respect to the number of training instances. Headings Test 1 and Test 2 refer to the test datasets in Table 1. These datasets have in this case been appended to themselves in order to increase the number of training instances, while keeping the concept stable.

The first set of size-up experiments looks on the algorithm's performance with respect to the number of data instances. For each dataset an initial sample of 10000 instances has been taken. Then this sample has been appended to itself in a vertical direction as explained above. The runtime for different sizes of data has been recorded and is plotted in Fig. 4 versus the data size. Please note that an initial sample of 10000 instances may seem small. However, considering the usage of 100 base classifiers would increase the sample in the memory so that the Parallel Random Prism system has in fact to deal with 1000000 data instances for a 10000 instance input sample.

In general we can observe a nice size-up that is close to being linear with respect to the number of training instances. These results clearly support the theoretical average linear behaviour.

The second set of size-up experiments looks at the algorithm's performance with respect to the number of features. The data has been appended to itself in a horizontal direction as explained earlier in this section. Again, the number of training instances is increasing by factor 100 due to the use of 100 base classifiers. The runtime for different sizes of data has been recorded and is plotted in Fig. 5 versus the data size.

Note that for this set of size-up experiments there is no setup with only one cluster node. The reason for this is that we used the original number of data features for both datasets, which simply exceeds the computational capabilities of one cluster node after the bagging procedure for 100 base classifiers.

In general we can observe a nice size-up that is close to being linear with respect to the number of features. These results clearly support the theoretical average linear behaviour.

The speed-up factors recorded for Parallel Random Prism, on both test datasets and for different numbers of cluster nodes (up to the 10 available) are

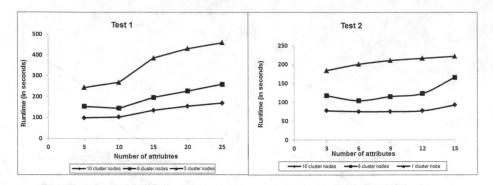

Fig. 5. Size up behaviour of Parallel Random Prism with respect to the number of features. Headings Test 1 and Test 2 refer to the test datasets in Table 1. These datasets have in this case been appended to themselves in order to increase the number of attributes, while keeping the concept stable.

displayed in Fig. 6. The theoretical ideal speed-up factors are plotted as a dashed line. It can be seen that the speed-up factors achieved are very close to the ideal linear case. This almost ideal speed-up has been verified by linear regression equations also depicted in Fig. 6. There is a small discrepancy between the ideal case and the actual speed-up factors, the more cluster nodes are used. However, this discrepancy is expected and can be explained by the non parallel part of Parallel Random Prism as mentioned in the previous section, which is the term $\sum_{i=1}^{b} T_{asm,i}$ and the communication overhead, which is $T_{comdat} \cdot p$ in the equation for the speed-up of Parallel Random Prism. It is expected that there will be an upper limit of the number of cluster nodes that are beneficial to reducing the

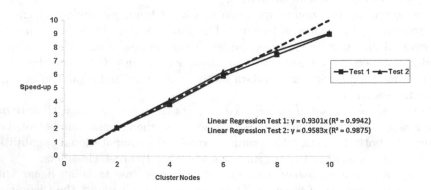

Fig. 6. The Speed-up factors for of Parallel Random Prism. The dashed line represents the theoretical ideal speedup. Linear regression equations and R^2 are displayed for the two test cases.

runtime. However, considering the low discrepancy after using 10 cluster nodes suggests that the impact of $\sum_{i=1}^{b} T_{asm,i}$ and $T_{comdat} \cdot p$ is not very high and thus the experiments are far from using the maximum number of cluster nodes that are still beneficial to lowering the runtime. This is consistent with the theoretical speed-up analysis in the previous section. Please note that the theoretical and empirical analysis presented in this paper focuses on the algorithm rather than the version of MapReduce being used. If the sample constructed constructed for the R-PrismTCS classifier is bigger than the HDFS block size additional communication overhead will be incurred and the less speedup can be achieved. The samples constructed in the experiments outlined in this paper were not bigger than the HDFS block size.

Loosely speaking, Parallel Random Prism indeed exhibits an linear scalability with respect to the number of training instances and the number of features. Furthermore, the algorithm also shows a near linear speed-up factor.

The current implementation of Parallel Random Prism is bound in its maximum parallelism by the number of R-PrismTCS classifiers utilised. However, R-PrismTCS classifiers could also be parallelised. The Parallel Modular Classification Rule Induction (PMCRI) framework [19] for parallelising, amongst others, the PrismTCS [5] classifier, can be used for parallelising the R-PrismTCS classifier also. This is due to the similarity of the R-PrismTCS and PrismTCS classifiers. However, this is outside the scope of this paper.

6   Conclusions

This paper presented work on a novel, well-scaling ensemble classifier called Parallel Random Prism. Ensemble classifiers exhibit a very high predictive accuracy compared with standalone classifiers, especially in noisy domains. However, this increase in performance is at the expense of computational efficiency due to data replication and the induction of multiple classifiers. Thus ensemble classifiers applied on modest size training data already challenge the computational hardware. Section 2 highlighted alternative base classifiers to decision trees (on which most ensemble classifiers are based), in particular the Prism approach. The PrismTCS standalone classifier often outperforms decision trees when applied to noisy data, and hence is a good candidate base classifier for ensemble classifiers. Section 2 proposed the Random Prism ensemble learner with the PrismTCS based R-PrismTCS base classifier. It summarised results concerning classification accuracy and gave an initial empirical estimate of Random Prism's runtime requirements. Section 3 also highlighted a parallel version of Random Prism using the Hadoop implementation of the MapReduce programming paradigm. Essentially multiple R-PrismTCS base classifiers are executed concurrently on p computing nodes in a Hadoop cluster. The only aspects of Random Prism that are not parallelised are the inexpensive combining procedure of the individual classifiers and the distribution of the original training data over the cluster. Section 4 gave a theoretical complexity analysis of Random Prism and a theoretical scalability analysis of Parallel Random Prism. The parallel version of Random Prism was examined in terms of its runtime with respect to the number of computing nodes used. In general a close to linear scalability was expected, as the main part of the workload, the base classifier induction was parallelised. However, the data communication to the cluster nodes at the beginning and the combining procedures were not parallelised, hence an upper limit of beneficial computing nodes was expected. Section 5 further supported the theoretical analysis with empirical results. In these results Parallel Random Prism's linear scalability with respect to the number of training instances and features was confirmed. These results also showed that Parallel Random Prism exhibits an almost ideal speed-up for up to 10 cluster nodes with a slightly increasing deterioration the more cluster nodes are utilised. The results suggested that there is an upper limit (due to the non-parallel parts of Parallel Random Prism). However, the results also suggested that the cluster is far away from its maximum number of beneficial cluster nodes.

References

1. Hadoop (2014). http://hadoop.apache.org/
2. Bacardit, J., Krasnogor, N.: The infobiotics PSP benchmarks repository. Technical report (2008)
3. Bache, K., Lichman, M.: UCI machine learning repository (2013)
4. Bramer, M.A.: Automatic induction of classification rules from examples using N-Prism. In: Bramer, M., Macintosh, A., Coenen, F. (eds.) Research and Development in Intelligent Systems XVI, pp. 99–121. Springer-Verlag, London (2000)
5. Bramer, M.A.: An information-theoretic approach to the pre-pruning of classification rules. In: Musen, M.A., Neumann, B., Studer, R. (eds.) Intelligent Information Processing. IFIP, vol. 93, pp. 201–212. Springer, Boston (2002)
6. Breiman, L.: Bagging predictors. Mach. Learn. **24**(2), 123–140 (1996)
7. Breiman, L.: Random forests. Mach. Learn. **45**(1), 5–32 (2001)
8. Cendrowska, J.: PRISM: an algorithm for inducing modular rules. Int. J. Man Mach. Stud. **27**(4), 349–370 (1987)
9. Chan, P., Stolfo, S.J.: Meta-Learning for multi strategy and parallel learning. In: Proceedings of Second International Workshop on Multistrategy Learning, pp. 150–165 (1993)
10. Dean, J., Ghemawat, S.: Mapreduce: simplified data processing on large clusters. Commun. ACM **51**, 107–113 (2008)
11. Grandvalet, Y.: Bagging equalizes influence. Mach. Learn. **55**(3), 251–270 (2004)
12. Han, J., Kamber, M., Pei, J.: Data Mining: Concepts and Techniques. The Morgan Kaufmann Series in Data Management Systems. Elsevier, Amsterdam (2011)
13. Hennessy, J.L., Patterson, D.A.: Computer Architecture: A Quantitative Approach, 3rd edn. Morgan Kaufmann, San Mateo (2003)
14. Ho, T.K.: Random decision forests. In: International Conference on Document Analysis and Recognition, vol. 1, p. 278 (1995)
15. Hwang, K., Briggs, F.A.: Computer Architecture and Parallel Processing. McGraw-Hill Book Co., New York (1987). International edition
16. Liu, T., Rosenberg, C., Rowley, H.A.: Clustering billions of images with large scale nearest neighbor search. In: Proceedings of the Eighth IEEE Workshop on Applications of Computer Vision, WACV 2007, Washington, DC, USA, p. 28. IEEE Computer Society (2007)

17. Panda, B., Herbach, J.S., Basu, S., Bayardo, R.J.: Planet: massively parallel learning of tree ensembles with mapreduce. Proc. VLDB Endow. **2**, 1426–1437 (2009)
18. Quinlan, R.J.: C4.5: Programs for Machine Learning. Morgan Kaufmann, San Francisco (1993)
19. Stahl, F., Bramer, M.: Computationally efficient induction of classification rules with the PMCRI and J-PMCRI frameworks. Knowl.-Based Syst. **35**, 49–63 (2012)
20. Stahl, F., Bramer, M.: Random prism: a noise-tolerant alternative to random forests. Expert Syst. **31**(4), 411–420 (2013)
21. Stahl, F., Bramer, M., Adda, M.: Parallel rule induction with information theoretic pre-pruning. In: Bramer, M., Ellis, R., Petridis, M. (eds.) Research and Development in Intelligent Systems XXVI, pp. 151–164. Springer, London (2010)
22. Stahl, F., May, D., Bramer, M.: Parallel random prism: a computationally efficient ensemble learner for classification. In: Bramer, M., Petridis, M. (eds.) Research and Development in Intelligent Systems XXIX, pp. 21–34. Springer, London (2012)
23. Tlili, R., Slimani, Y.: A hierarchical dynamic load balancing strategy for distributed data mining. Int. J. Adv. Sci. Technol. **39**, 29–48 (2012)
24. Witten, I.H., Frank, E.: Data Mining: Practical Machine Learning Tools and Techniques: Practical Machine Learning Tools and Techniques. The Morgan Kaufmann Series in Data Management Systems. Elsevier Science, Amsterdam (2011)

Performance Analysis of Adapting a MapReduce Framework to Dynamically Accommodate Heterogeneity

Jessica Hartog(✉), Renan DelValle, Madhusudhan Govindaraju,
and Michael J. Lewis

Department of Computer Science,
State University of New York (SUNY) at Binghamton,
Binghamton, NY 13902, USA
{jhartog1,rdelval1,mgovinda,mlewis}@binghamton.edu
http://www.cs.binghamton.edu

Abstract. When data centers employ the common and economical practice of upgrading subsets of nodes incrementally, rather than replacing or upgrading all nodes at once, they end up with clusters whose nodes have *non-uniform processing capability*, which we also call *performance-heterogeneity*. Popular frameworks supporting the effective MapReduce programming model for Big Data applications do not flexibly adapt to these environments. Instead, existing MapReduce frameworks, including Hadoop, typically divide data evenly among worker nodes, thereby inducing the well-known problem of stragglers on slower nodes. Our alternative MapReduce framework, called MARLA, divides each worker's labor into sub-tasks, delays the binding of data to worker processes, and thereby enables applications to run faster in performance-heterogeneous environments. This approach does introduce overhead, however. We explore and characterize the opportunity for performance gains, and identify when the benefits outweigh the costs. Our results suggest that frameworks should support finer grained sub-tasking and dynamic data partitioning when running on some performance-heterogeneous clusters. Blindly taking this approach in homogeneous clusters can slow applications down. Our study further suggests the opportunity for cluster managers to build performance-heterogeneous clusters by design, if they also run MapReduce frameworks that can exploit them.

1 Introduction

Scientists continue to develop applications that generate, process, and analyze large amounts of data. The MapReduce programming model helps express operations on Big Data. The model and its associated framework implementations, including Hadoop [1], successfully support applications such as genome sequencing in bioinformatics [2,3], and catalog indexing of celestial objects in

This work was supported in part by NSF grant CNS-0958501.

A. Hameurlain et al. (Eds.): TLDKS XX, LNCS 9070, pp. 108–130, 2015.
DOI: 10.1007/978-3-662-46703-9_5

astroinformatics [4], by splitting data across processing nodes, applying the same operation on each subset, and aggregating results.

When frameworks split data evenly across nodes, and when the `map` and `reduce` functions are applied uniformly, the frameworks implicitly assume that constituent nodes possess similar processing capability. When they do not, straggler processes result and performance suffers [5,6].

We refer to clusters whose nodes exhibit *non-uniform processing capability* as being *performance-heterogeneous*. Performance heterogeneity can result from data center administrators upgrading subsets of nodes incrementally, rather than replacing or upgrading all cluster nodes at once. This can result as funds become available incrementally, as older nodes fail or become obsolete, and as new faster processors continue to emerge. FutureGrid [7] and NERSC [8] exemplify *performance-heterogeneous* clusters. The FutureGrid test-bed is a geographically distributed set of heterogeneous nodes that vary significantly in terms of processor speeds, number of cores, available memory, and storage technologies. NERSC's Carver cluster includes a mix of Intel Nehalem quad-core processors, Westmere 6-core processors, and Nehalem-EX 8-core processors, for a total of 9,984 cores.

Hadoop [1], the de facto standard MapReduce framework, can perform poorly in performance-heterogeneous environments [5,6,9,10]. To improve performance, MapReduce applications, in concert with supporting frameworks, must consider differences in processing capabilities of underlying nodes. Simply put, faster nodes should perform more work in the same time, eliminating or greatly reducing the need for applications to wait for straggler processes to finish [6,11]. Our MARLA MapReduce framework [9] supports partitioning of labor into sub-tasks, and does not rely on the Hadoop Distributed File System (HDFS) [12]. Instead, it uses a standard implementation of Network File System (NFS); therefore, data need not reside on worker nodes before a MapReduce application runs, and more capable nodes can eventually receive and process more data. MARLA therefore does not require significant local storage space on worker nodes, but does require data movement (via NFS or some other underlying file system) at runtime.

In this paper, we configure a cluster to exhibit varying degrees of performance-heterogeneity, and test the effectiveness of splitting MapReduce applications with several degrees of granularity. Using smaller sub-tasks increases the opportunity to react to performance-heterogeneity, but also requires that the application pause more often to wait for data to arrive. Our experiments help identify the circumstances under which the benefits of fine-grained subtasking and delayed data partitioning outweigh the associated costs. We vary cluster nodes to include two and three different levels of processing capability, and configure different percentages of nodes at each level. For each cluster environment, we divide application labor into different granularities of subtasks, to help identify the best strategy for task distribution on clusters with different characteristics.

This paper makes the following contributions:

- It demonstrates how incremental upgrades of a cluster can affect performance of MapReduce applications that do not respond to cluster performance-heterogeneity. Application developers do not typically reap the performance improvements that cluster providers purportedly pay for.

- It identifies an approach for MapReduce frameworks to improve performance on clusters that contain nodes with non-uniform processing capabilities.
- It provides evidence that upgrades to a cluster that do not improve all nodes of the cluster uniformly can have a range of impacts on the turnaround time of MapReduce applications, suggesting that data center managers should carefully consider upgrades. These considerations should be made based upon both the techniques employed by the MapReduce framework to respond to heterogeneity, and the applications the framework runs most frequently.

The paper proceeds as follows: Sect. 2 describes related work, and Sect. 3 provides relevant background on our MARLA MapReduce framework, including the mechanisms for dividing and sub-dividing tasks at runtime. Section 4 then describes our testbed and experiments. Section 5 includes and analyzes results from experiments running on clusters containing two levels of processing nodes in varying percentages. Section 6 describes results for clusters that exhibit three levels of node capability. Sections 8 describes our plans for future work.

This work is an extension of the conference publication in the IEEE BigData Conference, Research Track [13]. The significant extensions in this submission are the following: Sect. 5.2 has been added for a detailed discussion on the performance effect of Progressive Granularity Changes. Figure 2 shows the execution times when we follow a two tasks per worker splitting rule. During these tests we incrementally perform upgrades on a subset of the nodes. Figure 3 shows the results when we follow a two tasks per worker scenario as the cluster is incrementally upgraded. In particular these results are presented relative to the execution time of an un-upgraded cluster. Figure 4 shows these same relative results when we follow a three tasks per worker splitting rule. Additionally we consider the impact of all of our experimentation relative to the data size involved. These results are considered in Fig. 12 and discussed in Sect. 7.

2   Related Work

Zaharia et al. [5] and Xie et al. [6] address MapReduce job scheduling in heterogeneous clusters. During speculative execution, Hadoop's *straggler* mechanism starts duplicate tasks when it discovers slow nodes, but this strategy falls short of solving the problem in clusters with increased performance-heterogeneity. Fadika et al. [10] show that Hadoop's straggler mitigation scheme also falls short in non-dedicated clusters with third-party load.

The LATE scheduler [5] allows Hadoop to speculatively execute the task that the framework expects to complete furthest into the future. LATE relies on HDFS for data placement and therefore can not delay the binding of data to worker processes; this restriction limits the tasks that may benefit from speculative execution.

Xie et al. [6] profile cluster node capabilities and skew data partitioning accordingly; slow nodes receive less work than faster nodes. This static profiling suffers when "surprise" third-party loads begin or end in the middle of a MapReduce job, thereby altering a node's ability to complete work compared to the profile-based prediction. Furthermore, when faster nodes receive more work and subsequently fail, the application stalls for longer than when slower nodes fail.

Ahmad et al. [11] notice that Hadoop's speculative execution favors local tasks over remote tasks, and speculatively execute remote tasks only near the end of the map phase. The authors' Tarazu enhancement suite re-distributes speculative execution of remote tasks based on an awareness of network communication. Tarazu monitors this communication to determine whether the map phase or the shuffle phase creates the bottleneck. In contrast, our work delays distributing data until just before workers need it, instead of making and then reconsidering binding decisions. In addition, Tarazu considers clusters with two classes of hardware, wimpy (Atom) nodes and brawny (Xeon) nodes. We find, as shown by Nathuji et al. [14], that clusters more often have levels of hardware that exhibit more closely-related performance than those considered for Tarazu. Our work analyzes the scenario where the difference between worker nodes is a more realistic depiction of the data center upgrade process described by Nathuji et al.

Our work studies how well a delayed task-to-worker binding of application data to worker nodes allows a MapReduce framework to make efficient use of performance-heterogeneous clusters, and the extent to which the strategy introduces overhead in homogeneous clusters. We believe this paper to be unique in varying both the granularity of data splits (and therefore the number of tasks), and also the performance-heterogeneity of the underlying cluster.

3 Deferred Binding of Tasks

This paper characterizes the performance of delayed mapping of data and tasks to worker nodes in the MARLA MapReduce framework.[1] This section describes important MARLA features and distinguishes MARLA from Hadoop, primarily with respect to how the two frameworks operate on performance-heterogeneous clusters. We have described MARLA in more detail elsewhere [9], including its performance improvements on load-imbalanced clusters.

Clusters whose nodes possess non-uniform processing capabilities (some nodes faster than others) undermine Hadoop's strategy of partitioning data equally across nodes and applying `map` and `reduce` methods uniformly. Workers on fast nodes finish their work quickly but must wait for straggler workers on slower nodes before the application completes.

MARLA works directly with existing cluster file systems instead of relying on the Hadoop Distributed File System (HDFS) [12]. MARLA instead focuses solely on `map` and `reduce` task management. MARLA uses a networked file system (e.g. NFS) to decouple data management from the framework, allowing the framework and the file system to address their separate concerns independently. MARLA specifically targets high performance scientific compute clusters, such as those at the National Energy Research Scientific Computing (NERSC)

---

[1] MARLA stands for "MApReduce with adaptive Load balancing for heterogeneous and Load imbalAnced clusters."

Center [8]. To run Hadoop and HDFS, these HPC centers typically partition their clusters and dedicate sub-parts for exclusive use by Hadoop [15]. MARLA can instead operate on existing shared file systems such as NFS or GPFS [16]. This feature increases the number of nodes available for MapReduce jobs, removes the requirement that individual nodes contain significant local storage, and enables MARLA to support scientific applications that require POSIX compliance.

The MARLA `Splitter` manages framework I/O. Framework configuration parameters drive and determine the division of application input into chunks. Different configuration parameters specify (i) the number of tasks, and (ii) the number of cores on each worker node. Workers request tasks and receive all associated input chunk data. To facilitate processing in a heterogeneous environment, MARLA allows the user to configure a number of tasks for the data to be split into. This parameter defines how many data chunks the input should be divided into, which allows the user to adopt a bag-of-tasks approach to combating heterogeneity. After the `Splitter` divides the tasks into input data chunks, it sub-divides those chunks into as many sub-tasks as there are cores on each worker node, a value defined by a framework parameter. This is done to facilitate multi-threading on worker nodes. When a worker node requests a task, the file handle gets passed as an argument, and the file system ensures that the worker node can access the file.

Hadoop instead splits and replicates data based on block size, and places it based on node storage capacity, among other factors. Data placement influences the nodes on which workers complete tasks, often well before the application runs. Although tasks can migrate from one node to another at the request of the Master, the system's implicit preference toward local tasks makes it difficult for Hadoop's straggler mitigation technique to keep up with the non-uniform processing capability of the cluster nodes when only portions of the cluster have been upgraded [6,11].

MARLA's `TaskController`, or `Master`, makes the user's `map` and `reduce` code available to workers, and starts and stops MapReduce jobs. The `Task Controller` monitors task progress on behalf of worker nodes, and resubmits failed tasks to the `FaultTracker`. The `FaultTracker` monitors tasks for failure, issuing a "strike" against any node that fails on a task that a worker on another node successfully completes. Three strikes relegate a worker to a `blacklist`, precluding it from further participation in the job.

Originally, the slowest MapReduce tasks, straggler tasks, limited and determined the turnaround time of larger MapReduce jobs. Causes of straggler tasks include less capable node hardware, external load, and variances in input chunk data, some may require more processing than others. To adapt to these challenges without making assumptions based on static profiling, MARLA supports the bag-of-tasks model to combat both static and dynamic heterogeneity.

In this paper we characterize the performance of this bag-of-tasks approach within a MapReduce framework. We identify beneficial framework configurations for adapting to performance-heterogeneous clusters. Assigning increasing numbers of tasks per node allows frameworks to divide data and tasks to better match node capabilities, but invites overhead.

4 Experimental Setup and Overview

Our experiments run on the Binghamton University Grid and Cloud Computing Research Laboratory experimental research cluster, which comprises the following components:

- 1 *Master* node running a 4 core Intel Xeon 5150 @ 2.66 GHz and 8 GB RAM
- 24 *Baseline* nodes - 4 core Intel Xeon 5150 @ 2.66 GHz and 8 GB RAM
- 24 *Faster* nodes - 8 core Intel Xeon E545 @ 2.33 GHz and 8 GB RAM
- 12 *Fastest* nodes - 32 core Intel Xeon E5-2670 @ 2.60 GHz and 126 GB RAM

Each node runs 64-bit Linux 2.6.32 and shares an NFS server. To emulate clusters that evolve as described by Nathuji et al. [14], who report that data centers perform partial upgrades of their compute and storage infrastructures approximately every two years, we model incremental upgrades by enabling different portions of the cluster containing different combinations of the three classes of machines.

We do not include performance data for Hadoop as it does not support deferred binding of tasks. In our earlier work, we compared Hadoop with our MARLA framework for load imbalanced and fault-tolerance scenarios [9]. The comparison shows that MARLA and Hadoop had a similar performance profile for processing floating point data in a homogeneous cluster. However, in 75-node cluster with 600 cores, in which 75 % of the nodes have third-party CPU and memory loads, MARLA takes 33 % less time than Hadoop to process 300 million matrices. For the widely used MapReduce benchmark of processing a 0.6 TB file for word frequency count, Hadoop and MARLA were tested for fault tolerance. In this test, a 32-node cluster progressively lost 6, 8, 10, 12, 14, and 16 nodes. The results showed that MARLA consistently performed better than Hadoop when faced with loss of nodes.

In this paper, our experiments multiply matrices containing random floating point values. The CPU-intensity of matrix multiplication emulates the characteristics and requirements of many Big Data applications. The differences between Baseline, Faster, and Fastest nodes lie primarily in processor speeds and the number of cores; therefore, CPU-intensive applications highlight this difference most effectively. We report (i) the average time for ten runs of each experiment, and (ii) the number of 33×33 matrices that are multiplied.

We design and run experiments on a cluster that utilizes a centralized file system(NFS). We limit the scope of this paper to the realm of NFS for two reasons. The first is based on our prior work MARIANE [15], in which we discuss how it is often the case that HPC environments are unable to utilize the MapReduce paradigm because of the burdens imposed by HDFS. The MARLA framework utilizes the same code-base as MARIANE as it was also designed with such HPC environments in mind. A comparison of how the use of HDFS has an effect on the performance of a MapReduce framework in such an environment was previously considered in [15] and is omitted here due to space constraints. The second reason we restrict our experiments to use of a centralized data store is because of evidence that suggests that many companies, like Facebook, use

NFS alongside HDFS when processing Big Data [17]. Since HDFS does not support late-binding of tasks to workers, and that is the aspect of this framework we wish to study, we limit our study to an NFS-based environment.

4.1   Clusters with Two Levels of Nodes

The first set of experiments varies the cluster configuration, the split granularity (that is, the number of tasks-per-node into which the framework splits the problem), and the input data size. In particular, we run tests for all combinations of the following:

- *Cluster configuration*: 16-node clusters with some Baseline nodes and some Faster nodes, varying the percentages of each in increments of four nodes, or 25 % of the cluster nodes.[2]
- *Split granularity*: We vary the number of tasks per node from one to four. To utilize the upgraded nodes most effectively, the number of cores parameter of the MARLA framework is defined as eight. Recall that this parameter defines how many sub-tasks to attribute to each task.
- *Problem size*: We use input matrices of size 33×33 randomly generated floating point values, multiplying 500 K, 750 K, 1 M, 1.25 M, 1.5 M, 1.75 M, 2 M, and 2.25 M matrices during execution of the various MapReduce jobs.

Section 5 contains results for this set of experiments.

4.2   Clusters with Three Levels of Nodes

The second set of experiments studies the effect of introducing the third class of Fastest nodes. We vary a 24-node cluster to contain all Baseline nodes, and then a variety of upgrade combinations. In particular, we vary the number of Faster nodes from zero to twenty-four, in increments of two. We simultaneously vary the number of Fastest nodes from zero to twelve, in increments two. We use tuple notation $< b, f, t >$ to indicate the number of nodes at the $< b = Baseline, f = Fast, t = Fastest >$ levels. We run tests for all tuples $< b, f, t >$ in the following set: $\{< b, f, t > \mid b \in [0, 24], f \in [0, 24], t \in [0, 12]; 2b, 2f, 2t \in \mathbf{N}; b + f + t = 24\}$.

In this configuration, we also vary the number of cores per worker alongside the number of tasks. This is done to identify what happens when the number of cores in the configuration file is not reflective of the actual number of cores on the most powerful of the nodes. To do this we consider splitting the tasks into 8 sub-tasks as we did for the previous experiments; we also consider splitting the tasks into 32 sub-tasks in an effort to take full advantage of the Fastest nodes. As with the previous set of experiments, we also vary the number of tasks. We vary this parameter in the same manner as the previous set of experiments, from one to four times the number of nodes in the cluster. Section 6 contains results for this third set of experiments.

---

[2] We do not use the Fastest node configuration for this set of experiments.

5   Variable Data Size Through Upgrade

This section describes results from tests that vary three different aspects of a MapReduce matrix multiply application running over MARLA. In particular:

- Increasing the *split granularity*, the number of tasks per worker node into which the original data set is split, provides more opportunity for Faster nodes to receive and complete more work in smaller chunks than slower nodes. In a 16 node cluster, results describe sets of runs with data split into 16 tasks (1 per node), 32 tasks (2 per node), 48 tasks (3 per node), and 64 tasks (4 per node).
- Altering the *performance-heterogeneity* of the cluster influences the degree to which the system requires straggler mitigation. Results describe sets of runs on a homogeneous system of all Baseline nodes (labeled "0 % Faster" in figures), a system with 25 % of the system upgraded to Faster nodes, systems with 50 % and 75 % Faster nodes, and a homogeneous system of 100 % Faster nodes.
- Varying the *problem size* ensures that trends exist as computational requirements of the application increase. Experiments set the size of matrices at 33×33 floating point numbers, and set the number of such matrices in the input data at 500 K, 750 K, 1 M, 1.25 M, 1.5 M, 1.75 M, 2 M, and 2.25 M matrices.

Four split granularities, five performance-heterogeneity levels, and eight input set sizes translate to 160 different tests. Graphs depict the averages of ten runs of each test. We plot portions of the data in several different ways to explore trends and highlight results that provide insight.

5.1   Traditional Coarse-Grained Splits

Figure 1 plots only the data for the most coarse grain split granularity of one task per worker node. This split mirrors the default behavior in Hadoop and explicitly disallows straggler mitigation because all nodes (no matter their capability) receive exactly one task at the outset of the application. Each group of five bars corresponds to a different problem size along the x-axis, the y-axis reflects execution time, and each bar corresponds to a different performance-heterogeneity (or upgrade level). Larger problem sizes take longer to finish, and clusters with 75 % and 100 % upgraded nodes outperform less capable clusters. However, a homogeneous cluster with all Baseline nodes, and clusters with 25 % and 50 % upgraded nodes all perform the same.

To understand this behavior, consider an example. Suppose we have N worker nodes and we assign $N + 1$ approximately equal sized tasks to each of them. In order for this running time to be comparable to the case where we have N tasks for N nodes, we would need a cluster configured in such a way that the fastest node is nearly twice as fast as the slowest node. In this scenario, the fastest node takes two tasks of equal size, and the slowest node takes one task of that same size. This implies that the execution time of the job is not related simply to the speed of the slowest node, but to the speed of the fastest node relative to the slowest node.

Expanding this example shows us that in order for our cluster to be able to achieve a performance improvement with $3N$ tasks per worker, the fastest node would have to be able to compute at least one of the slowest node's tasks; meaning that the fastest node would have to complete three tasks before the slowest node could finish two tasks. Note that the turnaround time in this case will then depend on the ability of the fastest node to complete four tasks, but that it is sufficient to complete three tasks before the slowest node completes two tasks. This is because once three tasks have been completed by the fastest node it will be free to request, and receive, more work from the Master which will prevent the slowest node from receiving that same work. In this scenario, the fastest worker node would have to be just over 1.5 times the speed of the slowest worker. In addition to this, there would need to be enough faster nodes in the cluster to be able to prevent all of the slower nodes from requesting an additional (third) task.

Because of this, for a traditional coarse-grain data split, initial upgrades to the cluster (even upgrading half of the cluster to machines with faster processors and twice as many cores) does not improve matrix multiplication performance. Overall application performance depends on stragglers on slower nodes, and the coarse grain split precludes straggler mitigation. Upgrading most (75 %) or all of the cluster to Faster nodes does improve performance.

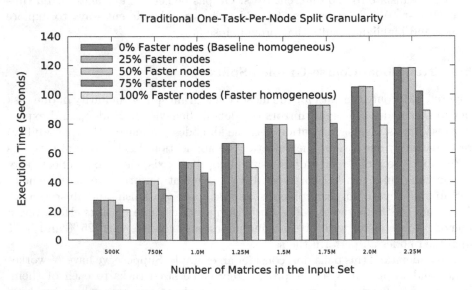

Fig. 1. Execution time for the traditional one-task-per-worker initial data split, for different problem sizes (groups of bars along the x-axis) and cluster upgrade levels (one bars in each group, as per the in-graph legend).

5.2   Progressive Granularity Changes

In order to analyze what happens as we move from coarse granularity to fine granularity with respect to the number of tasks, we perform experiments for each multiple of the number of worker nodes as we move from one task per node to four tasks per node. The results of this class of experiments follows are similar to those seen in Fig. 1 and the analysis provided in Sect. 5.1.

Doubling the Number of Tasks. In this set of experiments, we consider what happens when we double the number of tasks from one task per worker to two. These results are presented in Fig. 2. When we compare these results with those found in Fig. 1 and described in Sect. 5.1, they are very similar. The largest degree of difference between the two sets of experiments is 3.77 %. The average degree of difference between a one task per worker setup and the two task per worker setup is only 1.72 %. The increase in execution time is as a result of the overhead associated with worker nodes having to request additional work.

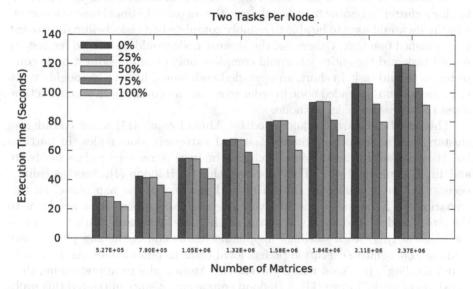

Fig. 2. This graph illustrates the execution times of our workload when we follow a two tasks per worker splitting rule. During these tests we incrementally perform upgrades on a subset of the nodes. On the X-axis is the number of matrices multiplied during the test. On the Y-axis is the execution time in seconds.

To illustrate the effects of the overhead, we consider the change in execution time between one task per worker and two tasks per worker considering file size. The percentage difference is 2.91 % on average for the smallest file size tested, but this difference steadily decreases as low as 1.01 % as the file sizes increase. Since this difference is not as prominent for the larger file sizes, we determine that the overhead associated with requesting additional work is relatively constant and does not depend on problem size. This tells us that the percentage overhead associated becomes amortized. From this we can conclude that as long as the file size is reasonably large, the cost of adding more tasks from the same data will not produce a heavy negative impact on our execution times provided the adaptability to heterogeneity is necessary.

Further, we expect similar performance for the one task per node and two tasks per node schemas in most cases. The reason that we expect this is because two tasks per node does not allow much room for adaptability to heterogeneity. To illustrate the inability to adapt at this level of taks granularity, we present Fig. 3. In the figure, the execution time of workloads is presented relative to their execution time on the original (unupgraded) cluster. The trend of the data presented is that the execution times for the slightly upgraded clusters(25 % and 50 % upgraded) are relatively consistent. These results also indicate a slight increase in execution time for smaller file sizes relative to larger file sizes. This illustrates both the overhead and the inability to adapt to heterogeneity at this level of task granularity. In order to realize heterogeneity adaptability from such a small difference in the number of tasks, the degree of heterogeneity would have to be high. In particular, for a cluster to be able to utilize the creation of one additional task per worker, a fast node would have to be able to reliably complete two tasks before the slowest node finished one task. Otherwise, the slowest node would be able to request its second task and the entire job would complete only once the slowest node completes its second task. In short, an upgraded node would have to be roughly twice as fast as an non-upgraded node in order to see an improvement in execution time when there are two tasks per node.

This has been partially addressed by Ahmad et al. [11] when considering clusters that have both extremely fast and extremely slow nodes. In particular, they consider a heterogeneous cluster of Intel Xeon server class hardware and Intel Atom hardware. They discover that in Hadoop [1], "work stealing" occurs, and is especially a problem toward the end of the map phase. In this scenario, the Xeon nodes speculatively execute tasks whose data are local to the Atom nodes. The non-local status of the data associated with the task is the cause of this "work stealing" happening at the end of the map phase, since Hadoop's speculative execution prefers local tasks to remote ones. As a result of "work stealing", the Xeon nodes prevent the Atom nodes from preforming their fair share of work. Tarazu [11], a Hadoop enhancement suite mitigated this problem by adding in communication aware speculative execution of tasks. However, this late map phase "work stealing" is not a problem in our framework. Due to the data visibility afforded to MARLA by use of a networked file system, the concept of remote tasks does not exist. Additionally, MARLA has no preference for local tasks over remote tasks, as all data is visible to all nodes. The Tarazu enhanced Hadoop has not been analyzed within the context of upgrading clusters as we have presented here; it focuses on the disparity between computation capabilities of Xeon and Atom based hardware, a drastic difference. We believe that a single node being upgraded to a node whose hardware is slightly more powerful is a more plausible scenario for existing data centers, as opposed to replacing one *brawny* node with eight *wimpy* ones.

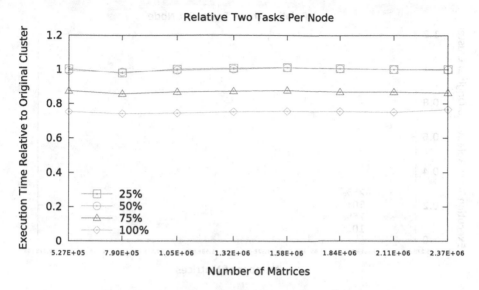

Fig. 3. This graph illustrates the overhead results of our experiments when we follow a two tasks per worker splitting rule. In particular, this graph shows the execution time of this rule relative to the execution time of a traditional data-split rule. During these tests we incrementally perform upgrades on a subset of the nodes. On the X-axis is the number of matrices multiplied during the test. On the Y-axis is the execution time of a two task per worker scenario relative to a one task per worker scenario.

Further Splitting Tasks. The results presented here correspond to what happens when the number of tasks available is three times the number of worker nodes. We look at these results explicitly, as well as comparing them to the results obtained in previous sections.

As with the previous granularity shift, we expect some deviation from the previous results because three tasks per node allows slightly more room to adapt to heterogeneity. From our results, the amount of overhead increases as we increase the number of tasks. This is expected because additional return trips to the master node are required to be assigned more work. This introduces stalling between tasks, which reduces turn around time. In particular when these results are compared to those presented in the previous section, the additional overhead as a result of generating yet more tasks can be seen. In this case we see a maximum overhead of 4.90 % and an average overhead of 1.88 %. Additionally, it is again confirmed that overhead is amortized as the problem size grows, ranging from 3.19 % overhead as we move from two to three tasks per worker for the smallest problem size to 0.48 % overhead for the largest problem size.

Next consider the results seen in Fig. 4. Here we expect to see similar results to that of Fig. 3. The data presented in this figure displays a slight change between a 25 % upgraded cluster and a 50 % upgraded cluster, a trend which is not seen in Fig. 3. This shows that while still not entirely able to adapt to this particular level of performance-heterogeneity, three tasks per worker shows slight performance

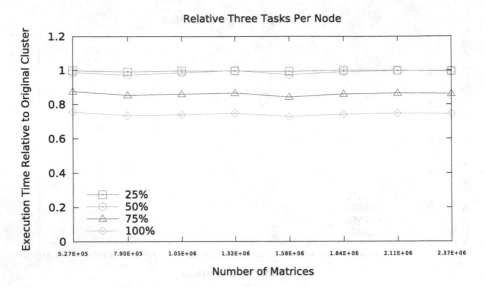

Fig. 4. This graph displays the relative results of our experiments when we follow a three tasks per worker splitting rule. During the experiments, we incrementally perform upgrades on a subset of the cluster. On the X-axis is the number of matrices multiplied during the experiment. On the Y-axis is the execution time in seconds of the MapReduce job relative to the time it took on the un-upgraded cluster.

improvements as smaller sections of the cluster are upgraded. This indicates that further increasing the number of tasks will likely have a more dramatic impact on turnaround time for these smaller percentage upgrade scenarios. This is something we consider in the next section.

Note that in the data presented thus far our cluster is not heterogeneous enough, nor the task granularity small enough, to see an improvement in performance using the configurations presented. The reason we have not yet seen performance improvements in most upgrade scenarios tested is because the upgraded nodes are not fast enough as to be able to take over the execution of all additional tasks that would be assigned to the stock (original) nodes when assuming all nodes will process the same number of tasks.

5.3   Finer-Grained Splits

Figure 5 plots data for the same set of tests as Fig. 1, for the finest granularity of the initial data split. This provides the most potential for Faster nodes to complete initial small assignments quickly and then retrieve more data and execute more tasks than slower nodes. In this case the Baseline homogeneous cluster (0 % Faster nodes) performs worst across all problem sizes, and the Faster homogeneous (100 % Faster) cluster performs best, two unsurprising results. The other three clusters, however, perform very similarly to one another across all problem sizes, despite the disparity between the number of upgraded nodes.

For a finer-grain data split, MARLA improves performance when the first 25 % of the cluster is upgraded, but subsequent upgrades to 50 % and 75 % do not yield performance gains. Only when the entire cluster runs Faster nodes do we see the next level of application performance improvement.

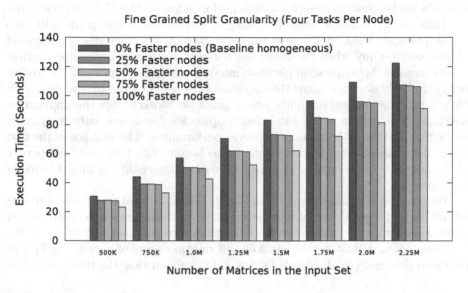

Fig. 5. This graph displays the results of our experiments when we follow a four tasks per worker splitting rule across our cluster as we incrementally perform upgrades. On the X-axis is the number of matrices multiplied during the test. On the Y-axis is the relative time each incremental upgrade takes with respect to the un-upgraded cluster.

We plotted but did not include results for the 32-tasks (2 per node) and 48-tasks (3 per node) versions of Figs. 1 and 5. The two omitted graphs plot data whose values closely approximates the data for Fig. 1. For example, runtimes are only slightly longer in all cases for the 2 tasks-per-node experiments (on average, values are 1.75 % longer and each individual value is within 4 % of its counter-part). The small increase reflects the small overhead of worker nodes requesting extra work rather than receiving it in the initial split. Figure 6, described next, adequately demonstrates the similarity of the data for the omitted graphs.

5.4   Matrices per Second

As problem sizes grow linearly (e.g. the x-axis in Figs. 1 and 5, the average runtime for each set of tests also grows linearly. To view more data in one place, and to highlight the effect of performance-heterogeneity and split granularity across all tests, Fig. 6 plots the average number of matrices multiplied per second, for all six cluster configurations paired with all four split granularities. Bars corresponding to the Baseline homogeneous (0 % Faster) and the 25 % and

122   J. Hartog et al.

50 % upgrades reflect similar runtimes for splits of one, two, and three tasks per worker, with a small decrease in slope reflecting overhead. Similarly, all four splits perform better at 75 % Faster and Homogeneous (100 %) Faster upgrade levels, across all task split granularities, including 4 tasks per node. With the finest grain split that we tested, performance on the intermediate (25 % and 50 % upgrade levels) clusters closely matches performance on the 75 % upgrade level.

Thus, an application developer using a traditional coarse-grain split into 1 task per node would not benefit from any incremental upgrades of subsets of cluster nodes. Only when the entire cluster contains Faster nodes does performance increase. Splitting an application into too few tasks (even 2 or 3 per worker node) similarly does not allow the application to benefit from partial upgrades. Only when the application splits into 4 tasks per worker does the application developer benefit from incremental cluster upgrades. Even then, only an upgrade of the first and last 25 % of nodes improves performance. The upgrade of the first 25 % allows straggler mitigation strategies to become effective, and the upgrade of the last 25 % helps reduce the appearance of stragglers by turning the cluster homogeneous.

We plot Fig. 6's data differently in Fig. 7. The downward trend across results within each of the four set of bars depicts the overhead associated with worker nodes having to retrieve more work, rather than receiving one initial task. In the two homogeneous clusters (the leftmost and rightmost sets of bars in Fig. 7), this overhead does not pay dividends for any split granularities; the trend continues

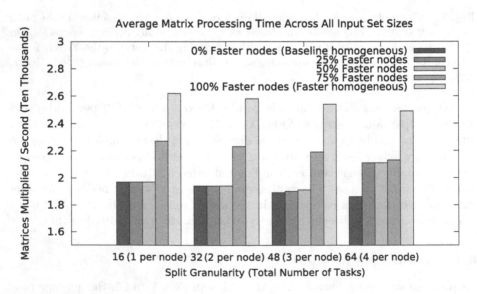

Fig. 6. Average number of matrices processed per second; averaged results across all eight problem sizes. The X-axis displays split granularity in terms of the number of tasks into which the problem is split. Y-axis displays the number of 33×33 matrices multiplied per second in units of ten thousand. The graph includes sets of bars for six different cluster configurations.

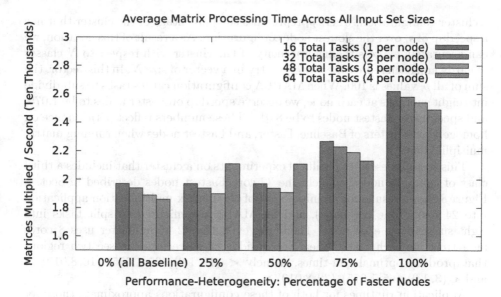

Fig. 7. Average number of matrices processed per second; averaged results across all eight problem sizes. The X-axis displays performance heterogeneity in terms of the percentage of the cluster that has been upgraded to Faster nodes. The Y-axis displays the number of 33×33 matrices multiplied per second in units of ten thousand. The graph includes sets of bars for four different split granularities.

through all four bars in both cases. Likewise, it does not pay dividends for a cluster with 75 % of its nodes upgraded. Within the 25 % and 50 % upgrade levels, only the rightmost bar is taller, illustrating the need for enough (4) tasks per node in the split to realize improved performance from the first 25 % of nodes being upgraded.

Conclusions: Cluster managers should not necessarily expect application performance to improve at all due to partial upgrades, especially when the MapReduce framework employs a traditional one-task-per-worker data split. Our results in as displayed in Figs. 6 and 7 suggest that even MapReduce frameworks that attempt to mitigate the effect of stragglers through the creation of additional tasks may succeed only in adding overhead, and not decreasing runtimes when they do not provide an adequate number of additional tasks. Such frameworks *can*, however, reap the benefits of partial upgrades with sufficient split granularities. In our tests, upgrading the first 25 % of nodes allowed MARLA to mitigate the effect of stragglers well enough to have matrix multiply perform as well as a more capable cluster that included 75 % Faster nodes.

6   Variability Between Upgrades

We introduce the following notation to facilitate discussion of this section's experiments and results. A series of tuples, $< (p_i, s_i) >$, describes the heterogeneity of a cluster configuration, where p_i represents the percentage of the cluster that has a speedup of s_i over the slowest node configuration. As a result of this notation, we can accurately express the heterogeneity of the cluster with respect to N classes of hardware, each represented by one entry in a vector of size N. In this vector, the sum of all p_i values is 100. When MARLA configuration causes tasks to sub-divide into eight subtasks at each node, we observe speedup on Faster nodes to be 1.075, and speedup on Fastest nodes to be 8.010. These numbers reflect performance on homogeneous clusters of Baseline, Faster, and Fastest nodes when running matrix multiplication.

This section describes results of experiments on a cluster that includes a third class of compute nodes, namely the 32-core Fastest nodes described in Sect. 4. Figure 8 shows results for an initial split of the matrix multiplication application into 24 tasks (one per node), and for MARLA configured to split tasks into eight subtasks at each node. Therefore, even the 32 node cluster uses 8 cores at a time for each task. When we consider these results, we see two regions that produce optimal run-times, namely $< (19, 1.0), (65, 1.075), (16, 8.010) >$ and $< (3, 1.0), (65, 1.075), (32, 8.010) >$.

Application runtimes for both of these configurations approximate those for the Faster homogeneous cluster configuration, which appears in the lower right corner of Fig. 8, with 100 % Faster nodes and 0 % Fastest nodes. Even for a coarse grained task split of one task per node on a cluster configuration that does not take full advantage of the Fastest nodes, run times improve.

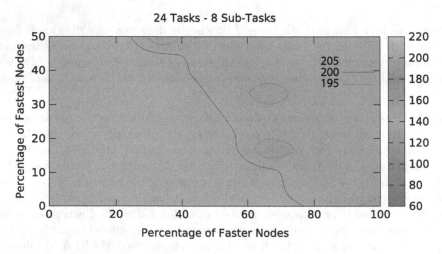

Fig. 8. This contour plot shows the effects of varying two kinds of nodes within a cluster with respect to computation time. In this case, the effect of 24 tasks in a 24 node cluster that assumes 8 sub-tasks for each task. The X-axis shows the percentage of the cluster that has been upgraded to Faster nodes, while the Y-axis shows the percentage of the cluster that has been upgraded to Fastest nodes. Impossible points have been interpolated. The solid lines indicate the trends in the data.

Figure 9 shows results for an initial task split of 72 tasks, or three per worker. Again, MARLA splits tasks into 8 subtasks at each node. Figure 9 shows that some upgrades result in performance degradation. In particular, configurations $< (52, 1.0), (32, 1.075), (16, 8.010) >$ and $< (20, 1.0), (64, 1.075), (16, 8.010) >$ underperform surrounding data points. In this case, Faster nodes request additional work that they cannot complete to improve turnaround time, because requests arrive after the new Fastest nodes have started executing additional tasks. The new tasks on Faster nodes then increase the turnaround time as the framework waits for them to finish. In other configurations, the Fastest nodes can complete these tasks because they constitute a higher percentage of the cluster and are able to get to these tasks before the Faster nodes can.

Comparing Figs. 8 and 9 shows that a split granularity of 72 tasks instead of 24 enables MARLA to adapt to cluster upgrades more efficiently. The difference in performance between these two figures illustrates that with a finer task granularity, upgrades to fewer nodes can still lead to faster execution times.

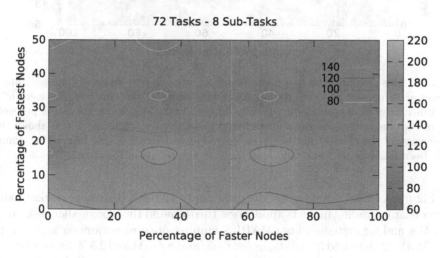

Fig. 9. This contour plot shows the effects of varying two kinds of nodes within a cluster with respect to computation time. In this case, the effect of 72 tasks in a 24 node cluster that assumes 8 sub-tasks for each task. The X-axis shows the percentage of the cluster that has been upgraded to Faster nodes, while the Y-axis shows the percentage of the cluster that has been upgraded to Fastest nodes. Impossible points have been interpolated. The solid lines indicate the trends in the data.

We also consider configurations where MARLA divides tasks into 32 subtasks. Figure 10 indicate that when too few tasks exist, Baseline nodes incur the overhead of 32 subtasks on a 4 core machine. This effect appears in the time difference at configurations $< (19, 1.0), (65, 1.075), (16, 8.010) >$ and $< (3, 1.0), (65, 1.075), (32, 8.010) >$ relative to the corresponding points in Fig. 8. The best performance is achieved in a larger range of configurations when each node processes 8 sub-tasks instead of 32. Therefore, the one-task per worker heuristic fails when a MapReduce configuration does not match the cluster topology. Furthermore, MARLA could improve by adapting to a cluster's topology without sacrificing the late binding of tasks to workers; we plan to study this as future work.

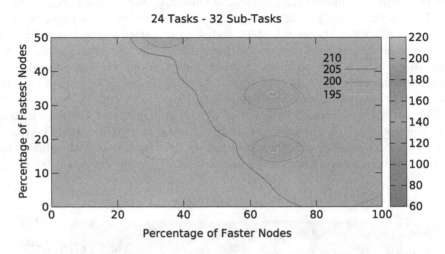

Fig. 10. This contour plot shows the effects of varying two kinds of nodes within a cluster with respect to computation time. In this case, the effect of 24 tasks in a 24 node cluster that assumes 32 sub-tasks for each task. The X-axis shows the percentage of the cluster that has been upgraded to Faster nodes, while the Y-axis shows the percentage of the cluster that has been upgraded to Fastest nodes. Impossible points have been interpolated. The solid lines indicate the trends in the data.

Figure 11 shows results of dividing work onto 72 tasks (three per worker), and shows that upgrading impacts application turn-around time for smaller task granularities and for systems whose MARLA number-of-cores parameter is set properly. With 72 tasks and 32 sub-tasks per task, and more than 12.5 % Fastest nodes, execution time drops below 100 s. Further, configurations that split into 32 nodes perform better than when tasks split into only 8 subtasks, because the Fastest nodes can use all 32 cores. In this case, performance improves more effectively when the most powerful nodes in the cluster are using effectively utilized.

This section's results indicate:

- The one task per worker heuristic combats *performance-heterogeneity* for the configurations we tested, with three discrete levels of worker performance.
- A mis-configuration of a MapReduce framework that is not fully aware of cluster topology can reduce the number of configurations that provide improved performance as the cluster is upgraded.
- The addition of more tasks to the pool of tasks that needs to be completed allows for a MapReduce framework to be configured so that it takes full advantage of the Fastest nodes in the cluster and still sees improved turn-around time for most cluster configurations.

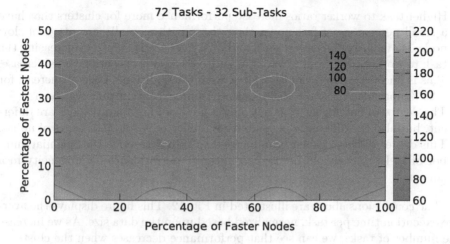

Fig. 11. This contour plot shows the effects of varying two kinds of nodes within a cluster with respect to computation time. In this case, the effect of 72 tasks in a 24 node cluster that assumes 32 sub-tasks for each task. The X-axis shows the percentage of the cluster that has been upgraded to Faster nodes, while the Y-axis shows the percentage of the cluster that has been upgraded to Fastest nodes. Impossible points have been interpolated. The solid lines indicate the trends in the data.

7   Conclusions

As we discussed in [9], we are able to accommodate heterogeneity in a cluster by increasing the number of tasks associated with each worker node. Thus far using experimentation on variable data sizes, variable degrees of heterogeneity in the cluster, and various data partitioning rules we are able to provide the following results:

– As the processing data size grows 4.5 fold, the amount of overhead produced as a result of an increased number of tasks decreases, resulting in performance improvement only when the file size is large. In the case of a four-task-per worker ratio, the overall execution time increases by an average of 7.553 % in the case of the smallest file, and decreases by an average of 1.661 % in the case of the largest file. Therefore, frameworks should consider heterogeneity mitigation using a bag-of-tasks mechanism only when the file size is large.
– An increase in task granularity can provide performance improvements even in clusters that do not have a high degree of heterogeneity. For example, increasing task granularity from two tasks per worker to four tasks per worker generates, on average a 3.13 % improvement in execution time across our runs executed using the largest input file. In particular, improvements are seen in as little as a 25 % cluster upgrade in the case of four tasks per node; whereas improvements are not seen until a 75 % upgrade for the two tasks per node case.

- Higher task to worker ratios increase performance more for clusters that have a small percentage of fast nodes than those with a small percentage of slow nodes. In fact, for the largest data and a 75 % upgraded cluster, increasing the task to worker ratio from two to four caused a 3.03 % execution time increase. This is due to the overhead associated with the additional tasks. Whereas, for a 25 % upgraded cluster a 10.36 % decrease in execution time was seen.
- The degree of heterogeneity is not only a factor of how many nodes are different, but also the difference in computing ability of the various types of nodes. This degree of heterogeneity can be used to help determine the optimial number of tasks that should be used to mitigate performance-heterogeneity in a cluster.

The conclusions above are illustrated in Fig. 12. This figure displays the average execution time per task, normalized based upon the data size. As we increase the number of tasks, we can see that performance decreases when the cluster is homogeneous due to the additional overhead associated with these tasks. Performance improvements are not seen even though there are upgrades to the cluster, as in the two and three tasks per worker cases, since the degree of heterogeneity physically provided by these upgrades is small. Despite the additional overhead associated with generation of four tasks per node, we can see performance improvements based upon the degree of heterogeneity within the cluster.

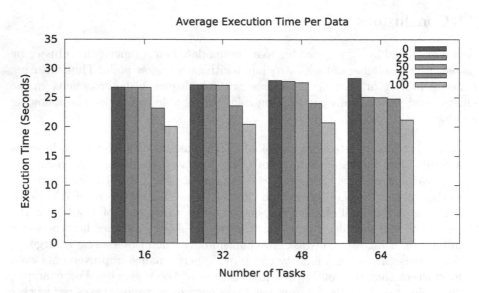

Fig. 12. This graph displays the results of our experiments as we increase the number of tasks per worker and as we incrementally perform upgrades to subsets of the cluster. The data here is normalized based upon data size, with the average execution time of data per configuration presented on the Y-axis. On the X-axis is the number of tasks assigned for the job in our 16 node cluster configuration.

The degree of performance-heterogeneity in a cluster influences MapReduce application performance. Some MapReduce frameworks can use relatively few upgraded nodes for straggler mitigation and improved performance. But not all upgrades influence performance equally. For example, applications that may benefit significantly from upgrades to the first 25 % of nodes, may see no further improvements in upgrades of an additional 25 % and even 50 % of nodes. MARLA's fine grained splitting of jobs into a larger number of smaller tasks, and further splitting each task into one sub-task per core (on the cluster node with the most cores) yields the best results for clusters with the most performance-heterogeneity. For homogeneous clusters, however, having many tasks and sub-tasks introduces overhead to tackle a straggler problem that is less pronounced. Clusters with as few as three different classes of nodes can exhibit particular configurations that support significantly improved performance, but not every upgrade automatically leads to requisite performance gains.

8   Future Work

Our future work will encompass many facets of MapReduce and the processing of large pieces of data. In addition to this work, we will run further experiments to determine how the results presented here apply to other classes of applications. We will confirm this within both heterogeneous and homogeneous settings for memory, storage, and the network interconnect between nodes. Once we have explored many classes of application, we intend to use all of the information collected to define a mathematical model that will help determine the optimal data-split configuration for a static cluster and a given class of workload. Development of such a model will encourage use of MARLA in data centers and HPC environments with centralized data stores who currently cannot get the full benefit of Hadoop due to its early binding of tasks.

Another future direction is to use the insights gathered from this work towards achieving energy efficiency with respect to our MapReduce framework in a heterogeneous, non-dedicated cluster. Our future work seeks to develop an efficient MapReduce framework that can dynamically assess the energy consumption of worker nodes. We believe that our work should not require nodes to be outfitted with expensive power meters as such a requirement will make this framework impractical for many potential consumers. The results discussed in this work will lead us toward development of an energy-aware, efficient, elastic, dynamic MapReduce framework that can be deployed on any number of nodes.

References

1. Apache Hadoop. http://hadoop.apache.org
2. 1000 Genomes: A Deep Catalog of Human Genetic Variation. http://www.1000genomes.org

3. McKenna, A., Hanna, M., Banks, E., Sivachenko, A., Cibulskis, K., Kernytsky, A., Garimella, K., Altshuler, D., Gabriel, S., Daly, M., DePristo, M.A.: The genome analysis toolkit: a mapreduce framework for analyzing next-generation dna sequencing data. Genome Res. **20**, 1297–1303 (2010)

4. Starr, D.L., Bloom, J.S., Brewer, J.M., Butler, N., Clein, C.: A map/reduce parallelized framework for rapidly classifying astrophysical transients. In: Astronomical Data Analysis Software and Systems XIX, Series, vol. 434. ASP Conference Series (2010)

5. Zaharia, M., Konwinski, A., Joseph, A.D., Katz, R., Stoica, I.: Improving mapreduce performance in heterogeneous environments. In: Proceedings of the 8th USENIX Conference on Operating Systems Design and Implementation, Series, OSDI 2008, pp. 29–42. USENIX Association, Berkeley (2008). http://dl.acm.org/citation.cfm?id=1855741.1855744

6. Xie, J., Yin, S., Ruan, X., Ding, Z., Tian, Y., Majors, J., Manzanares, A., Quin, X.: Improving mapreduce performance through data placement in heterogeneous hadoop clusters. In: IPDPS Workshops, pp. 1–9 (2010)

7. The FutureGrid Resource Project: An XSEDE Resource Provider. https://portal.futuregrid.org/about

8. National Energy Research Scientific Computing Center. http://nersc.gov

9. Fadika, Z., Dede, E., Hartog, J., Govindaraju, M.: Marla: mapreduce for heterogeneous and load imbalanced clusters. In: 2012 12th IEEE/ACM International Symposium on Cluster, Cloud and Grid Computing (CCGrid), pp. 49–56, May 2012

10. Fadika, Z., Dede, E., Govindaraju, M., Ramakrishnan, L.: Benchmarking mapreduce implementations for application usage scenarios. In: IEEE/ACM International Workshop on Grid Computing, pp. 90–97 (2011)

11. Ahmad, F., Chakradhar, S.T., Raghunathan, A., Vijaykumar, T.: Tarazu: optimizing mapreduce on heterogeneous clusters. ACM SIGARCH Comput Archit. News **40**(1), 61–74 (2012)

12. HDFS. http://hadoop.apache.org/docs/hdfs/r0.22.0/hdfs_design.html

13. Hartog, J., DelValle, R., Govindaraju, M., Lewis, M.: Configuring a mapreduce framework for performance-heterogeneous clusters. In: Proceedings of the 2013 IEEE Big Data 2014 Conference, Research Track, Series, BigData 2014, Anchorage, AL, USA (2014)

14. Nathuji, R., Isci, C., Gorbatov, E.: Exploiting platform heterogeneity for power efficient data centers. In: Fourth International Conference on Autonomic Computing, ICAC 2007, p. 5. IEEE (2007)

15. Fadika, Z., Dede, E., Govindaraju, M., Ramakrishnan, L.: Mariane: mapreduce implementation adapted for HPC environments. In: IEEE/ACM International Workshop on Grid Computing, pp. 82–89 (2011)

16. General Parallel File System. http://www-03.ibm.com/systems/software/gpfs

17. Thusoo, A., Sarma, J.S., Jain, N., Shao, Z., Chakka, P., Anthony, S., Liu, H., Wyckoff, P., Murthy, R.: Hive: a warehousing solution over a map-reduce framework. Proc. VLDB Endowment **2**(2), 1626–1629 (2009)

An Overview of Cloud Based Content Delivery Networks: Research Dimensions and State-of-the-Art

Meisong Wang[1,2], Prem Prakash Jayaraman[2], Rajiv Ranjan[2],
Karan Mitra[3], Miranda Zhang[1,2], Eddie Li[1,2], Samee Khan[4],
Mukaddim Pathan[5], and Dimitrios Georgeakopoulos[6(✉)]

[1] Research School of Computer Science, ANU, Canberra, Australia
{u5454816,miranda.zhang,zheng.li}@anu.edu.au
[2] CSIRO DP&S Flagship, Canberra, Australia
{prem.jayaraman,rajiv.ranjan}@csiro.au
[3] Luleå University of Technology, SE-931 87 Skellefteå, Sweden
karan.mitra@ltu.se
[4] North Dakota State University, Fargo, USA
samee.khan@ndsu.edu
[5] Telstra Corporation, Melbourne, Australia
mukaddim.pathan@team.telstra.com
[6] Royal Melbourne Institute of Technology, Melbourne, Australia
dimitrios.georgakopoulos@rmit.edu.au

Abstract. Content distribution networks (CDNs) using cloud resources such as storage and compute have started to emerge. Unlike traditional CDNs hosted on private data centers, cloud-based CDNs take advantage of the geographical availability and the pay-as-you-go model of cloud platforms. The Cloud-based CDNs (CCDNs) promote content-delivery-as-a-service cloud model. Though CDNs and CCDNs share similar functionalities, introduction of cloud impose additional challenges that have to be addressed for a successful CCDN deployment. Several papers have tried to address the issues and challenges around CDN with varying degree of success. However, to the best of our knowledge there is no clear articulation of issues and challenges problems within the context of cloud-based CDNs. Hence, this paper aims to identify the open challenges in cloud-based CDNs. In this regard, we present an overview of cloud-based CDN followed by a detailed discussion on open challenges and research dimensions. We present a state-of-the-art survey on current commercial and research/academic CCDNs. Finally, we present a comprehensive analysis of current CCDNs against the identified research dimensions.

1 Introduction

The digital universe is doubling in size every two years. It is expected that the data we create and copy will reach 44 zettabytes by 2020 [19]. The global internet video traffic alone will comprise 79 percent of all Internet traffic in 2016, up from 66 percent in 2013 [18]. In our current Internet-driven world, consumers expect fast, always-on data access from anywhere and any device. As a result, content providers are expected to confront

© Springer-Verlag Berlin Heidelberg 2015
A. Hameurlain et al. (Eds.): TLDKS XX, LNCS 9070, pp. 131–158, 2015.
DOI: 10.1007/978-3-662-46703-9_6

with the challenge of delivering optimised and streaming content to application running on devices including tablets and smart-phones while ensuring high-speed access and superior performance. The major challenges that the emerging applications bring to the future internet [23] include the requirements of: (1) higher scalability, (2) higher capability, (3) higher quality of service (QoS), (4) stronger interactivity, (5) dealing with heterogeneity (e.g., device, network and application) and (6) security. Content delivery networks (CDNs) are often required to face the data deluge to efficiently and securely distribute content to a large number of online users. The growth of related technologies such as accelerated web performance, rich media content streaming, IPTV, management and delivery of user generated content over the last decade has led to the significant adoption of CDNs. Cisco has estimated that over half of the internet traffic generated will be carried out by content delivery networks by 2018.

A CDN is a distributed network of servers and file storage devices that replicates content/services (e.g. files, video, audio etc.) on a large number of surrogate systems placed at various locations, distributed across the globe. CDNs are highly flexible and aims to improve the quality and scalability of the services offered over the Internet by reducing the latency and efficiency of delivering contents to clients. The CDN maximises the bandwidth for accessing to data from clients throughout the network by strategically placing content replica(s) at geographically distributed locations. The concept of a CDN was conceived during the early days of Internet. By the end of 1990's before CDNs from Akamai and other commercial providers managed to deliver Web content (i.e., web pages, text, graphics, URLs and scripts) anywhere in the world, and at the same time meet the high availability and quality expected by their end users. Today, Akamai [22] delivers between fifteen to thirty percent of all Web traffic, reaching more than 4 Tb per second.

In today's dynamic Internet landscape, it is more important than ever for content and service providers to understand the requirements and demands of users. For instance, consider a video distribution services such as Netflix, YouTube and Quickflix. When delivering video content to geographically distributed subscribers, the video experience can vary depending on the delivery path to the subscriber. Studies [20, 21] show that, the sensitivity of subscribers to video quality issues can greatly impact the subscriptions to the services offered by the video distribution service providers.

Cloud computing is an emerging computing model where a myriad of virtualized ICT resources are exposed as web utilities, which can be invoked and released in an on-demand fashion [24, 25]. The concept of cloud computing is an immediate extension of many well researched domains such as virtualisation, distributed, utility, cluster, and grid computing. The most comprehensive, widely used and referred definition of cloud computing in the literature is presented in [16]. It defines cloud computing as "A model for enabling convenient, on-demand network access to a shared pool of configurable computing resources (e.g., networks, servers, storage, applications, and services) that can be rapidly provisioned and released with minimal management effort or service provider interaction". A number of public cloud providers including Amazon Web Services (AWS), Microsoft Azure, Salesforce.com and Google App Engine have been emerged to be very successful in the recent past. The advent of virtualization has led to the transformation of traditional data centres into flexible cloud infrastructure.

In the days before cloud, the main way to address issues regarding performance, availability and scale in CDN was for companies to physically replicate existing infrastructure in other geographical locations in order to decrease the physical distance between the end user and content servers. For example, deploy servers close to ISP gateways. This approach was not only expensive but companies had to determine the best replicate and server placement strategy [26]. The cloud model offers companies an alternative and less expensive way to expand infrastructure, in particular the ability to virtually scale across unlimited resources on demand without the need to buy expensive hardware. The cloud and CDN have both evolved to be complimentary utility platforms. The cloud provides virtually unlimited access to computational resources (processing, storage and network infrastructure) via array of physical servers deployed globally. Conversely, CDN provides an optimised repeatable delivery of content from servers to end users (one-to-many). Using the cloud and CDN together can deliver a holistic agile system that meets CDN demands and is economically viable. A cloud-based CDN architecture can provide the following advantages [27]:

- An elastic platform with ability to dynamically and easily scale capacity up and down.
- Hides the infrastructure complexity from CDN applications and content provides.
- Enable a QoS driven performance management.
- Open standard approach to tap into the capabilities of public clouds to scale during peak demand.

A few studies [4, 23, 28–32] in the past have investigated CDN presenting overview and technical challenges in designing and implementing effective CDNs. Most of the work has focused on commercial CDNs that work over private data centres. With the current trends and advances in cloud computing and the mutual advantages that can be leveraged by cloud and CDN, in this paper, we present a comprehensive study of Cloud CDNs. We present a state-of-the art survey on current commercial and research driven Cloud CDNs. We then present an analysis of current Cloud CDN based on a comprehensive taxonomy. We finally identify the opportunities in the Cloud CDN area.

2   Content Delivery Network and Cloud Computing

2.1   Content Delivery Network

An overview of a typical CDN architecture is presented in Fig. 1. Depending on application and content type the architecture of CDNs may vary However, all CDN architectures mainly comprise of an origin server, a request redirecting mechanism and a large number of surrogate cache servers namely Point of Presence (POP).

1. **Origin server:** is a powerful storage system that contains all the content and/or the metadata of all the content. To achieve high performance of the whole CDN, the content in the origin server are pushed to the POP servers (surrogate servers) that are located at different geographical locations across the globe.
2. **POP servers:** are distributed in a large numbers at diverse areas in a CDN. The main function of pop server is to offer the content based on user request. When the content is not available locally, the pop server should pull it from the origin server and store it

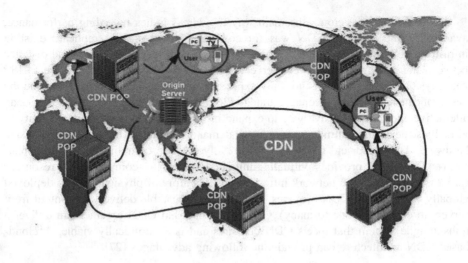

Fig. 1. The architecture of a Content Delivery network

Table 1. CDN Request Redirecting mechanisms

Global Server Load Balancing	Global awareness
	Smart authoritative DNS
DNS-based request routing	
HTTP redirection	
URL rewriting	URL modification
	Automation through scripts
Anycasting	IP anycast
	Application level anycast
CDN Peering	Centralized directory model
	Distributed Hash Table
	Flooded request model
	Document routing model

for the next probable requirement; as it might be possible that the same/other user(s) in the region will require the content. Prefetching [2] is another important functionality provided by the POP server where it fetches the content that clients may be interested in from the origin server thereby reducing the chance of traffic congestion especially during the high demand. Needless to say, prefetching needs to predict the users' preferential contents by synthesizing and analysing the historical information such as access logs. It is evident that this kind of prefetching techniques may require statistical data mining algorithms to determine what content to prefetch.

3. **Request Redirecting mechanism:** One of the functions of a CDN is to dynamically redirect clients to the most optimal servers based on several QoS parameters such as server load, latency, network congestion, client access networks, and proximity etc. There are a variety of methods that can be used to implement this mechanism as presented in Table 1 [3].

Global Server Load Balancing (GSLB): aims to optimize resource use, maximize throughput, minimize response time, and avoid overload of any one of the resources. The capabilities that allow global server load balancing include global awareness and smart authoritative domain name service (DNS). In GSLB, services nodes are aware of information and status of other service nodes. This provides intermediate switching nodes to be globally aware. To make use of the global awareness, intermediate switches act as smart authoritative DNS, each switching between the best surrogate servers.

DNS-based request-routing: is widely used in the Internet. DNS based request-routing is also used in many CDNs because of its ubiquity as a directory service. DNS servers handle the domain name of the desired web site or content. The client initiates a name lookup in a local DNS server, which is supposed to return the address of a surrogate server near the client. If local DNS cache misses, it forwards the name lookup to the DNS root server. DNS root server returns the address of the authoritative DNS server for the web site. The Authoritative DNS server then returns the address of a surrogate server near the client based on specialized routing, load monitoring and Internet mapping mechanism. Finally, the client retrieves the content from the designated surrogate server. A number of studies have examined and reported the performance and effectiveness of DNS [33, 34].

HTTP Redirection: takes advantage of the HTTP protocol's redirection feature. This mechanism builds on special Web servers that can inspect a client request and chooses the most suitable surrogate server and redirect the client to those servers. This approach provides the flexibility of managing replication with finer granularity (e.g., at page level). However, it does pose significant overheads due to the introduction of extra messages round trips.

URL Rewriting: can be one of the best and quickest ways to improve the usability and search friendliness. A rewrite engine is software located in a Web application framework running on a Web server that modifies a web URL's appearance. Many framework users have come to refer to this feature as a "Router". This modification is called URL rewriting. For example, request for web sites with images, the router can rewrite the URLs of the images to point to the best surrogate servers.

Anycasting: is a new routing technology based on the Ipv6. It is a methodology in which datagrams from a single sender are routed to the topologically nearest node in a group of potential receivers, though it may be sent to several nodes, all identified by the same destination address. CDNs may use anycast for routing user request to their distribution centres or DNS.

CDN Peering: is a methodology where clients provide resources; the client can also use these resources based on their requirements. This means that unlike client-server systems, the content serving capacity of peer-to-peer networks can actually increase as more users begin to access the content (especially with protocols such as Bittorrent that require users to share). This property is one of the major advantages of using P2P networks because it makes the setup and running costs very small for the original content distributor. To locate the content in CDN peering [34], a centralised directory model, distributed hash table, flooded request model or document routing model can be used. In centralised P2P file-sharing service, a large server is used to provide directory service. The P2P application contacts the directory service, informing the directory service of its IP address and the names of objects in its local disk that it is making available for sharing. When an active peer obtains a new object or removes one, it informs the directory server, which then updates its database. In a distributed hash table, peers are indexed through hashing keys and are found through complex queries within a distributed system. This approach is good in performing load balancing and offloading loads to less-loaded peers. The flooded request model is simple but scales poorly. When a node wants to find a resource on the network, which may be on a node it does not know about, it could simply broadcast its search query to its immediate neighbours. If the neighbours do not have the resource, it then asks its neighbours to forward the query. This is repeated until the resource is found or all the nodes have been contacted, or perhaps a network-imposed hop limit is reached.

2.2 Cloud Computing

Cloud computing [35, 36] assembles large networks of virtualised ICT services such as hardware resources (such as CPU, storage, and network), software resources (such as databases, application servers, and web servers) and applications. The advent of virtualization has led to the transformation of traditional data centres into flexible cloud infrastructure [44, 45]. With the benefit of virtualization, data centres progressively provide flexible online application service hosting [17] such as: web hosting, search, e-mails, and gaming. Largely, virtualization provides the opportunity to achieve high availability of applications in data centres at reduced costs. In industry, these services are referred to as Infrastructure as a Service (IaaS), Platform as a Service (PaaS), and Software as a Service (SaaS) [46, 47]. Cloud computing services are hosted in large data centres, often referred to as data farms, operated by companies such as Amazon [10], Apple, Google, and Microsoft [8]. Cloud computing gives developers the ability to marshal virtually infinite computing and storage based on amount of data to be processed and stored; and number of people to be notified in real time. Cloud-based ICT resources can be acquired under pay-per-use models and as needed, instead of requiring upfront investments in resources that may never be used optimally. As defined by National Institute of Standards and Technology [16], the five essential characterises of cloud computing are:

- On-demand self-service.
- Broad network access.
- Resource pooling.
- Rapid elasticity.
- Measured service.

Another important characteristic of cloud computing that is gaining significant momentum is Quality of Service (QoS) driven service delivery. For reliable and efficient management of application performance hosted on the *aaS layers, system administrators have to be fully aware of the compute, storage, networking resources, application performance and their respective quality of service (QoS). QoS parameters (e.g., latency, renting cost, throughput, etc.) play an important role in maintaining the grade of services delivered to the application consumer and administrator as specified and agreed upon in the Service Level Agreement (SLA) document. The SLA guarantees scope and nature of an agreed QoS performance objective (also referred to as the QoS targets) that the cloud application consumer and administrators can expect from cloud service provider(s).

Though the notion of virtually unlimited resources is true in many aspects, there are practical limitations to the realisation of this concept. For example, how to automatically provision new resources as the demand for the service increases. Previous work on resource provisioning in distributed computing environments [7, 37] enables its users to manually modify the hardware resources of their running job flows.

3 Cloud CDNs

CDNs have made a significant impact on how content is delivered via the Internet to the end-users [21]. Traditionally content providers have relied on third-party CDNs to deliver their content to end-users. With the ever changing landscape of content types e.g. moving for standard definition video to high definition to full high definition, it is a challenge for content providers who either supplement their existing delivery networks with third-party providers or completely rely on them to understand and monitor the performance of their service. Moreover, the performance of the CDN is impacted by the geographical availability of the third-party infrastructure. A cloud CDN (CCDN) provides a flexible solution allowing content providers to intelligently match and place content on one or more cloud storage servers based on coverage, budget and QoS preferences [23]. The key implication is economies of scale and the benefits delivered by the pay-as-you-go model. Using clouds the content providers have more agility in managing situations such as flash crowds avoiding the need to invest in infrastructure development.

As stated previously, clouds provide the end users with virtually infinite pool of compute and storage resources with no capital investment in terms of hardware and software. Therefore, CCDN systems can be very valuable in data processing and delivery of content over the Internet. The main advantage of such a system would be that they provide a cheaper means of hosting and deploying multi-tiered applications that can scale based on the usage demands. Further clouds offer not only cheaper content storage and distribution functionality, but also compute functionality such that application and data processing can also be performed on clouds. Lastly, cloud offers pay-as-you-model whereby the end-users can start and terminate the cloud resources based on the amount of money they are willing to spend hosting their services without entering into a complex contract with the cloud provider. Migration from traditional client/server based CDNs to cloud computing model is a major transformation that introduces great opportunities and challenges. The major advantages and opportunities introduced by CCDNs include:

1. *Pay-as-you-go CCDN model:* CCDN allows the users to consume the delivery content using a pay-as-you-go model. Hence, it would be much more cost-effective than owning the physical infrastructure that is necessary for the users to be the part of CDN.
2. *Increased point-of-presence:* The content is moved closer to users with relative ease in the CCDN system than the traditional CDN due to the omnipresence of cloud. The Cloud-based content delivery network can reduce the transmission latency as it can rent operating resources from the cloud provider to increase the reach and visibility of the CDN on-demand.
3. *CCDN Interoperability:* CDN interoperability has emerged as a strategic important concept for service providers and content providers. Interoperability of CDNs via the cloud will allow content providers to reach new markets and regions and support nomadic users. E.g., instead of setting up an infrastructure to serve a small group of customers in Africa, taking advantage of current cloud providers in the region to dynamically host surrogate servers.
4. *Support for variety of CCDN application:* The cloud can support dynamic changes in load. This will facilitate the CDNs to support different kinds of applications that have unpredictable bursting traffic, predictable bursting traffic, scale up and scale down of resources and ability to expand and grow fast.

However, while cloud-based CDNs [5, 7] have made a remarkable progress in the past five years, they are still limited in a number of aspects. For instance, moving into the cloud might carry some marked security and performance challenges that can impact the efficiency and productivity of the CDN thus affecting the client's business. Further, current CCDNs are more suited to distributing static content such as audio, video and text. They are not well suited to serving dynamic content-based applications such as collaborative audio-video processing and streaming. Moreover, CDNs are usually owned by private and telecommunication companies making these services costly to the end-users as they have to enter in legal contract to use CDN services. A categorical list of technical issues and challenges in CCDN system is presented in Fig. 2 and the following sections.

3.1 Dynamic Content Management

CDNs are designed for streaming staged content but do not perform well in situations where content is produced dynamically. This is typically the case when content is produced, managed and consumed in collaborative activities. For example, an art teacher may find and discuss movies from different film archives; the students may then edit the selected movies. Parts of them may be used in producing new movies that will be sent to the students' friends for comments and suggestions. Current CDNs do not support such collaborative activities that involve dynamic content creation.

3.2 Content Creation

Traditional CDNs are not designed to manage content (e.g., find and play high definition movies). This is typically done by CDN applications [42, 43]. For example, CDNs do not provide services that allow an individual to create a streaming music video service combining music videos from an existing content source on the Internet (e.g., YouTube), his/her personal collection, and from live performances he/she attends using his/her smart phone to capture such content. This can only be done by an application managing where and when the CDN will deliver the video component of his/her music program. With CCDN, the end-user will act as both content creator and consumer. CCDN needs to support this feature inherently. User-generated content distribution is emerging as one of the dominant forms in the global media market.

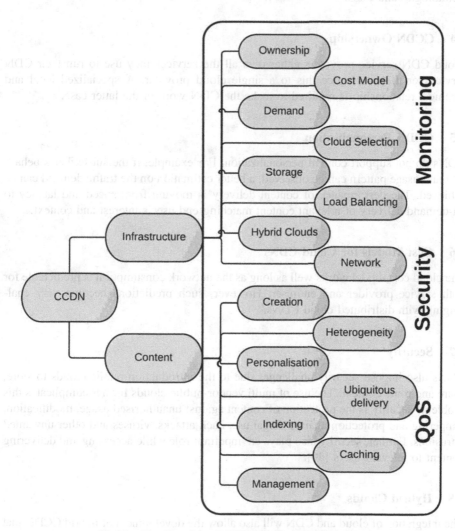

Fig. 2. Classification of CCDN challenges and issues

3.3   Content Heterogeneity

Existing Web 2.0 technologies currently support the authoring of structured multimedia content (e.g., web pages linking images, sounds, videos, and animations). The CCDNs will need to extend and broaden existing Web 2.0 strengths with a new environment aimed at supporting the creation and consumption of interactive multimedia content (e.g., interactive audio and video), as well as other novel forms of multimedia content (e.g., virtual and augmented reality) that are currently not supported by existing Web 2.0 technologies and tools.

3.4   CCDN Ownership

Cloud CDN service providers either own all the services they use to run their CDN services or they outsource this to a single cloud provider. A specialized legal and technical relationship is required to make the CDN work in the latter case.

3.5   CCDN Personalisation

CDNs do not support content personalization. For example, if the subscriber's behaviour and usage pattern can be observed, a better estimation on the traffic demand can be achieved. The performance of content delivery is moving from speed and latency to on-demand delivery of relevant content matching end-user's interest and context.

3.6   Cost Models for Cloud CDNs

The cloud cost model works well as long as the network consumption is predictable for both service provider and end-user. However, such predictions become very challenging with distributed cloud CDNs.

3.7   Security

CDNs also impose security challenges due to the introduction public clouds to store, share and route content. The use of multi vendor public clouds further complicates this problem. Security is the protection of content against unauthorised usage, modification, tampering and protection against illegal use, hack attacks, viruses and other unwanted intrusions. Further, security also plays an important role while accessing and delivering content to relevant users [40].

3.8   Hybrid Clouds

The integration of cloud and CDN will also allow the development of hybrid CCDN that can leverage on a combination and private and public cloud providers. E.g. the content provider can use a combination of cloud service platforms offered by Microsoft Azure and Amazon AWS to host their content. Depending on the pay-as-you go model, the content provider can also move from one cloud provider to another. However, achieving a hybrid model is very challenging due to various CCDN ownership issues and QoS issues.

3.9 CCDN Monitoring

The CCDNs can deliver end-to-end QoS monitoring by tracking the overall service availability and pinpoint issues. Clouds can also provide additional tools for monitoring specific content e.g. video quality monitoring. However, developing a CCDN monitoring framework is always a challenge.

3.10 CCDN QoS

With the notion of virtually unlimited resources offered by the cloud, quality for service plays a key role in CCDNs to maintain a balance between service delivery quality and cost. Defining appropriate SLA's to enforce QoS and guarantee service quality is very important and is also challenging. Further, the notion of hybrid clouds further complicate CCDN QoS challenges due to the involvement of multiple cloud providers with varying SLAs. CCDNs must accommodate highly transient, unpredictable users behaviour (arrival patterns, service time distributions, I/O system behaviours, user profile, network usage, etc.) and activities (streaming, searching, editing, and downloading).

3.11 CCDN Demand Prediction

It is critical that CCDNs are able to predict the demands and behaviours of hosted applications, so that it can manage the cloud resources optimally. Concrete prediction or forecasting models must be built before the demands and behaviours of CDN applications can be predicted accurately. The hard challenge is to accurately identify and continuously learn the most important behaviours and accurately compute statistical prediction functions based on the observed demands and behaviours such as request arrival pattern, service time distributions, I/O system behaviours, user profile, and network usage.

3.12 CCDN Cloud Selection

The diversity of offering by Cloud providers make cloud section to host CDN components a complex task. A practical question to be addressed is: how well does a cloud provider perform compared to the other providers? For example, how does a CDN application engineer compare the cost/performance features of CPU, storage, and network resources offered by Amazon EC2, Microsoft Azure, GoGrid, FelxiScale, Terre-Mark, and RackSpace. For instance, a low-end CPU resource of Microsoft Azure is 30 % more expensive than the comparable Amazon EC2 CPU resource, but it can process CDN application workload twice as quickly. Similarly, a CDN application engineer may choose one provider for storage intensive applications and another for computation intensive CDN applications. Hence, there is need to develop novel decision making framework that can analyse existing cloud providers to help CDN service engineers in making optimal selection decisions.

3.13   Ubiquitous Content Delivery

Content delivery services will interact with the network and appropriately adjust its QoS as needed to deliver content to a specific user based on content and user requirements for maintaining its integrity, the device the user is using, his/her location, and the service contracts. This is a requirement for CCDNs with the growing complexity in media types, end-user access devices and intermediate network architectures.

3.14   Flexible Content Storage, Compression, and Indexing

Cloud storage resources allow content producers to store content on virtualized disks and access them anytime from any point on the Internet. These storage resources are different from the local storage (for example, the local hard drive) in each CPU resource (e.g., Amazon EC2 instance types), which is temporary or non-persistent and cannot be directly accessed by other instances of CPU resources. Multiple storage resource types are available for building content orchestrator. Naturally, the choice of a particular storage resource type stems from the format (e.g., structured vs. unstructured) of the content. For instance, Azure Blob (https://azure.microsoft.com/en-us/) and Amazon S3 (http://aws.amazon.com/) storage resources can hold video, audio, photos, archived email messages, or anything else, and allow applications to store and access content in a very flexible way. In contrast, NoSQL (Not Only SQL) storage resources have recently emerged to complement traditional database systems [12]. Amazon SimpleDB, Microsoft Azure Table Storage, Google App Engine Datastore, MongoDB, and Cassandra are some of the popular offerings in this category.

   Though cloud environments are decentralized by nature, existing CDN application architecture tends to be designed based on centralized network models. It is worth noting that none of the existing cloud storage resources exposes content indexing APIs. It is up to the CDN application designer to come-up with efficient indexing structure that can scale to large content sizes to help end-users find and retrieve relevant content effectively and efficiently. To facilitate new and better ways of content delivery using CCDNs, advanced distributed algorithms need to be developed for indexing, browsing, filtering, searching and updating the vast amount of information.

3.15   Other Challenges

Apart from the above CCDN specific challenges, there are also several important factors specific to the CDN in a CCDN that affect the performance of service within the cloud infrastructure. These include [1]:

- *Network proximity:* reduces the response time for improving the customers' experience about the services offered via the CDN.
- *Load balancing:* improves the capability of the whole network by decreasing the flash crowd situation i.e., it distributes the load to different nodes in a network such that response times and system throughput improve.

- *Local caching:* fetches the content for the customer from the origin server and stores it in a local server closer to the customer. This technique helps in significantly reducing the response time.
- *Request redirecting:* plays a very pivotal role in the performance of a CDN service as it redirects the customer's request to the nearest cache server.

4   CCDNs Architecture and Services

Technically, architectures of CCDNs in existence are various in terms of the correlation between CDN and Cloud. For instance, some CCDNs adopt the cloud-based store as their origin server. In this kind of CCDNs, the general mechanism is similar as the traditional CDNs'. Other architecture includes Master/Slave mechanism [4]. Specifically, in this kind of CCDNs [4, 14, 15, 23, 39] the functionality of master node is managing, monitoring and provisioning slave nodes on demand. The slave nodes combine the functions of POP servers. The data is replicated in the master nodes which act as the origin server. When the slave node has to get some contents users require, it only needs to communicate with the master node to fetch the content. A typical CCDN architecture is presented in Fig. 3. As depicted in the Fig. 3, the POPs are distributed across multiple cloud providers while the master node/origin server is responsible to orchestrate the entire CDN functionality. Based on demand from various geographical locations and QoS constraints, the master node will fire new slave POP nodes in close proximity to origin of user requests.

Cloud-based CDNs offer a large number of additional services compared to traditional CDNs. These include:

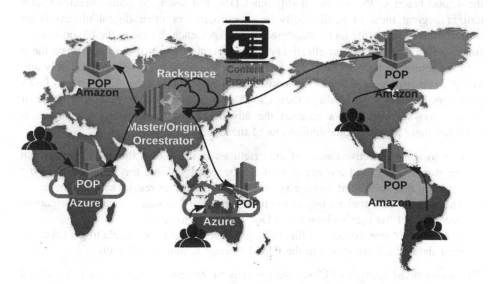

Fig. 3. Cloud CDN typical architecture

Cloud Security. The Cloud-based CDN providers can combine CDN security with the performance of cloud-based distributed infrastructures to keep their customers' websites both high performance and secure. The following aspects are some instances of services the providers may provide in this area:

1. Data Security: The Cloud-based CDN providers can apply and support advanced standards and methods of security like PCI compliance, secure socket layer, and digital rights management to offer the protection of their customers' data.
2. High Availability: The providers offer the Cloud-based delivery of robust website and application functionality in a high-performance manner.
3. Cloud DDoS Protection: It means the protection of websites via DDoS mitigation. The CDN can support proactive monitoring and alerting.
4. Regulatory Compliance: The Cloud-based CDN enhance the CDN infrastructures and services to meet the requirement of industrial and governmental standards for protecting the customers' personal or financial information.

Cloud-Based DNS. The Domain Name System (DNS) is a very important Internet infrastructure that enables visitors to reach their website. DNS redirection has a very crucial role to play in a Content Delivery Network, for it enables the users to get the content they want from the available nearest surrogate server to reduce the response time. Fetching the users' preferential content form the optimal cache server can not only improve the performance but reduce the chance of traffic congestion especially during the rush time. Actually, DNS redirection is one of the mainly two techniques the most CDN providers adopt in their architecture to achieve the aim of redirecting the clients to the nearest surrogate server, the other is URL re-writing.

Cloud Storage. Taking advantage of Cloud Storage is a significant difference between the Cloud-based CDN and the traditional CDN. For users, to Store, maintain, and deliver a great mess of media, software, documents, or other digital objects is an essential part of ensuring an outstanding online experience. By using the Cloud storage functionality, the clients can effectively store a great amount of data and serve these data to the users who need such data in different locations over the world reliably and fastly. Furthermore, it is a very economical option. Though most Cloud-based CDN providers in today's world allege their Cloud storage designed for reliability, scale or speed, anyway they always mention the advantages of Cloud storage as more as possible, there are also some limitations of the Cloud storage [6]:

1. Due to some defective causes of the machines in the Cloud, the users' data which are stored in a Cloud Storage system can be corrupted and this would lead to the situation that the Cloud Storage system returns incorrect results to the users.
2. The attacker may make a bug in the user's programs to steal valuable information, even control the user's client to do Dos attacks or to spam.
3. In some rush time, because of the traffic jam, users might not be able to get access to their data which are stored in the Cloud storage system accidentally.

The above disadvantages of Cloud storage may be extremely impossible, if the Cloud Storage system is robust, well-management, well-designed etc. However, the first importance of the fact is that when these bad events happen, it will be very difficult to find that who should be responded for that among the Cloud provider, the CDN provider and the Customer when something goes wrong. As a consequence, it would be necessary to build an accountable Cloud system which means it is easy to find whose false when some mistakes happen in such kind of Cloud system. Implementing data mining algorithms to analyze the log system is a good choice to address this problem.

Cloud Load Balancer. The Cloud load balancer provides the customers the flexibility to manage their content delivery strategy. This service enables customers to specify content delivery policies based on real-time conditions and user targets. The typical cloud load balancing technology manages the customers' application traffic and makes decisions of where to route it. When a node in the Cloud system fails, a health check process will remove it from rotation to keep maximum availability of the whole system. The Cloud load balancer service should follow the pay-as-you-go model as well in term of the hours the customers use, number of current connections and bandwidth [7].

Cloud Orchestrator. Cloud orchestration service offers enhanced flexibility and elasticity of CCDN as it manages public and private cloud resources using the pay-as-you-go model. Cloud orchestration operations include: (i) production: create and edit; (ii) storage: uploading and scaling of storage space; (iii) keyword-based content tagging and searching and (iv) distribution: streaming and downloading. At Cloud service level, the orchestrator capabilities span across a range of operations such as selection, assembly, deployment of cloud resources to monitoring their run-time QoS statistics (e.g., latency, utilization, and throughput). The orchestrate supports deployment, configuration and monitoring of content and cloud resources deployed across hybrid cloud platforms using web-based widgets. These widgets hide the underlying complexity related to cloud resources and provide an easy do-it-yourself interface for content management. The cloud orchestration service is also responsible to manage the cloud resources based on service providers SLAs.

5 Existing Cloud-Based CDNs

The current landscape of CCDNs leverages the flexibility of the cloud to easily and quickly distribute content across the internet. The CCDNs landscape diversifies into two primary forms namely web site content distribution and media distribution. Web site content focuses mostly on serving static pages with a combination of text and other media content while the media delivery CCDNs are dedicated to deliver high speed video form content providers such as Netflix. The majority of the system use the architecture presented in Fig. 3 with proprietary implementation of cloud storage architecture, security, DNS, load balancer, CDN orchestrator and indexing mechanisms. In this section, we will analyse the current state-of-the are in commercial and academic/research based CCDN solutions.

5.1   Rackspace Cloud Files

RackSpace offers "Cloud Files" [9] as a Cloud-based CDN service where the customers can use virtually unlimited and on-demand cloud storage and high speed content delivery over the Internet all over the world. The high-level architecture of Cloud Files is shown in Fig. 4. As "Cloud Files" is a cloud based system, it offers pay-as-you-go model which means that the users only need to pay for the amount of storage and network bandwidth based on the actual usage. The "Cloud Files" takes advantage of the Akamai Content Delivery Network to deliver the content worldwide. Akamai CDN is one of the largest CDN providers in the world and has a large number of surrogate servers around the world so that the content access latency is significantly minimized even if the customers are far away from the origin server. In terms of content hosting, Cloud Files make use of OpenStack for file storage functionality. The Cloud Files supports API to that cloud and CDN resources can be managed programmatically. The Cloud Files system uses Time-to-Live (TTL) timers to manage content that change dynamically. The dynamic content to be shared using the CDN are associated with a CDN-enabled container. The TTL of the container navigates to each file in the container. When the TTL expires, the edge servers (POPs) will synchronise with the origin server to update the changed content. It is not possible to have a TTL associate with each individual file within a CDN-enabled container.

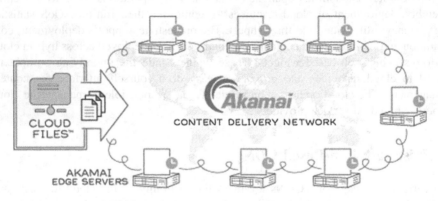

Fig. 4. Architecture of rackspace cloud files

5.2   Amazon CloudFront

Amazon offers CloudFront as a content delivery service that can be integrated with their widely popular Amazon Elastic Cloud Compute service [10]. Similar to Rackspace, CloudFont is also offered as a pay-as-you-go model and supports both static and dynamic content delivery along with live media streaming functionality. Using Cloud-Front, the customers can store their content on the origin servers, or use the Amazon's Cloud Store service (Amazon S3).The customers can use simple APIs or the AWS

Management Console to register their origin servers with Amazon CloudFront. When the customer has more than one server, he/she can use URL pattern matching to find which origin server has the content, and the customer can assign one of those origin servers as the default server. The most significant feature of Amazon's CloudFront is that it can be co-operated with several other Amazon Cloud Services. The architecture of interactions between Amazon CloudFront and other AWS services is presented in Fig. 5. One of the major difference between Rackspace Cloud Files and Amazon CloudFront is that Rackspace utilizes Akamai CDN service that offers 219 CDN edge locations worldwide compared to only 32 CDN edge locations offered by Amazon. The Cloud-Front enables handing of dynamic content while delivering web content that change for each end-user. It uses the concept of URL pattern matching which has to be defined for the dynamic content being served to control the cache behaviour. When a URL match succeeds for a dynamic content request, the corresponding cache behaviour is invoked.

5.3 MetaCDN

MetaCDN [11] is another content delivery provider that offers two kinds of CDN services: one for static content (e.g., websites) acceleration, and another for live multimedia streaming. Unlike other CDN providers that have their own global distributed system, MetaCDN take advantage of existing storage clouds and compute technology to support its own services. Contrary to cloud providers such as Amazon and Rackspace that offer diverse kind of additional services using their own infrastructure, MetaCDN offers its services by integrating the offerings from several other public cloud providers worldwide, thereby having in excess of 120 edge locations across the world for static content delivery. In case of live streaming, they also have more than 40 edge servers located around the world. As a consequence, MetaCDN is clearly illustrates the power and value of combining the Cloud with the CDN for optimized content delivery over the Internet. Figure 6 presents an overview of MetaCDN architecture [11].

The MetaCDN platform uses connectors to interface with public cloud storage providers such as Amzaon S3, Limelight networks. The connector has the basic sets of operations that are supported by most cloud storage providers. The MetaCDN also have a number of core components responsible for functioning of the service. These include the MetaCDN manager, QoS monitor, Allocator, Database and Load redirector. The allocator selects the optimal service provider. The QoS monitor keeps track of cloud storage performance and the CDN Manager tracks each user's current deployments. The database is used to store vital user and cloud storage mapping information and finally the Load Redirector is responsible for distribute end-user requests to appropriate POP servers. The MetaCDN system also provides user interfaces and APIs to configure system via the web and programmatically.

5.4 Limelight Orchestrate: Limelight Networks

Limelight [13] is one of the biggest CDN providers in the world and offers services such as cloud storage, web acceleration and media delivery. There are some typical

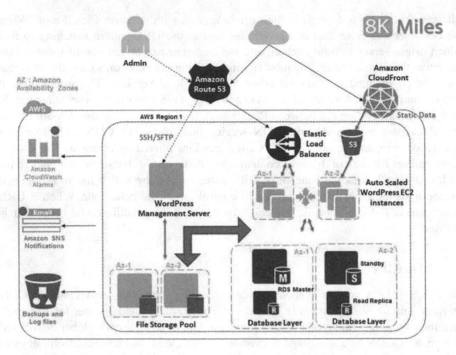

Fig. 5. Integration between the CloudFront and other Amazon services

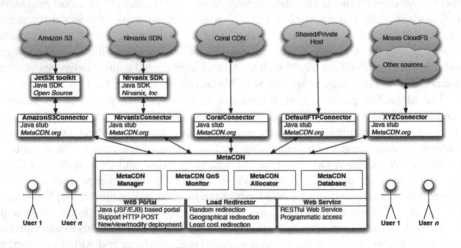

Fig. 6. METACDN architecture

products the Limelight offer like "Deep Insight" which gives the customers analytic data which would be helpful for them to make business decisions. The Limelight orchestrate is a content delivery network offered by Limelight networks. This service is one of the world's largest CDN. The Limelight orchestrate service features cloud

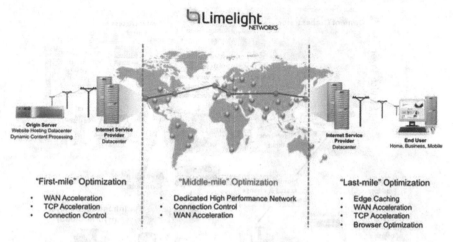

Fig. 7. Limelight Orchestrate – Overview (source: http://www.esg-global.com/lab-reports/limelight-orchestrate-performance/)

storage, content control, security, traffic direction and mobile device content delivery. The cloud part of the system take advantage of Limelight networks cloud storage service. Figure 7 presents an overview of the orchestrate service.

5.5 MediaWise Cloud

The MediaWise cloud [14, 15] offers a novel cloud orchestration framework where any user can become a CDN provider. As in MetaCDN, the MediaWise cloud leverages multiple cloud providers and offers pay-as-you-go model. The end user can select any public cloud provider simultaneously (e.g., Amazon and Rackspace) based on SLA, price and QoS requirements to leverage services such as compute, storage and content distribution at significantly lower costs. The main highlight of this approach is that a customer is not locked to any particular cloud and CDN provider. Compared to other cloud-based CDNs, another major highlight of the MediaWise cloud is that it supports dynamic content delivery to enable collaborative activities such as collaborative content creation, indexing, storage and retrieval [38].

Figure 8 shows the reference architecture of MediaWise cloud. As can be seen in this figure, the MediaWise cloud consists of a several components. These include: content orchestrator, hybrid clouds, content access portal and the content management portal. Using the content management portal, the users (content producers) can add, delete or update content on any public clouds (e.g., Amazon and Rackspace). This content is then available to the end users via the content access portal. As mentioned previously, the MediaWise Cloud supports dynamic content creation and delivery. Using this functionality, several users using the MediaWise clouds create multimedia content together

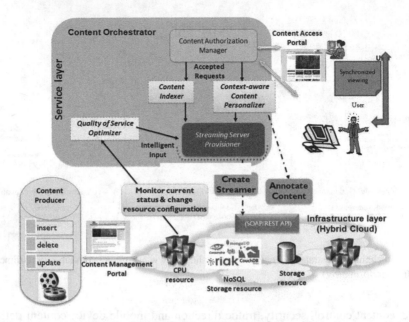

Fig. 8. The MediaWise Cloud architecture [14]

via the content access/management portal. This dynamic content can also be annotated using keywords for efficient indexing, search and retrieval. As soon as the request the content is generated from a user(s), it is forwarded it to the MediaWise Cloud content orchestrator (MCCO) [39].

MCCO is the heart of MediaWise cloud. It monitors hybrid clouds and provide mechanisms for QoS-aware cloud selection, scheduling and admission control. For example, as soon as the use request comes from the end user (via the content access portal) for content processing and delivery, the MCCO decides which virtual machine (VM) to provision out of several VMs running on several public clouds. This decision is based on the type of request and the QoS status of the VM on a particular public cloud. Hence, the MediaWise cloud offers QoS-based content placement, delivery as well as compute functionality that is critical in matching end-user SLAs.

5.6   Codeen

Codeen is an academic CDN test-bed developed at Princeton university (http://codeen. cs.princeton.edu/). It is primarily used to support services delivered the Planet Lab project, a global research networks that supports developments of new network services. Codeen has many proxy nodes distributed at various planet lab node locations. The proxy perform the role of POPs and request redirectors. A number of related projects that use the Codeen CDN include web-based content distribution service, name lookup, synchronisation tools, activity monitoring and visualisation tools. A Codeen user sets their cache to a nearby high bandwidth plant lab node location. Request to the codeen node at the location is directed to the most appropriate member of the planet lab system that has a cached copy of the file. This file is forwarded to the client. However, this system lacks support for dynamic content distribution.

5.7   Comodin

COMODIN (COoperative Media On-Demand on the InterNet) is an academic CDN providing streaming media service on current Internet infrastructure [41]. COMODIN enables a collaborative experience while streaming media content via the Internet. For examples, a group of users can coordinate the state of a media file (e.g. play, pause etc.). COMODIN follows a two layer architecture comprising of a base plane and a distributed set of playback components. The system employs IP-multicast to stream data across multiple clients. This academic CDN focuses more on content control collaboratively rather than content creation or distribution.

5.8   CoDaaS: An Experimental Cloud-Centric Content Delivery
Platform for User-Generated Contents

CoDaaS [42] is a cloud-centric content delivery system focused on distributing user-generated content in the most economical fashion while respecting the Quality-of-Service (QoS) requirements. It enables on-demand virtual content delivery to a targeted set of users. The system is built of hybrid cloud environments. Figure 9 presents an architecture overview of the CoDaaS system.

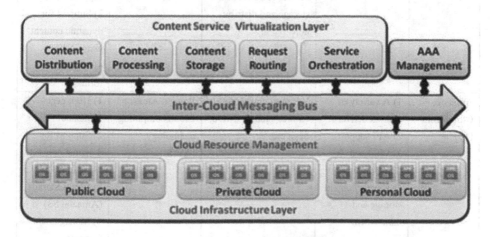

Fig. 9. CoDaaS system architecture

The CoDaaS architecture consists of three layers namely the cloud layer, the content service virtualizations layer and the security layer. The cloud layer comprises the hybrid cloud from which resources are used to develop a content distribution overlay. It also has a set of media rendering engines, managerial and service orchestration function. The content service visualization does the operation of content distribution, processing, storage and routing. This layer performs the function of a typical CDN. The security

Table 2. Commercial CDNs service analysis

CDN Provider Name	Services	Customers	Technology	Characteristics
Akamai [5]	Delivering static, dynamic content and streaming media.	A variety of corporations, such as Rackspace and HP	1) Distributing a large number of surrogate servers 2) Utilizing DNS system 3) BGP (Border Gateway Protocol)	1) Solving the problem of flash crowd 2) The commercial CDN leader 3) Superior load balance system.
Rackspace Cloud Files [9]	1) CDN 2) API for programmatic access 3) File storage	A variety of corporations such as Metro Trains Melbourne, Kogan Australia Private users for file storage and distributions.	1) Powered by Open Stack	1) Global presence using Akamai CDN 2) Large file support 3) Support for dynamic content using API 4) High Performance
Amazon CloudFront [10]	1) A variety of content delivery 2) API support 3) Wildcard CNAME support 4) Private content storage and manaement	Various commercial entities such as IMDb, Sega etc.	Related Amazon Cloud computing technology (AWS)	1) High performance 2) Support for dynamic content using low TTL 3) Cloud Storage (Amazon S3) 4) Management Console

CDN Provider Name	Services	Customers	Technology	Characteristics
Accellion (www.accellion.com)	1) On-demand content transfer solution for exchanging content safely 2) Sending large attachments (gigabyte-sized) 3) Online desktop	Industries, such as Media production, healthcare, consumer goods	1) SeOS (SmartEdge Operating System) 2) SFTA (Secure File Transfer Appliances)	1) Handling large sized files effectively 2) Backup and Recovery Solutions
EdgeStream (http://www2.edgestream.com/es/)	1) IPTV streaming. 2) Video on-demand.	Network providers, Telco's, CDNs, ISPs, content owners and so on	1) Congestion Tunnel Through 2) Continuous Route Optimization	1) High quality of video streams
CloudFlare (https://www.cloudflare.com/features-cdn)	1) Web site content acceleration 2) Web site analytics 3) CDN to support web acceleration	Numerous commercial entities including eHarmony, CISCO, QuickSilver and GOV.UK This service is offered as both free and as pay-as-you-go.	1) 28 data centres around the world 2) CloudFlare optimizer to reduce page service latency 3) Security 4) Analytics for web page content serving .	1) High performance 2) Works with static and dynamic web content 3) Interoperates with other CDNs
MetaCDN [11]	1) Multi CDN 2) Live content streaming 3) Video on demand and video encoding	Many organisation and universities including Sony, The University of Melbourne and Harvard Business School.	1) CDN with 120+ POPs 2) Based on public cloud platforms 3) Uses API connectors to interface with public	1) Fast 2) Reliable

CDN Provider Name	Services	Customers	Technology	Characteristics
			cloud providers	
Mirror Image (http://www.mirror-image.com/)	1) application logic 2) Content Delivery 3) Streaming Media Delivery (video on demand, multi screen, live streaming)	Creative, Open System, and SiteRock to name a few.	1) Patented global dynamic delivery network 2) Edge computing to run application closer to end-users 3) Device optimisations	1) Automatic elastic Scalability 2) Low latency 3) Worldwide coverage 4) Strong SLAs
MaxCDN (http://www.maxcdn.com)	1) Web Content delivery solutions 2) API support for total automation 3) Real time analytics	1,000 customers, 200 large websites including Garmin, Kodak, The Washington times.	1) HTTP Caching 2) Automatic provisioning.	1) Support for static and dynamic content 2) Multi-path network 3) Super POPs 4) Web-based control panel

module is responsible to ensure authorized, authenticated and accountable access to resources across hybrid clouds. Finally, the inter-cloud messaging bus is employed to integrate all participating components into an integrated media application.

6   Analysis of CCDNs Current State-of-the-Art

As mentioned in the previous section, most commercial CCDNs follow an identical architecture. In the previous section, we presented some of the most popular commercial CCDN architectures and a few academic CDNs. In this section, we will present a twofold comprehensive analysis of commercial CCDNs based on services offered and research dimensions. The services analysis is based on the following characteristics (1) target audience; (2) services; (3) technology and characteristics. The research dimensions used for analysis presented in Sect. 3 are (1) Hybrid cloud support; (2) Content creation and management; (3) Content personalization; (4) Quality of Service; (5) Indexing; (6) Cloud Selection; (7) Content Type. For academic CCDNs we only focus on the research dimensions (Tables 2 and 3).

Table 3. Commercial CDNs research dimensions analysis

CDN Provider name	Hybrid cloud support	Content creation and management	Personalisation (User/Device)	QoS	Indexing	Cloud selection	Content type
Akamai [5]	No	Partial content management	No/Yes	Yes	Title and Keyword	Not applicable	Web (static and dynamic) and Media
LimeLight Networks [13]	No	Publish content using web interface	No/Yes	Yes	Title and Keyword	Not applicable	Web (static and dynamic) and Media
Rackspace Cloud Files [9]	No	Mainly content storage and distribution using Akamai	No	Yes. Using Akamai	No	Not applicable	Cloud store for any type of content
Amazon CloudFront [10]	No	Publish content using web interface and APIs	No/Yes	Yes	Title and Keyword	Not applicable	Web (static and dynamic) and Media
Accellion (www.accellion.com)	No	Mainly file sharing and mobile collaboration	No/yes	No	No	Not applicable	Cloud store for any type of content
EdgeStream (http://www2.edgestream.com/es/)	No	Support to publish content by providers	No/Yes (edge stream enabled device)	Yes	Title and Keyword	Not applicable	Video streaming
CloudFlare (https://www.cloudflare.com/features-cdn)	No	No	No/yes	Yes	Title and Keyword	Not applicable	Web site content acceleration
MetaCDN [11]	Yes	Interface to upload content (cannot orchestrate new content from existing content)	No/Yes	Yes	Title and Keyword	Yes.	Web (static) and various content media types (video, audio, images etc.)
Mirror Image (http://www.mirror-image.com/)	No	Dynamic content publishing support	No/Yes	Yes	Title and Keyword	Not applicable	Mostly video (live streaming, video on demand)
MaxCDN (http://www.maxcdn.com)	No	Only serve web pages (static and dynamic)	No/Yes	No	No	Not applicable	Web site acceleration
MediWise Cloud [14, 15]	Yes	Yes. Group of users can create content from existing content.	Yes/Yes	Yes	Title, keyword and video context across clouds	Yes	Video, audio and images
CODEEN (http://codeen.cs.princeton.edu/)	No	Specifically used content storage and distribution	No/No	No	No	Not applicable	Any content
COMODIN [41]	Yes	Partially. Group of users can control media collaboratively	No/No	No	No	No	Video, audio and images
CoDaaS [42]	Yes	Yes. Support for user-generated content	No/Yes	Yes	Name	No	Video, audio and images

7 Conclusion

Cloud-based CDNs have gained significant importance due to the wide-spread avail-ability and adoption of cloud computing platforms. The integration of Cloud and CDN has mutual benefits allowing content to be efficiently and effectively distributed in the Internet using a pay-as-you-go model promoting the content-as-a-service model. We identified the key challenges and research dimensions that need to be addressed in the cloud-based CDN space. We have presented a state-of-the-art survey on existing commercial and academic cloud CDN solutions. Finally, we provided a comprehensive analysis of commercial and academic cloud CDNs against the service they offer and the research dimensions identified in this paper.

Our findings show that current cloud CDN providers are mostly based on one cloud platform and lacks support for the emerging form of content distribution namely dynamic user-generated content. Since, the solutions are based on a single cloud providers, the services lack consideration for cost models when taking advantage of cloud content storage spaning multiple cloud providers. Further, most commercial and few academic solutions do not support personalisation at user level. We believe, the future of CCDN will be based around the need to support user created content and ability to support hybrid cloud platforms and addressing the challenges such as QoS, SLA, costing introduced by hybrid clouds.

References

1. Wang, L., Pai, V., Peterson, L.: The effectiveness of request redirection on CDN robustness. web.cs.wpi.edu/~rek/DCS/D04/CDN_Redirection.ppt. Accessed 09 October 2014
2. Pallis, G., Vakali, A.: Insight and perspectives for content delivery networks. Commun. ACM **49**(1), 101–106 (2006)
3. Pathan, A.K., Buyya, R.: A taxonomy and survey of content delivery networks. Technical Report, GRIDS-TR-2007-4, Grid Computing and Distributed Systems Laboratory, The University of Melbourne, Australia, 12 Feb 2007
4. Li, L., Ma, X., Huang, Y.: CDN cloud: A novel scheme for combining CDN and cloud computing. In: 2013 International Conference on Measurement, Information and Control (ICMIC), vol. 01, pp. 687, 690, 16–18 August 2013
5. Akamai Technologies, Inc. (2014). www.akamai.com
6. A case for the Accountable Cloud. http://aws.amazon.com/cn/cloudfront/
7. Krauter, K., Buyya, R., et al.: A taxonomy and survey of grid resource management systems for distributed computing. Softw. Pract. Exp. (SPE) **32**, 135–164 (2002)
8. Microsoft Azure Cloud Services. http://www.windows.azure.com. Accessed 09 October 2014
9. Rackspace Cloud Files. http://www.rackspace.com.au/cloud/files. Accessed 06 August 2014
10. Amazon CloudFront. http://aws.amazon.com/cloudfront/. Accessed 09 October 2014
11. Broberg, J., Buyya, R., Tari, Z.: MetaCDN: Harnessing 'Storage Clouds' for high performance content delivery. J. Netw. Comput. Appl. **32**(5), 1012–1022 (2009). ISSN: 1084-8045. http://dx.doi.org/10.1016/j.jnca.2009.03.004
12. NoSQL. http://nosql-database.org/. Accessed 06 August 2014

13. Limelight Orchestrate CDN. http://www.limelight.com/services/orchestrate-content-delivery. html. Accessed 06 August 2014
14. Georgakopoulos, D., Ranjan, R., Mitra, K., Zhou, X.: MediaWise - Designing a smart media cloud. In: Proceedings of the International Conference on Advances in Cloud Computing (ACC 2012), Banglore, India, 26–28 July (2012). http://arxiv.org/ftp/arxiv/papers/1206/ 1206.1943.pdf
15. Ranjan, R., Mitra, K., Georgakopoulos, D.: MediaWise cloud content orchestrator. J. Internet Serv. Appl. **4**, 2 (2013)
16. Mell, P., Grance, T.: The NIST definition of cloud computing (draft). NIST special publication, vol. 800, p. 145 (2011)
17. Gong, C., Liu, J., Zhang, Q., Chen, H., Gong, Z.: The characteristics of cloud computing. In: 2010 39th International Conference on Parallel Processing Workshops (ICPPW), pp. 275–279 (2010)
18. Cisco: Cisco Visual Networking Index: Forecast and Methodology, 2013–2018. http://www. cisco.com/c/en/us/solutions/collateral/service-provider/ip-ngn-ip-next-generation-network/ white_paper_c11-481360.html. Accessed 09 October 2014
19. IDC: Data Growth, Business Opportunities, and IT Imperatives. http://www.emc.com/ leadership/digital-universe/2014iview/executive-summary.htm. Accessed 09 October 2014
20. Akamai: The Importance of Delivering A Great Online Video Experience. http://www. akamai.com/dl/reports/jupiter_onlinevideoexp.pdf. Accessed: 09 October 2014
21. IneoQuest: The Case for Leveraging the Cloud for Video Service Assurance. http://www. ineoquest.com/wp-content/uploads/2013/10/Whitepaper_Cloud_Services.pdf. Accessed 09 October 2014
22. BigData & CDN: http://www.slideshare.net/pavlobaron/bigdata-cdnoop2011-pavlo-baron. Accessed 07 March 2014
23. Yin, H., Liu, X., Min, G., Lin, C.: Content delivery networks: A bridge between emerging applications and future IP networks. Network, IEEE, **24**(4), 52, 56, July–August 2010
24. Wang, L., Kunze, M., Tao, J., Laszewski, G.: Towards building a cloud for scientific applications. Adv. Eng. Softw. **42**(9), 714–722 (2011)
25. Wang, L., Fu, C.: Research advances in modern cyber infrastructure. New GenerComput. **28** (2), 111–112 (2010)
26. Mastin, P.: Is the cloud a CDN killer. http://cloudcomputing.sys-con.com/node/2628667. Accessed 07 March 2014
27. Compton, K.: Marching towards cloud CDN. http://blogs.cisco.com/sp/marching-towards-cloud-cdn/. Accessed 07 March 2014
28. Peng, G.: CDN: Content distribution network. Technical Report TR-125, Experimental Computer Systems Lab, Department of Computer Science, State University of New York, Stony Brook, NY, 2003. http://citeseer.ist.psu.edu/peng03cdn.html
29. Vakali, A., Pallis, G.: Content delivery networks: Status and trends. IEEE Internet Comput., 68–74. IEEE Computer Society, November–December 2003
30. Dilley, J., Maggs, B., Parikh, J., Prokop, H., Sitaraman, R., Weihl, B.: Globally distributed content delivery. IEEE Internet Comput. **6**(5), 50–58 (2002)
31. Kung, H.T., Wu, C.H.: Content networks: Taxonomy and new approaches. In: Park, K., Willinger, W. (eds.) The Internet as a Large-Scale Complex System. Oxford University Press (2002)
32. Wen, Y., Zhu, X., Rodrigues, J.J.P.C., Chen, C.W.: Cloud mobile media: Reflections and outlook. IEEE Trans. Multimedia **16**(4), 885, 902, June 2014
33. Shaikh, A., Tewari, R., Agrawal, M.: On the effectiveness of DNS-based server selection. In: Proceedings of IEEE INFOCOM, Anchorage, AK, USA, pp. 1801–1810, April 2001

34. Mao, Z.M., Cranor, C.D., Boughs, F., Rabinovich, M., Spatscheck, O., Wang, J.: A precise and efficient evaluation of the proximity between web clients and their local DNS servers. In: Proceedings of the USENIX 2002 Annual Technical Conference, Monterey, CA, USA, pp. 229–242, June 2002

35. Armbrust, M., et al.: A view of cloud computing. Commun. ACM Mag. **53**(4), 50–58 (2010). doi:10.1145/1721654.1721672. ACM Press

36. Patterson, D.A.: Technical perspective: The data center is the computer. Commun. ACM Mag. **51**(1), 105–105 (2008). ACM Press

37. Hui, L.: Realistic workload modeling and its performance impacts in large-scale eScience grids. IEEE Trans. Parallel Distrib. Syst. **21**, 480–493 (2010)

38. Wang, C., Ranjan, R., Zhou, X., Mitra, K., Saha, S., Meng, M., Georgakopopulos, D., Wang, L., Thew, P.: A cloud-based collaborative video story authoring and sharing platform. CSI J. Comput. **1**(3), 66–76 (2012)

39. Ranjan, R., Mitra, K., Saha, S., Georgakopoulos, D., Zaslavsky, A.: Do-it-yourself content delivery network orchestrator. In: Wang, X., Cruz, I., Delis, A., Huang, G. (eds.) WISE 2012. LNCS, vol. 7651, pp. 789–791. Springer, Heidelberg (2012)

40. Zhang, X., Du, H., Chen, J.-Q., Lin, Y., Zeng, L.-J.: Ensure data security in cloud storage. In: 2011 International Conference on Network Computing and Information Security (NCIS), vol. 1, pp. 284, 287, 14–15 May 2011

41. Russo, W., Mastroianni, C., Palau, C.E., Fortino, G.: CDN-Supported collaborative media streaming control. IEEE MultiMedia **14**(2), 60–71 (2007)

42. Jin, Y., Wen, Y., Shi, G., Wang, G., Vasilakos, AV.: CoDaaS: An experimental cloud-centric content delivery platform for user-generated contents. In: 2012 International Conference on Computing, Networking and Communications (ICNC), pp. 934, 938, 30 Jan – 2 Feb 2012

43. Li, H., Zhong, L., Liu, J., Li, B., Xu, B.: Cost-effective partial migration of VoD services to content clouds. In: 2011 IEEE International Conference on Cloud Computing (CLOUD), pp. 203, 210, 4–9 July 2011

44. Wang, L., Chen, D., Zhao, J., Tao, J.: Resource management of distributed virtual machines. IJAHUC **10**(2), 96–111 (2012)

45. Wang, L., Jie, W.: Towards supporting multiple virtual private computing environments on computational Grids. Adv. Eng. Softw. **40**(4), 239–245 (2009)

46. Wang, L., von Laszewski, G., Younge, A.J., He, X., Kunze, M., Tao, J., Cheng, F.: Cloud computing: A perspective study. New Generation Comput. **28**(2), 137–146 (2010)

47. Wang, L., Chen, D., Yangyang, H., Ma, Y., Wang, J.: Towards enabling cyberinfrastructure as a service in clouds. Comput. Electr. Eng. **39**(1), 3–14 (2013)

Author Index

Printed in the United States
By Bookmasters